STUDY GUIDE for use with

Third Canadian Edition

MACROECONOMICS

COLANDER
ROCKERBIE
RICHTER

Prepared by
Oliver Franke
Athabasca University

David C. Colander
Middlebury College

Douglas Copeland
Johnson County Community College

Jenifer Gamber

 McGraw-Hill Ryerson

Toronto Montréal New York Burr Ridge Bangkok Bogotá Caracas Lisbon London
Madrid Mexico City Milan New Delhi Seoul Singapore Sydney Taipei

The McGraw-Hill Companies

McGraw-Hill Ryerson

Study Guide for use with
Macroeconomics
Third Canadian Edition

ISBN: 0-07-095102-0

1 2 3 4 5 6 7 8 9 10 CP 0 9 8 7

Printed and bound in the Canada

Statistics Canada information is used with the permission of the Minister of Industry, as Minister responsible for Statistics Canada. Information on the availability of the wide range of data from Statistics Canada can be obtained from Statistics Canada's Regional Offices, its World Wide Web site at <http://www.statcan.ca>, and its toll-free access number 1-800-263-1136.

Publisher: Lynn Fisher
Developmental Editor: Maria Chu
Economics Editor: Ron Doleman
Senior Marketing Manager: Kelly Smyth
Sales Manager: Megan Farrell
Supervising Editor: Jaime Smith
Senior Production Coordinator: Madeleine Harrington
Page Layout: First Image Design
Cover Design: Dianna Little
Cover Image: © Glen Allison/Getty Images
Printer: Canadian Printco, Ltd.

Contents

Preface

We wrote this study guide to help you do well in your economics courses. Even using a great book like the Colander textbook, we know that studying is not all fun. The reality is: most studying is hard work and a study guide won't change that. Your text and lectures will give you the foundation for doing well. So the first advice we will give you is:

1. Read the textbook.
2. Attend class.

We cannot emphasize that enough. Working through the study guide will not replace the text or lectures; this study guide is designed to help you retain the knowledge from the text and classroom by practicing the tools of economics. It is not an alternative to the textbook and class; it is **in addition to them**.

Having said that, we should point out that buying this guide isn't enough. You have to *use* it. Really, if it sits on your desk, or even under your pillow, it won't do you any good. Osmosis only works with plants. This study guide should be well worn by the end of the semester with dog-eared pages, scribbles beneath questions, and some pages even torn out. It should look used.

WHAT CAN YOU EXPECT FROM THIS BOOK?

This study guide concentrates on the terminology and models in your text. It does not expand upon the material in the textbook; it reinforces it. It primarily serves to give you a good foundation to understanding principles of economics. Your professor has chosen this study guide for you, suggesting that your economics exams are going to focus on this kind of foundational understanding. You should be sure of this: if your professor is going to give you mainly essay exams, or complex questions about applying the foundations (like the more difficult end-of-chapter questions in your textbook), this study guide will not be enough to ace that exam.

To get an idea of what your exams will be like, ask your professor to take a look at these questions and tell the class whether they are representative of the type of questions that will be on the exam. And if they will differ, how.

HOW SHOULD YOU USE THIS STUDY GUIDE?

As we stated above, this book works best if you have attended class and read the textbook. Ideally, you were awake during class and took notes, you have read the textbook chapters more than once, and have worked through some of the questions at the end of the chapter. (So, we're optimists.)

Just in case the material in the book isn't fresh in your mind, before turning to this study guide, it is a good idea to refresh your memory about the material in the text. To do so:

1. Read through the margin comments in the text; they highlight the main concepts in each chapter.
2. Turn to the last few pages of the chapter and reread the chapter summary.
3. Look through the key terms, making sure they are familiar. (O.K., we're not only optimists, we're wild optimists.)

Even if you do not do the above, working though the questions in the study guide will help to tell you whether you really do know the material in the textbook chapters.

STRUCTURE OF THE STUDY GUIDE

This study guide has two main components: (1) a chapter-by-chapter review and (2) pretests based upon groups of chapters.

Chapter-by-chapter review

Each chapter has eight elements:

1. A chapter at a glance: A brief exposition and discussion of the learning objectives for the chapter.
2. A test of matching the terms to their definitions.
3. Multiple choice questions.
4. Short-answer questions keyed to the learning objectives.
5. Problems and applications.
6. A brain teaser.
7. Potential essay questions.
8. Answers to all questions.

Each chapter presents the sections in the order that we believe they can be most beneficial to you. Here is how we suggest you use them:

Chapter at a Glance: These should jog your memory about the textbook and lecture. If you don't remember ever seeing the material before, you should go back and reread the textbook chapter. The numbers in parentheses following each learning objective refer to the page in the text that covers that objective. Remember, reading a chapter when you are thinking about a fantasy date is almost the same as not having read the chapter at all.

Match the Terms and Concepts to Their Definitions: Since the definitions are listed, you should get most of these right. The best way to match these is to read the definition first, and then find the term on the left that it defines. If you are not sure of the matching term, circle that definition and move on to the next one. At the end, return to the remaining definitions and look at the remaining terms to complete the matches. After completing this part, check your answers with those in the back of the chapter and figure our what percent you got right. If that percent is below the grade you want to get on your exam, try to see why you missed the ones you did and review those terms and concepts in the textbook.

Multiple Choice Questions: The next exercise in each chapter is the multiple choice test. It serves to test the breadth of your knowledge of the text material. Multiple choice questions are not the final arbiters of your understanding. They are, instead, a way of determining whether you have read the textbook and generally understood the material.

Give the answer that most closely corresponds to the answer presented in your text. If you can answer these questions you should be ready for the multiple choice part of your exam.

Work through all the questions in the test before grading yourself. Looking up the answer before you try to answer the questions is a poor way to study. For a multiple choice exam, the percent you answer correctly will be a good predictor of how well you will do on the test.

You can foul up on multiple choice questions in two ways. You can know too little and you can know too much. The answer to knowing too little is obvious: Study more, that is, read the chapters more carefully (and maybe more often). The answer to knowing too much is more complicated. Our suggestions for students who know too much is not to ask themselves "What is the answer?" but instead to ask "What is the answer the person writing the question wants?" Since, with these multiple choice questions, the writer of many of the questions is the textbook author, ask yourself: "What answer would the textbook author want me to give? Answering the questions in this way will stop you from going too deeply into them and trying to see nuances that aren't supposed to be there.

For the most part, questions in this study guide are meant to be straightforward. There may be deeper levels at which other answers could be relevant, but searching for those deeper answers will generally get you in trouble and not be worth the cost.

If you are having difficulty answering a multiple choice question, make your best guess. Once you are familiar with the material, even if you don't know the answer to a question, you can generally make a reasonable guess. What point do you think the writer of the question wanted to make with the question? Figuring out that point and then thinking of incorrect answers may be a way for you to eliminate wrong answers and then choose among the remaining options.

Notice that the answers at the end of the chapter are not just the lettered answers. We have provided an explanation for each answer as to why the right one is right and why some of the other choices are wrong. If you miss a question, read that rationale carefully. If you are not convinced, or do not follow the reasoning, go to the page in the text referred to in the answer and reread the material. If you are still not convinced, see the caveat on the next page.

Short-Answer Questions: The short-answer questions will tell you if you are familiar with the learning objectives. Try to answer each within the space below each question. Don't just read the questions and assume you can write an answer. Actually writing an answer will reveal your weaknesses. If you can answer them all perfectly, great. But, quite honestly, we don't expect you to be able to answer them all perfectly. We only expect you to be able to sketch out an answer.

Of course, some other questions are important to know. For example, if there is a question about the economic decision rule and you don't remember that it excludes past costs and benefits, you need more studying. So the rule is: Know the central ideas of the chapter; be less concerned about the specific presentation of those central ideas.

After you have sketched out all your answers, check them with those at the end of the chapter and review those that you didn't get right. Since each question is based upon a specific learning objective in the text, for those you didn't get right, you may want to return to the textbook to review the material covering that learning objective.

Problems and Applications: Now it's time to take on any problems in the chapter. These problems are generally more difficult than the short-answer questions. These problems focus on numerical and graphical aspects of the chapter.

Working through problems is perhaps one of the best ways to practice your understanding of economic principles. Even if you are expecting a multiple choice exam, working through these problems will give you a good handle on using the concepts in each chapter.

If you expect a multiple choice exam with no problems, you can work through these fairly quickly, making sure you understand the concepts being tested. If you will have a test with problems and exercises, make sure you can answer each of these questions accurately.

Work out the answers to all the problems in the space provided before checking them against the answers in the back of the chapter. Where our answers differ from yours, check to find out why. The answers refer to specific pages in the textbook so you can review the text again too.

Most of the problems are objective and have only one answer. A few are interpretative and have many answers. Some questions can be answered in different ways than provided. If you cannot reconcile your answer with those in the answer section, check with

your professor. Once you are at this stage, worrying about different interpretations, you're ahead of most students and, most likely, prepared for the exam.

A Brain Teaser: This section consists of one problem that is generally one step up in the level of difficulty from the "Problems and Applications" exercises or is a critical thought question. It is designed to provide a challenge to those few students who have studied the way we have suggested.

Potential Essay Questions: These questions provide yet another opportunity to test your understanding of what you have learned. Answering these questions will be especially helpful if you expect these types of questions on the exams. We have only sketched the beginning to an answer to these. This beginning should give you a good sense of the direction to go in your answer, but be aware that on exam a more complete answer will be required.

Questions on Appendices: In the chapters, we have included a number of questions on the text appendices. To separate these questions from the others, the letter A precedes the question number. They are for students who have been assigned the appendices. If you have not been assigned them (and you have not read them on your own out of your great interest in economics) you can skip these.

Answers to All Questions: The answers to all questions appear at the end of each chapter. They begin on a new page so that you can tear out the answers and more easily check your answers against ours. It cannot be emphasized enough that the best way to study is to answer the questions yourself first, and then check out the answers. Just looking at the questions and the answers may tell you what the answers are but will not give you the chance to see where your knowledge of the material is weak.

Pretests

Most class exams cover more than one chapter. To prepare you for such an exam, multiple choice pretests are provided for groups of chapters. These pretests consist of 25-40 multiple choice questions from the selected group of chapters. These questions are identical to earlier questions so if you have done the work, you should do well on these. It is suggested that you complete the entire exam before grading yourself.

We also suggest taking these under test conditions. Specifically,

Use a set time period to complete the exam.
Sit at a hard chair at a desk with good lighting.

Each answer will tell you the chapter on which the question is based, so if you did not cover one of the chapters in the text for your class, don't worry if you get that question wrong. If you get a number of questions wrong from the chapters your class has covered, worry.

There is another way to use these pretests which we hesitate to mention, but we're realists so we will. That way is to forget doing the chapter-by-chapter work and simply take the pretests. Go back and review the material you get wrong.

However you use the pretests, if it turns out that you consistently miss questions from the same chapter, return to your notes from the lecture and reread your textbook chapters.

A FINAL WORD OF ADVICE

That's about it. If you use it, this study guide can help you do better on the exam by giving you the opportunity to use the terms and models of economics. However, we reiterate one last time: The best way to do well in a class is to attend every class and read every chapter in the text as well as work through the chapters in this study guide. Start early and work consistently. Do not do all your studying the night before the exam.

David Colander
Douglas Copeland
Jenifer Gamber
Oliver Franke

ECONOMICS AND ECONOMIC REASONING

CHAPTER AT A GLANCE

Chapter 1 introduces students to the discipline called economics – the study of how individuals, firms, and governments make optimal choices from among a set of alternatives when facing scarce resources. Human beings coordinate their wants and desires, given the decision-making mechanisms, social customs, and political realities of society.

Central to the study of economics is making choices. Everyday, we are faced with deciding what to do among the alternatives present. An optimal choice requires that some sort of criteria be derived to determine when a choice is the best choice for the decision maker. Economic analysis utilizes a variety of criteria depending upon the nature of the decisionmaker. This could be in terms of maximizing satisfaction for a consumer, maximizing profit for firms, or maximizing some sort of social welfare for governments. In making choices, there are two defining principles – the fact that our society has limited resources and that every one in society has unlimited wants and desires. The dilemma becomes how to as efficiently as possible utilize our scarce resources in order to satisfy as many wants and desires as possible. In any decision making process, choices have to be made and there is a cost to us for making one choice over another. In economics, this cost is called opportunity cost.

Understanding economics allows us to become more aware of our surroundings and to more fully understand why certain things happen, and why people and firms react in certain ways. We will see that the behaviour of various groups or economic entities in our economy will be influenced by many factors – economic, political, legal, social, and historical. Economics has a role to play in sociology, history, and politics, just as sociology, history, and politics have roles to play in economics.

The discipline of economics is based on theories and principles, many of which are only generalizations – only true under certain circumstances.

This is due to the fact that the real world is a very complex place and economics attempts to simplify our society in order to better understand all of the intricate workings of our economy. Yet, our society is so complicated and people and firms all react differently that theories can only explain a portion of the behaviour. Despite the economic generalizations being simplified and abstract representations of the real world, they can based on actual data and facts. Even with this shortcoming, economic theories, models and principles are very important to understanding the workings of the economy, to solve specific economic problems and to achieve specific economic goals.

Economic theory is divided in two broad categories – microeconomics and macroeconomics. Microeconomic theory considers economic reasoning and behaviour of individuals and firms. Macroeconomics studies the economy as a whole and considers broad economic aggregates such as inflation, unemployment, business cycles, and economic growth.

This review is based upon the learning objectives that open the chapter.

1a. Economics is the study of how individuals, firms, and governments make optimal choices from among a set of alternatives when facing scarce resources. (4)

1b. An optimal choice requires that some sort of criteria be used to determine when a choice is the best choice for the decisionmaker. Economics assumes that decisionmakers face scarce resources when making their choices. (5)

2. If the marginal benefits of doing something exceed the marginal costs, do it. If the marginal costs of doing something exceed the marginal benefits, don't do it. This is known as the economic decision rule. (6)

You really need to think in terms of the marginal, or "extra" benefits (MB) and marginal, or "extra" costs (MC) of a course of action.

Economic decision rule:
If MB>MC ⇒ <u>Do more of it</u> because "it's worth it."

If MB<MC ⇒ <u>Do less of it</u> because "it's not worth it."

NOTE: The symbol " ⇒ " means "implies" or "logically follows."

3.   Opportunity cost is the basis of cost/benefit economic reasoning; it is the benefit forgone, or the cost of the next-best alternative to the activity you've chosen. In economic reasoning, that cost is less than the benefit of what you've chosen. (7)

Opportunity cost ⇒ "What must be given up in order to get something else." Opportunity costs are often "hidden." You need to take into consideration <u>all</u> costs when making a decision.

4.   Economic reality is controlled by economic forces, social forces and political forces: (8-10)

What happens in a society can be seen as the reaction and interaction of these 3 forces.

- Economic forces (the invisible hand);
  These are the market forces of demand, supply, and prices, etc.

- Social and cultural forces;
  Social forces can prevent economic forces from becoming market forces.

- Political and legal forces.
  Political and legal forces affect decisions too.

5.   3 important definitions: (11-12)

- An economic model is a set of simple assumptions about how decisionmakers behave that simplifies the real world so that decisions can be explained using economics.

- Economic principles form the key assumptions in economics that are common to all economic models.

- The invisible hand is a market economy, through the price mechanism, will allocate resources efficiently.

6.   Microeconomics considers economic reasoning from the viewpoint of individuals and builds up to the analysis of the whole economy; macroeconomics considers economic reasoning from the aggregate, or whole, and builds down into components. (13)

Microeconomics (micro) is concerned with some particular segment of the economy.

Macroeconomics (macro) is concerned with the entire economy.

7a. *Positive economics* is the study of what is, and how the economy works. (15)

Deals with "what is" (objective analysis).

7b. *Normative economics* is the study of what the goals of the economy should be. (15)

Deals with "what ought to be" (subjective analysis).

7c. The *science of economics* is the application of the knowledge learned in positive economics to the achievement of the goals determined in normative economics. (15)

The art of economics is sometimes referred to as "policy economics."

"Good" policy tries to be objective. It tries to weigh all the benefits and costs associated with all policy options and chooses that option in which the benefits outweigh the costs to the greatest degree.

See also, Appendix A: "The Language of Graphs"

In Appendix A, remember 2 types of relationships:

- *Direct (Positive) Relationship*: expressed as an upward sloping curve.

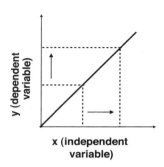

Note: as x increases, y increases; as x decreases, y decreases.

- *Inverse (Negative) Relationship*: expressed as a downward sloping curve.

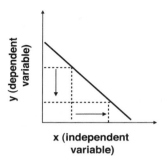

Note: as x increases, y decreases; as x decreases, y increases.

MATCHING THE TERMS
Match the terms to their definitions

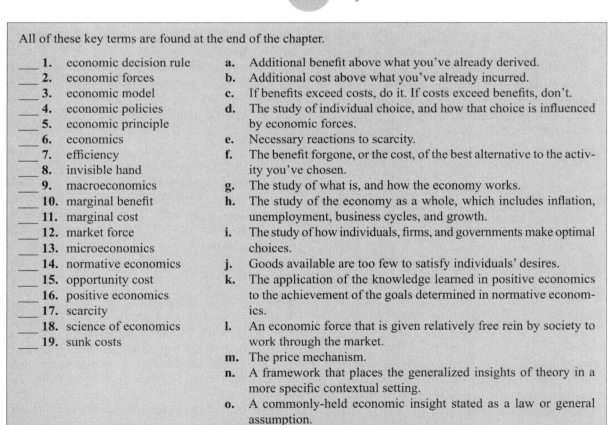

All of these key terms are found at the end of the chapter.

____ 1. economic decision rule	**a.** Additional benefit above what you've already derived.
____ 2. economic forces	**b.** Additional cost above what you've already incurred.
____ 3. economic model	**c.** If benefits exceed costs, do it. If costs exceed benefits, don't.
____ 4. economic policies	**d.** The study of individual choice, and how that choice is influenced by economic forces.
____ 5. economic principle	**e.** Necessary reactions to scarcity.
____ 6. economics	**f.** The benefit forgone, or the cost, of the best alternative to the activity you've chosen.
____ 7. efficiency	**g.** The study of what is, and how the economy works.
____ 8. invisible hand	**h.** The study of the economy as a whole, which includes inflation, unemployment, business cycles, and growth.
____ 9. macroeconomics	**i.** The study of how individuals, firms, and governments make optimal choices.
____ 10. marginal benefit	**j.** Goods available are too few to satisfy individuals' desires.
____ 11. marginal cost	**k.** The application of the knowledge learned in positive economics to the achievement of the goals determined in normative economics.
____ 12. market force	
____ 13. microeconomics	
____ 14. normative economics	**l.** An economic force that is given relatively free rein by society to work through the market.
____ 15. opportunity cost	**m.** The price mechanism.
____ 16. positive economics	**n.** A framework that places the generalized insights of theory in a more specific contextual setting.
____ 17. scarcity	**o.** A commonly-held economic insight stated as a law or general assumption.
____ 18. science of economics	
____ 19. sunk costs	**p.** Achieving a goal as cheaply as possible.
	q. Actions taken by government to influence economic events.
	r. Study of what the goals of the economy should be.
	s. Costs that have already been incurred and cannot be recovered.

● MULTIPLE CHOICE

Circle the one best answer for each of the following questions:

1. Economic reasoning
   a. provides a framework with which to approach questions.
   b. provides correct answers to just about every question.
   c. is only used by economists.
   d. should only be applied to economic business matters.

2. Scarcity could be reduced if
   a. individuals work less and want fewer consumption goods.
   b. individuals work more and want fewer consumption goods.
   c. world population grows and world production remains the same.
   d. innovation comes to a halt.

3. In the textbook, the authors focus on optimal choices rather than scarcity as the central point of the definition of economics because
   a. economics is not really about scarcity.
   b. scarcity involves coercion, and the author doesn't like coercion.
   c. choices have to be made to efficiently allocate scarce resources.
   d. the concept "scarcity" does not fit within the institutional structure of the economy.

4. In the Canadian economy, who is in charge of organizing and coordinating overall economic activities?
   a. Government.
   b. Corporations.
   c. No one.
   d. Consumers.

5. You bought stock A for $10 and stock B for $50. The price of each is currently $20. Assuming no tax issues, which should you sell if you need money?
   a. Stock A.
   b. Stock B.
   c. It doesn't matter which.
   d. You should sell an equal amount of both.

6. In deciding whether to go to lectures in the middle of the semester, you should
   a. include tuition as part of the cost of that decision.
   b. not include tuition as part of the cost of that decision.
   c. include a portion of tuition as part of the cost of that decision.
   d. only include tuition if you paid it rather than your parents.

7. In making economic decisions, you should consider
   a. marginal costs and marginal benefits.
   b. marginal costs and average benefits.
   c. average costs and average benefits.
   d. total costs and total benefits, including past costs and benefits.

8. In arriving at a decision, a good economist would say that
   a. one should consider only total costs and total benefits.
   b. one should consider only marginal costs and marginal benefits.
   c. after one has considered marginal costs and benefits, one should integrate the social and moral implications and reconsider those costs and benefits.
   d. after considering the marginal costs and benefits, one should make the decision on social and moral grounds.

9. In making decisions, economists primarily use
   a. monetary costs.
   b. opportunity costs.
   c. benefit costs.
   d. dollar costs.

10. The opportunity cost of reading Chapter 1 of the text
    a. is about 1/20 of the price you paid for the book because the chapter is about one twentieth of the price of the book.
    b. zero since you have already paid for the book
    c. has nothing to do with the price you paid for the book.
    d. is 1/20 the price of the book plus 1/20 the price of the tuition.

11. Rationing devices that our society uses include
    a. the invisible hand only.
    b. the invisible hand and social forces only.
    c. the invisible hand and political forces only.
    d. the invisible hand, the social forces, and political forces.

12. If at Female College there are significantly more females than males (and there are not a significant number of gays) economic forces
    a. will be pushing for females to pay on dates.
    b. will be pushing for males to pay on dates.
    c. will be pushing for neither to pay on dates.
    d. are irrelevant to this issue. Everyone knows that the males always should pay.

13. Individuals are prohibited from practicing medicine without a license. This is an example of
    a. the invisible hand.
    b. social forces.
    c. political forces.
    d. market forces.

14. Which of the following is most likely an example of a microeconomic topic?
    a. The effect of a flood in B.C. on the price of bottled water.
    b. How a government policy will affect inflation.
    c. The relationship between unemployment and inflation.
    d. Why an economy goes into a recession.

15. Which of the following is an example of a macroeconomic topic?
    a. The effect of a frost on the Florida orange crop.
    b. Wages of cross-country truckers.
    c. How the unemployment and inflation rates are related.
    d. How income is distributed in Canada.

16. The statement, "The distribution of income should be left to the market," is
    a. a positive statement.
    b. a normative statement.
    c. an science-of economics statement
    d. an objective statement.

17. "Given certain conditions, the market achieves efficient results" is an example of a
    a. positive statement.
    b. normative statement.
    c. art-of-economics statement.
    d. subjective statement.

A1. In the graph below, the point A represents
    a. a price of 1 and a quantity of 2.
    b. a price of 2 and a quantity of 2.
    c. a price of 2 and a quantity of 1.
    d. a price of 1 and a quantity of 1.

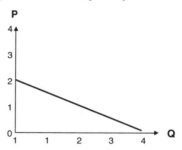

A2. The slope of the line in the graph below is
    a. 1/2.
    b. 2.
    c. minus 1/2.
    d. minus 2.

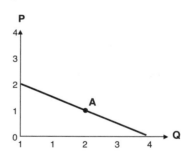

A3. At the maximum and minimum points of a nonlinear curve, the value of the slope is equal to
    a. 1.
    b. zero.
    c. minus 1.
    d. indeterminate.

A4. Which of the four lines in the graphs below has the larger slope?

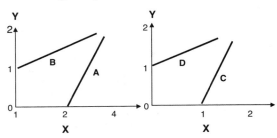

a. A.
b. B.
c. C.
d. A and C.

● SHORT-ANSWER QUESTIONS

1. What is economics?

2. State the economic decision rule.

3. Define opportunity cost.

4. What is the importance of opportunity cost to economic reasoning?

5. What is scarcity? What are two elements that comprise scarcity? How do they affect relative scarcity?

6. What is an economic force? What are the forces that can keep an economic force from becoming a market force?

7. How does microeconomics differ from macroeconomics? Give an example of a macroeconomic issue and a microeconomic issue.

8. Define positive economics, normative economics, and the science of economics. How do they relate to one another?

● PROBLEMS AND APPLICATIONS

1. State as best you can:

a. The opportunity cost of going out on a date tonight with the date you made last Wednesday.

b. The opportunity cost of breaking the date for tonight you made last Wednesday.

c. The opportunity cost of working through this study guide.

d. The opportunity cost of buying this study guide.

2. Assume you have purchased a $15,000 car. The salesperson has offered you a maintenance contract covering all major repairs for the next 3 years, with some exclusions, for $750.

a. What is the opportunity cost of purchasing that maintenance contract?

b. What information would you need to make a decision based on the economic decision rule?

c. Based upon that information how would you make your decision?

3. State what happens to scarcity for each good in the following situations:

a. New storage technology allows college dining services to keep peaches from rotting for a longer time. (Good: peaches).

b. More students desire to live in single-sex dormitories. No new single-sex dormitories are established. (Good: single-sex dormitory rooms).

4. State for each of the following whether it is an example of political forces, social forces or economic forces at work:

a. Warm weather arrives and more people take Sunday afternoon drives. As a result, the price of gasoline rises.

b. In some states, liquor cannot be sold before noon on Sunday.

c. Minors cannot purchase cigarettes.

d. Many parents will send money to their children in college without the expectation of being repaid.

A BRAIN TEASER

1. Suppose you are a producer of handcrafted picture frames. The going market price for your frames is $250 a piece. No matter how many frames you sell your revenue per unit (equal to the selling price per unit) is constant at $250 per frame. However, your per unit costs of producing each additional picture frame are not constant. Suppose the following table summarizes your costs of producing picture frames. Use benefit/cost analysis to determine the most economical (profit maximizing) number of frames to produce given the price per unit and the cost schedule shown below. What are your total profits per week?

# of frames	Price	Total Cost
0	$250	$0
1	$250	$25
2	$250	$75
3	$250	$150
4	$250	$300
5	$250	$560

POTENTIAL ESSAY QUESTIONS

You may also see essay questions similar to the "Problems & Applications" and "Brain Teasers" exercises.

1. Respond to the following statement: "Theories are of no use to me because they are not very practical. All I need is the facts because they speak for themselves."

2. Canada is one of the wealthiest nations on earth, yet our fundamental economic problem is scarcity. How can this be?

3. Does economics help teach us how to approach problems, or does it give us a set of answers to problems?

4. Can we say that what is true for the part (micro) is necessarily true for the whole (macro)?

━━━━━━━━ ANSWERS ━━━━━━━━

MATCHING

1-c; 2-e; 3-n; 4-q; 5-o; 6-i; 7-p; 8-m; 9-h; 10-a; 11-b; 12-l; 13-d; 14-r; 15-f; 16-g; 17-j; 18-k; 19-s.

━━━━━━━━ ANSWERS ━━━━━━━━

MULTIPLE CHOICE

1. a   As discussed on page 6, the textbook authors clearly believe that economic reasoning applies to just about everything. This eliminates c and d. They also carefully points out that it is not the only reasoning that can be used; hence b does not fit. So the correct answer must be a.

2. b   On page 8 of the textbook, the author states that the problem of scarcity depends upon our wants and our means of fulfilling those wants. An implication of this is that scarcity could be reduced if individuals worked more and wanted less.

3. c   On page 4 of the textbook, the authors emphasize the human action as being the reason for focusing on coordination. They explicitly point out that scarcity is important, but that the concept of coordination is broader.

4. c   As discussed on page 9, the invisible hand of the market coordinates the activities and is a composite of many individuals rather than just any one individual. If you were tempted to say b, corporations, your instincts are right, but the "overall" eliminated that as a possible answer.

5. c   As is discussed on page 6 of the book, in making economic decisions you consider that only costs from this point on are relevant; historical costs have no relevance. Since the prices of the stocks are currently the same, it doesn't matter which you sell.

6. b   As discussed on page 6, in economic decisions, you only look at costs from this point on; sunk costs are sunk costs, so tuition can be forgotten. Economic decisions focus on forward-looking marginal costs and marginal benefits.

7. a   The economic decision rule is "If benefits exceed costs, do it." As is discussed on page 6 of the text, however, the relevant benefits and relevant costs to be considered are marginal (additional) costs and marginal benefits. The answer d is definitely ruled out by the qualifying phrase referring to past benefits and costs. Thus, only a is correct.

8. c   As the textbook points out on pages 6 and 7, economists use a framework of costs and benefits initially, but then later they add the social and moral implications to their conclusions. Adding these can change the estimates of costs and benefits, and in doing so can change the result of economic analysis, so there is an integration between the two. (This was a hard question which required careful reading of the text to answer correctly.)

9. b   As discussed on page 7 of the text, opportunity costs include measures of nonmonetary costs. The other answers either do not include all the costs that an economist would consider, or are simply two words put together. The opportunity costs include the benefit forgone by undertaking an activity.

10. c   As discussed on pages 7 and 8, the correct answer is that it has nothing to do with the price you paid since that is already paid, so a and d are wrong. The opportunity cost is not zero, however, since there are costs of reading the book. The primary opportunity cost of reading the book is the value of the time you're spending on it which is determined by what you could otherwise be doing with that time.

11. d   As discussed on page 9 of the text, all of these are rationing devices. The invisible hand works through the market and thus is focused on in economics. However, the others also play a role in determining what people want, either through legal means or through social control.

12. a As discussed on pages 9 and 10 of the text, if there are significantly more of one gender than another, dates with that group must be rationed out among the other group. Economic forces will be pushing for the group in excess quantity supplied (in this case women) to pay. Economic forces may be pushing in that direction even though historical forces may push us in the opposite direction. Thus, even if males pay because of social forces, economic forces will be pushing for females to pay.

13. c Laws are legal forces.

14. a As discussed on pages 13 and 14, macroeconomics is concerned with inflation, unemployment, business cycles and growth. Microeconomics is the study of individuals and individual markets.

15. c As discussed on pages 13 and 14, macroeconomics is concerned with inflation, unemployment, business cycles and growth. Microeconomics is the study of individuals. The distribution of income is a microeconomic topic because it is concerned with the distribution of income among individuals.

16. b As discussed on pages 15 and 16, this could be either a normative or an science-of-economics statement, depending on whether there is an implicit "given the way the real-world economy operates to best achieve the growth rate you desire." Since these qualifiers are not there, "normative" is the preferable answer.

17. a As discussed on page 15 this is a positive statement. It is a statement about *what is*, not about what should be.

A1. a As discussed in Appendix A, page 22 and 23, a point represents the corresponding numbers on the horizontal and vertical number lines.

A2. c As discussed on pages 22 to 23 of Appendix A, the slope of a line is defined as rise over run. Since the rise is -2 and the run is 4, the slope of the above line is minus 1/2.

A3. b As discussed on page 23 of Appendix A, at the maximum and minimum points of a curve the slope is zero.

A4. c As discussed in Appendix A, page 22, the slope is defined as rise over run. Line C has the largest rise for a given run so c is the answer. Even though, visually, line A seems to have the same slope as line C, it has a different coordinate system. Line A has a slope of 1 whereas line B has a slope of 1/4. Always be careful about checking coordinate systems when visually interpreting a graph.

ANSWERS

SHORT-ANSWER QUESTIONS

1. Economics is the study of how individuals, firms, and government make optimal choices from among a set of alternatives when facing scarce resources. (4)

2. If the marginal benefits of doing something exceed the marginal costs, do it. If the marginal costs of doing something exceed the marginal benefits, don't do it. (6)

3. Opportunity cost is the benefit forgone by undertaking an activity. It is the benefit forgone of the next best alternative to the activity you have chosen. Otherwise stated, it is what must be given up in order to obtain something else. (7)

4. Opportunity cost is the basis of cost/benefit economic reasoning. In economic reasoning, opportunity cost is less than the benefit of what you have chosen. (7)

5. Scarcity occurs when there are not enough goods available to satisfy individuals' desires. (8)

6. An economic force is the necessary reaction to scarcity. All scarce goods must be rationed in some way. If an economic force is allowed to work through the market, that economic force becomes a market force. The invisible hand is the price mechanism, the rise and fall of prices that guides our actions in a market. Social and political forces can keep economic forces from becoming market forces. (8-9)

7. Microeconomic theory considers economic reasoning from the viewpoint of individuals and builds up while macroeconomics considers economic reasoning from the aggregate and builds down. Microeconomics studies things like household buying decisions such as how much of one's income to save and how much to consume. Macroeconomics studies things like the unemployment rate, inflation and growth. (13-14)

8. Positive economics is the study of what is and how the economy works. Normative economics is the study of what the goals of the economy should be. The science of economics is the application of the knowledge learned in positive economics to the achievement of the goals one has determined in normative economics. (15)

ANSWERS

PROBLEMS AND APPLICATIONS

1. a. The opportunity cost of going out on a date tonight that I made last Wednesday is the benefit forgone of the best alternative. If my best alternative was to study for an economics exam, it would be the increase in my exam grade that I would have gotten had I studied. Many answers are possible. (7-8)

b. The opportunity cost of breaking the date for tonight that I made last Wednesday is the benefit forgone of going out on that date. It would be all the fun I would have had on that date. Other answers are possible. (7-8)

c. The opportunity cost of working through this study guide is the benefit forgone of the next-best alternative to studying. It could be the increase in the grade I would have received by studying for another exam, or the money I could have earned if I were working at the library. Many answers are possible. (7-8)

d. The opportunity cost of buying this study guide is the benefit forgone of spending that money on the next-best alternative. Perhaps it is the enjoyment forgone of eating two pizzas. Other answers are possible. (7-8)

2. a. The opportunity cost of purchasing the maintenance contract is the benefit I could receive by spending that $750 on something else like new tires. (7-8)

b. I would need to know the benefit of the maintenance contract to assess whether the cost of $750 is worthwhile. (7-8)

c. For me, the benefit of the maintenance contract is the expected cost of future repairs that would be covered and the peace of mind of knowing that future repairs are covered by the contract. The cost is the opportunity cost of using the $750 in another way. If the benefit exceeds the cost, do it. If the cost exceeds the benefit, do not do it. (7-8)

3. a. Scarcity will fall because fewer peaches will rot. (8)

b. Scarcity of single-sex dorm rooms will rise since the number of students desiring single-sex dorm rooms has risen, but the number available has not. (8)

4. a. This is an example of an economic force. (9)

b. This is an example of legal forces. Some U.S. states have laws, called blue laws, against selling liquor on Sundays altogether or selling it before noon. (9)

c. This is an example of a legal force. This is a federal law. (9)

d. This is an example of a social force. (9)

ANSWERS

ANSWERS

A BRAIN TEASER

1. The most economical (profit-maximizing) quantity of frames to produce is 4 frames. This is because the marginal benefit of producing frames (the revenue per unit–equal to the price per unit of $250)–exceeds the marginal (extra) cost of producing frames through the first 4 frames produced. The 5th frame should not be produced because the marginal benefit (the price received) is less than the marginal (extra) cost of production. You would be adding more to your costs than to your revenues and thereby reducing your profits. Your profit would total $700 per week.

(Q)	Price (P) Marginal Benefit	Total Cost (TC)	Marginal Cost	Total Revenue (TR=PQ)	Profit (TR–TC)
0	$250	$0	—	$0	$0
1	$250	$25	$25	$250	$225
2	$250	$75	$50	$500	$425
3	$250	$150	$75	$750	$600
4	$250	$300	$150	$1000	$700
5	$250	$560	$260	$1250	$690

POTENTIAL ESSAY QUESTIONS

The following are annotated answers. They indicate the general idea behind the answer.

1. Theories are practical because they are generalizations based on real world observations or facts. They enable us to predict and to explain real-world economic behavior. Because they are generalizations, they enable us to avoid unnecessary details or facts. The drawback, however, is that because they are generalizations, at times, there will be exceptions to the prediction we would generally expect to observe.

    Facts, on the other hand, do not always speak for themselves. One can often be overwhelmed by a large set of data or facts. Not until one systematically arranges, interprets and generalizes upon facts, tying them together, and distilling out a theory (general statement) related to those facts, do they take on any real meaning. In short, theory and facts are inseparable in the scientific process because theory gives meaning to facts and facts check the validity of theory.

2. Canada is still faced with scarcity because we are unable to have as much as we would like to have. Our resources (as vast as they are) are still scarce relative to the amount of goods and services we would like to have (indeed, our wants appear to be unlimited).

3. Economics is a methodology, or an approach to how we think about the world. It does not come to us equipped with a whole set of solutions to complex real-world problems. However, it may help shed some light on the complexities of real world issues helping us to find solutions.

4. No, not necessarily. For example, if one farmer has a "bumper-crop" year, an unusually large harvest, he will be better off. But, if all farmers experience the same thing, then the increased supply of the crop made available in the market will drive its price down and all farmers will be worse off.

THE ECONOMIC ORGANIZATION OF SOCIETY

● CHAPTER AT A GLANCE

Chapter 2 highlights the importance of economics in our society, to explain how our scarce resources are allocated and coordinated on order to solve problems facing any economy. These central problems are 1.) What, and how much, to produce, 2.) how to produce it, and 3.) for whom to produce it. How these economic problems are dealt with depends on the type of economic system that has been adopted by each society.

Two of the most important economic systems are market economy and command economy. A market economy is an economic system based on private property and the market. It gives private property rights to individuals, and relies on market forces to coordinate economic activity. A command economy is an economic system that places the ownership of private property in the hands of the state and coordinates all production planning with a central authority.

This chapter also develops a sample model to explain how an economy can get the most out of its scarce resources and satisfy as many wants and desires as possible. The production possibilities curve is useful in illustrating many important economic concepts such as opportunity cost, scarcity, choice, and the principle of increasing marginal opportunity cost.

The last part of the chapter introduces students to the concept of international trade in an attempt to further the discussion of what an economy needs to do in order to efficiently use its scarce resources and given technology. Key concepts such as specialization, comparative advantage, absolute advantage, and the division of labour will be introduced.

This review is based upon the learning objectives that open the chapter.

1. <u>A market economy</u> is an economic system based on private property and the market. It gives private property rights to individuals, and relies on market forces to coordinate economic activity. (26-27)

   A market economy ("market-oriented economy") is characterized by:
   (I) mainly private ownership of resources
   (II) market system solves the What? How? and For whom? problems.

   A market economy's <u>solutions</u> to the central economic problems:
   - *What to produce: what businesses believe people want, and what is profitable.*
   - *How to produce: businesses decide how to produce efficiently, guided by their desire to make a profit.*
   - *For whom to produce: distribution according to individuals' ability and/or inherited wealth.*

2a. <u>A command economy</u> is an economic system that places the ownership of private property in the hands of the state and coordinates all production planning with a central authority. (27)

   A command economy ("government-controlled economy") is characterized by:
   (I) government control over resources
   (II) government solves the What? How? and For whom? problems.

   <u>Communism</u> seeks to abolish all private property, aside from some consumer goods, and assigns all ownership of property to the state.

   Communism's solutions to the three problems:
   - *What to produce: what central planners believe is socially beneficial.*
   - *How to produce: central planners decide, based on what they think is good for the country.*
   - *For whom to produce: central planners distribute goods based on what they determine are individuals' needs.*

2b. A mixed economy is a blend of a market economy and a command economy, that is, both private markets and the government play important roles in the economy. (28)

3a. Remember this graph:

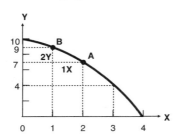

Production Possibilities Curve
Shows the trade-off (or opportunity cost) between two things.

The slope tells you the opportunity cost of good X in terms of good Y. In this particular graph, you have to give up 2 Y to get 1 X when you move from the combination of goods at point B to those at point A. (32-33)

3b . The principle of increasing marginal opportunity cost states that opportunity costs increase the more you concentrate on the activity. In order to get more of something, one must give up ever-increasing quantities of something else. (33)

The following production possibility curve and table demonstrate the principle of increasing marginal opportunity cost.

Production Possibility Curve

Production Possibility Table

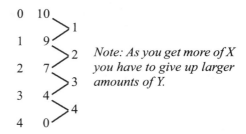

Opportunity cost of X

X	Y	(amount of Y which must be foregone)
0	10	1
1	9	2
2	7	3
3	4	4
4	0	

Note: As you get more of X you have to give up larger amounts of Y.

3c. Because decisions are contextual, what the production possibility curve for a particular decision looks like depends upon the existing institutions, and the analysis can be applied only in that institutional and historical context. (36-37)

The production possibility curve is an engine of analysis to make contextual choices, not a definitive tool to decide what one should do in all cases.

4. When individuals trade, using their comparative advantages, their combined production possibility curve shifts out. (37-39)

Specialization and trade based on comparative advantage is mutually beneficial to all involved.

Markets and trading make people better off.

To find the curve that shows the combined production possibilities for two people (assuming constant opportunity cost), do the following: (1) Find the amount of good A that can be produced if both produce good A. This is the A-axis intercept. (2) Find the amount of good B that can be produced if both produce good B. This is the B-axis intercept. (3) Determine the amount of each good A and B that can be produced if each person specializes and takes advantage of his or her comparative advantage. (4) Connect these three points and you've got it. As long as one person has a comparative advantage in one good, this curve will be bowed out.

See also, Appendix A: "The History of Economic Systems."

A1. Capitalism and socialism haven't existed forever. (45-46)

- In the eighth century, feudalism—an economic system based upon tradition—dominated.
- In the fifteenth century, feudalism gave way to mercantilism—an economic system in which government doles out the right to undertake certain economic activities.
- In the eighteenth century, mercantilism gave way to capitalism

MATCHING THE TERMS
Match the terms to their definitions

All of these key terms are found at the end of the chapter.

_____ **1.** absolute advantage

_____ **2.** allocative efficiency

_____ **3.** communism

_____ **4.** comparative advantage

_____ **5.** decision tree

_____ **6.** efficiency

_____ **7.** inefficiency

_____ **8.** input

_____ **9.** market economy

_____ **10.** NIMBY

_____ **11.** output

_____ **12.** principle of increasing marginal opportunity cost

_____ **13.** private property rights

_____ **14.** production possibility curve

_____ **15.** production possibility table

_____ **16.** productive efficiency

_____ **17.** socialism

a. Control a private individual or firm has over an asset or a right.

b. Getting less output from inputs which, if devoted to some other activity, would produce more output.

c. The result of an activity.

d. Economic system that seeks to maximize the welfare of its citizens.

e. Determines what output will be produced.

f. Represents Not In My Back Yard; a phrase used by people who may approve of a project, but don't want it to be near them.

g. Achieving a goal using as few inputs as possible.

h. The advantage that attaches to a resource when that resource is better suited to the production of one good than to the production of another good.

i. In order to get more of something, one must give up ever-increasing quantities of something else.

j. A curve measuring the maximum combination of outputs that can be obtained from a given number of inputs.

k. Achieving as much output as possible from a given amount of inputs or resources.

l. An economic system based on private property and the market in which, in principle, individuals decide how, what, and for whom to produce.

m. Table that lists the maximum combination of outputs that can be obtained from a given number of inputs for given resources and technology.

n. Visual description of sequential choices demonstrating that the cost of reversing your path rises the further one is along the path.

o. What you put into a production process to achieve an output.

p. A country produces a good that it can produce more of with the same amount of resource inputs.

q. Seeks to abolish all private property, aside from some consumer goods, and assign all ownership of property to the state.

r. An economic system based on private property and the market.

● MULTIPLE CHOICE

1. For a market to exist, you have to have
   a. public property rights.
   b. private property rights.
   c. a combination of public and private property rights.
   d. coordination rights.

2. In a market economy, individuals are encouraged to follow
   a. their own interests.
   b. their need to maximize profits.
   c. their own self-interest
   d. the wishes of the government.

3. In theory, a command economy is an economic system
   a. that places the ownership of private property in the hands of the state.
   b. is a blend of a market economy and socialism. ownership of the means of production.
   c. based on private property.
   d. based on markets.

4. A mixed economy is an economic system:
   a. that tries to organize society in the same ways as most families organize, striving to see that individuals get what they need.
   b. based on central planning and government ownership of the means of production.
   c. based on private property rights.
   d. based on markets.

5. In a market economy, the "what to produce" decision is made by
   a. consumers.
   b. the market.
   c. government.
   d. firms.

6. In a command economy, the "what to produce" decision is supposed to be made by
   a. what people want.
   b. what firms believe people want and will make a profit for firms.
   c. what government believes people want and what will make a profit for government.
   d. what central authorities want or what they believe is socially beneficial.

7. The Canadian economy today can best be described as
   a. socialist.
   b. pure capitalist.
   c. welfare capitalist.
   d. state socialist.

8. If the opportunity cost of good X in terms of good Y is 2Y, so you'll have to give up 2Y to get one X, the production possibility curve would look like
   a. a.
   b. b.
   c. c.
   d. a, b and c.

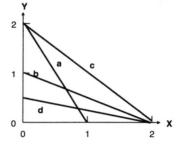

9. If the opportunity cost of good X in terms of good Y is 2Y, so you'll have to give up 2Y to get one X, the production possibility curve would look like
   a. a.
   b. b.
   c. c.
   d. d.

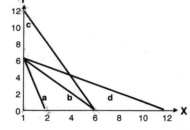

10. If the opportunity cost of good X in terms of good Y is 2Y, so you'll have to give up 2Y to get one X, the production possibility curve would look like
   a. a.
   b. b.
   c. c.
   d. a, b and c

11. If the opportunity cost is constant for all combinations, the production possibility frontier will look like

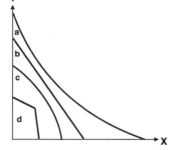

    a. a.
    b. b.
    c. c.
    d. d.

12. If the principle of increasing marginal opportunity cost applies at all points, the production possibility curve looks like

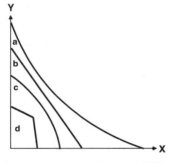

    a. a.
    b. b.
    c. c.
    d. d.

13. Given the accompanying production possibility curve, when you're moving from point C to B the opportunity cost of butter in terms of guns is

    a. 1/3.
    b. 1.
    c. 2.
    d. 3/2.

14. In the graph for question 14, in the range of points between A and B there is

    a. a high opportunity cost of guns in terms of butter.
    b. a low opportunity cost of guns in terms of butter.
    c. no opportunity cost of guns in terms of butter.
    d. a high monetary cost of guns in terms of butter.

15. In the accompanying production possibility diagram, point A would be

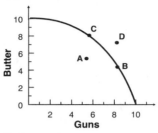

    a. an efficient point.
    b. a super-efficient point.
    c. an inefficient point.
    d. a non-attainable point.

16. A law about the growth of efficiency of computers states that computer chip technology doubles the efficiency of computers each year. If that holds true, which of the four arrows would demonstrate the appropriate shifting of the production possibility curve?

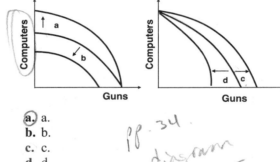

    a. a.
    b. b.
    c. c.
    d. d.

17. Say that methods of production are tied to particular income distributions, so that choosing one method will help some people but hurt others. Say also that method A produces significantly more total output than method B. In this case

    a. method A is more efficient than method B.
    b. method B is more efficient than method A.
    c. if method A produces more and gives more to the poor people, method A is more efficient.
    d. one can't say whether A or B is more efficient.

18. Productive efficiency
    a. relates to what output will be produced and who will get it.
    b. uses the most effective means to yield the maximum profits.
    c. is achieving as much output as possible from a given amount of inputs or resources.
    d. relates to the invisible hand.

19. If Canada and Japan have production possibility curves as shown in the diagram below, at what point would they most likely be after trade?
    a. A
    b. B
    c. C
    d. D

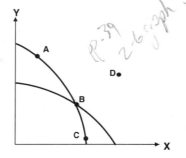

A1. In feudalism, the most important force was
    a. the price mechanism.
    b. cultural force.
    c. legal force.
    d. anarchy.

A2. In mercantilism, the guiding force is
    a. the price mechanism.
    b. legal force.
    c. cultural force.
    d. anarchy.

A3. Mercantilism evolved into capitalism because
    a. government investments did not pan out.
    b. the Industrial Revolution undermined the craft guilds' mercantilist method of production.
    c. the guilds wanted more freedom.
    d. serfs wanted more freedom.

A4. Marx saw the strongest tension between
    a. rich capitalists and poor capitalists.
    b. capitalists and government.
    c. capitalists and the proletariat.
    d. government and the proletariat.

A5. State socialism is an economic system in which
    a. business sees to it that people work for their own good until they can be relied upon to do that on their own.
    b. business sees to it that people work for the common good until they can be relied upon to do that on their own.
    c. government sees to it that people work for their own good until they can be relied upon to do so on their own.
    d. government sees to it that people work for the common good until they can be relied upon to do so on their own.

● SHORT-ANSWER QUESTIONS

1. What is a market economy? How does it solve the three central economic problems?

2. What is a command economy? In practice, how has it solved the three central economic problems?

3. Name the economic systems that have evolved from the eighth century to today in the order that they occurred.

4. How can markets coordinate economic decisions without the active involvement of government?

5. Design a grade production possibility curve of studying economics and English, and show how it demonstrates the concept of opportunity cost.

6. State the principle of increasing marginal opportunity cost.

7. What would the production possibility curve look like if opportunity cost were constant?

8. What happens to the production possibility curve with trade? Why does trade make individuals better off?

9. Why is the production possibility curve more useful in discussing small changes than in discussing changes in entire economic systems?

A1. Why did feudalism evolve into mercantilism?

A2. Why did mercantilism evolve into capitalism?

A3. Explain what is meant by the statement that capitalism has evolved into welfare capitalism.

PROBLEMS AND APPLICATIONS

1. Suppose a restaurant has the following production possibility table:

Resources devoted to pizza in % of total	Output of pizza in pies per week	Resources devoted to spaghetti in % of total	Output of spaghetti in bowls per week
100	50	0	0
80	40	20	10
60	30	40	17
40	20	60	22
20	10	80	25
0	0	100	27

a. Plot the restaurant's production possibility curve. Put output of pizza in pies on the horizontal axis.

b. What happens to the marginal opportunity cost as the output of bowls of spaghetti increases?

c. What would happen to the production possibility curve if the restaurant found a way to toss and cook pizzas faster?

d. What would happen to the production possibility curve if the restaurant bought new stoves and ovens that cooked both pizzas and spaghetti faster?

2. Suppose Ecoland has the following production possibilities table:

% resources devoted to production of guns	Number of guns	% resources devoted to production of butter	Pounds of butter
100	50	0	0
80	40	20	5
60	30	40	10
40	20	60	15
20	10	80	20
0	0	100	25

a. Plot the production possibility curve for the production of guns and butter. Put the number of guns on the horizontal axis.

b. What is the per unit opportunity cost of increasing the production of guns from 20 to 30? From 40 to 50?

c. What happens to the opportunity cost of producing guns as the production of guns increases?

d. What is the per unit opportunity cost of increasing the production of butter from 10 to 15? From 20 to 25?

e. What happens to the opportunity cost of producing butter as the production of butter increases?

f. Given this production possibility curve, is producing 26 guns and 13 pounds of butter possible?

g. Is producing 34 guns and 7 pounds of butter possible? Is it efficient?

3. Using the following production possibility tables and using production possibility curves, show how the United States and Japan would be better off specializing in the production of either food or machinery and then trading rather than producing both food and machinery themselves and not trading.

United States Production per year		Japan Production per year	
Tons food	1000 units machinery	Tons food	1000 units machinery
10	0	12.5	0
8	5	10	1
6	10	7.5	2
4	15	5	3
2	20	2.5	4
0	25	0	5

4. Assume that France can produce wine at 25 francs per bottle and can produce butter at 5 francs per pound. Assume that Italy can produce wine at 16,000 lire per bottle and butter at 10,000 lire per pound.

a. In terms of pounds of butter, what is the opportunity cost of producing wine in each country?

b. Who has the comparative advantage in producing butter?

c. Which country should most likely specialize in wine and which should specialized in butter?

◉ A BRAIN TEASER

1. Consider the production possibilities for an entire nation. Within any national economy, there are only two general kinds of products that can be produced–consumer products and capital products. Consumer products (e.g. food, clothes, medical services, etc ...) satisfy our wants directly when we use them and while we consume them. Capital products (e.g. machines, and other plant and equipment) satisfy our wants indirectly and in the future because they increase our productivity and help us produce even more products over time. Answer the following questions based on the production possibilities of consumer and capital products for a national economy shown in the graph below.

a. Between the production possibilities A and B, which would provide the greatest amount of current satisfaction? Why?

b. What is the opportunity cost of moving from point B to A?

c. Consider the choice of currently producing a relatively large amount of consumer products shown at point B (which means, given limited resources, relatively few capital products can be produced), compared to producing a relatively large amount of capital products now, shown at point A (which means relatively few consumer

products can be produced). Which of these two points (or combinations of consumer and capital goods production) do you think will increase the production possibilities (shift the curve to the right) the most over time giving rise to the greatest rate of economic growth? Why? *(Hint: Whenever workers have more capital, like factories and machinery to work with, then they become more productive.)*

◉ POTENTIAL ESSAY QUESTIONS

You may also see essay questions similar to the "Problems & Applications" and "Brain Teasers" exercises.

1. There has always been much political debate between "conservatives" and "liberals" in this country, as well as in other countries, over what constitutes the "appropriate" role for government to play in correcting for the problems of a market-oriented, capitalist economy.

    a. Is this controversy ever likely to go away? Why or why not?

    b. Could greater reliance upon positive economic analysis of "what is" as opposed to normative economic analysis of "what ought to be" help reduce some of this controversy?

2. Contrast capitalism's and socialism's solutions to the three economic problems.

3. What is a decision tree? What is its significance?

ANSWERS

MATCHING

1-p; 2-e; 3-q; 4-h; 5-n; 6-g; 7-b; 8-o; 9-r; 10-f; 11-c; 12-i; 13-a; 14-j; 15-m.;16-k;17-d.

ANSWERS

MULTIPLE CHOICE

1.   **b**   As discussed on page 27 and 28, markets require private property rights because these give people the framework within which they can trade and markets rely on trading. Markets also require government, but government and public property rights are not the same thing, which rules out a and c. And d is a throwaway answer.

2.   **c**   As discussed on pages 27, c represents a major characteristic of a market economy.

3.   **a**   As discussed on page 27, a is the correct answer. Answer b simply cannot exist, while c and d are characteristics of a market economy.

4.   **b**   As discussed on page 28, b is the correct answer. Answer a is a characteristic of the command economy, while c and d are characteristics of a market economy.

5.   **b**   In a market economy, firms decide what to produce based on what they think will sell. (26-27)

6.   **d**   As discussed on page 27, central authorities decide what to produce based upon what they believe society needs. We should point out that this is *ideally*; in practice, central authorities may not be concerned with society. Thus c is a possible answer, but the term "profit" makes it unacceptable. Central planners would not get profit—they might get rich, but it wouldn't be through profits.

7.   **c**   As discussed on pages 28 and 46, since in Canada the market is allowed to operate, but the government intervenes in determining distribution, Canada is best described as welfare capitalist.

8.   **a**   As discussed on pages 32-35, the production possibility curve tells how much of one good you must give up to get more of the other good; here you must give up 2Y to get one X, making a the correct answer.

9.   **c**   As discussed on pages 32-35, the production possibility curve tells how much of one good you must give up to get more of another good. Opportunity cost is a ratio; it determines the slope, not the position, of the ppc curve. Thus, the correct answer is c because the 12 to 6 trade-off reduces to a 2 to 1 trade-off.

10.   **d**   As discussed on pages 32-35, the production possibility curve tells how much of one good you must give up to get more of the other good. Opportunity cost is a ratio; it determines the slope, not the position, of the ppc curve. Since all have the same correct slope, all three are correct, so d is the right answer.

11.   **b**   As discussed on pages 30 and 31, if the opportunity costs are constant, the ppc is a straight line, so b must be the answer.

12.   **c**   As discussed on page 33, with increasing marginal opportunity costs, as you produce more and more of a good, you will have to give up more and more of the other good to do so. This means that the slope of the ppc must be bowed outward, so c is the correct answer. (See Figure 2-2, page 32 for an in-depth discussion.)

13.   **d**   As discussed on pages 30-32, the slope of the ppc measures the trade-off of one good for the other. Since moving from point c to b means giving up 3 guns for 2 pounds of butter, the correct answer is 3/2 or d.

14.   **b**   As discussed on pages 31-32, the flatter the slope, the higher the opportunity cost of the good measured on the vertical axis; alternatively, the flatter the slope the lower the opportunity cost of that good measured on the horizontal axis. In the AB range the slope is flat so guns have a low opportunity cost in terms of butter; one need give up only one pound of butter to get four guns.

15. c   As discussed on page 34 (See Figure 2-3), point A is an inefficient point.

16. a   As discussed on page 34 (See Figure 2-3), technological change that improves the efficiency of producing a good shifts the ppc out in that good, but not in the other good. So a is the correct answer.

17. d   The answer is "You can't say," as discussed on pages 34-37. The term "efficiency" involve *using the most effective means to yield the maximum benefits.* Without specifying one's goal, one cannot say what method is more efficient. The concept efficiency generally presumes that the goal includes preferring more to less, so if any method is more productive, it will be method A. But because there are distributional effects that involve making additional judgments, the correct answer is d. Some students may have been tempted to choose c because their goals involve more equity, but that is their particular judgment, and not all people may agree. Thus c would be incorrect, leaving d as the correct answer.

18. c   As discussed on page 33, productive efficiency deals with producing the most output for a given amount of scarce resources and a given level of technology. Answer a relates to allocative efficiency, while b is just wrong. Productive efficiency does not deal with profits.

19. d   As discussed in Figure 2-6 on page 39, with trade, both countries can attain a point outside each production possibility curve. The only point not already attainable is D.

A1. b   As discussed on page 41, in feudalism tradition reigned.

A2. b   As discussed on page 42, in mercantilism government directed the economy.

A3. b   See page 46.

A4. c   See pages 49-50. To the degree that government was controlled by capitalists, d would be a correct answer, but it is not as good an answer as c, which represents the primary conflict. Remember, you are choosing the answer that best reflects the discussion in the text.

A5. d   See page 51.

ANSWERS

SHORT-ANSWER QUESTIONS

1. A market economy is an economic system based on private property and the market. It gives private property rights to individuals, and relies on market forces to coordinate economic activity. In a market economy, businesses produce what they believe people want and think they can make a profit supplying. Businesses decide how to produce, guided by their desire to make a profit. Goods are distributed according to individuals' ability and/or inherited wealth. (26-27)

2. A command economy is an economic system that places the ownership of private property in the hands of the state and coordinates all production planning with a central authority. The central authorities decide what is to be produced, how much is produced, who is to produce it, and how it is to be distributed. (27)

3. Economic systems have evolved from feudalism (from the 8th to the 15th centuries) to mercantilism (from the mid-15th to the 18th centuries) to capitalism (from the 18th century to today). Economic systems are constantly evolving. (45-46)

4. The invisible hand — the price mechanism — guides the actions of suppliers and consumers to the general good. That is, competition directs individuals pursuing profit to do what society needs to have done. Markets coordinate economic decisions by turning self-interest into social good. (26-27)

5. The production possibility curve shows the highest combination of grades you can get with 20 hours of studying economics and English. The grade received in economics is on the vertical axis and the grade received in English is on the horizontal axis. The graph tells us the opportunity cost of spending any combination of 20 hours on economics and English. For example, the opportunity cost of increasing your grade in economics by 6 points is decreasing your English grade by 4 points (2/3 grade point reduction in English for one grade point improvement in Economics). (29-33)

6. The principle of increasing marginal opportunity cost states that in order to get more of something, one must give up ever-increasing quantities of something else. (33)

7. Such a production possibility curve would be a straight line connecting the maximum number of units that could be produced of each product if all inputs were devoted to one or the other good. (31-32)

8. By comparing individual production possibility curves, one can determine those activities in which each has a comparative advantage. By concentrating on those activities for which one has a comparative advantage and trading those goods for goods for which others have a comparative advantage, individuals can end up with a combination of goods not attainable without trade. The production possibility curve shifts out with trade. (28-39)

9. The production possibility curve is best used when discussing small changes because the relationships between costs and production can be assumed to remain constant. Changes in economic systems can change the relationships that affect costs in everyday decisions and in production. The text's example of how changing

from socialism to capitalism would affect the production possibility curve is a good example of how an analysis using just the production possibility curve can mask the probability that beneficial results of major structural changes may take many years. (36-37)

A1. Feudalism evolved into mercantilism as the development of money allowed trade to grow, undermining the traditional base of feudalism. Politics rather than social forces came to control the central economic decisions. (45-48)

A2. Mercantilism evolved into capitalism because the Industrial Revolution shifted the economic power base away from craftsmen toward industrialists and toward an understanding that markets could coordinate the economy without the active involvement of the government. (48-49)

A3. Capitalism has evolved into welfare capitalism. That is, the human abuses marked by early capitalist developments led to a criticism of the market economic system. Political forces have changed government's role in the market, making government a key player in determining distribution and in making the what, how, and for whom decisions. This characterizes the Canadian economy today. (46)

ANSWERS

PROBLEMS AND APPLICATIONS

1. a. The restaurant's production possibility curve is shown below. (29-32)

    b. The number of pizza pies that must be given up to make an additional bowl of spaghetti increases as the number of bowls of spaghetti produced increases. (32-33)

c. If the restaurant found a way to toss and cook pizzas faster, the production possibility curve would rotate out along the pizza axis as shown below. (34)

d. The production possibility curve would shift out to the right as shown in the figure below. (34)

2. a. The production possibility curve is a straight line as shown below. (29-35)

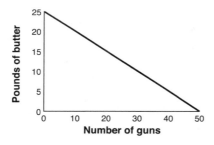

b. The opportunity cost of increasing the production of guns from 20 to 30 is 0.5 pounds of butter per gun. The opportunity cost of increasing the production of guns from 40 to 50 is also 0.5 pounds of butter per gun. (29-32)

c. The opportunity cost of producing guns stays the same as the production of guns increases. (29-32)

d. The opportunity cost of increasing the production of butter from 10 to 15 is 2 guns per pound of butter. The opportunity cost of increasing the production of butter from 20 to 25 is 2 guns per pound of butter. (29-32)

e. The opportunity cost of producing butter stays the same as the production of butter increases. (29-32)

f. Producing 26 guns and 13 pounds of butter is not attainable given this production possibility curve. We can produce 20 guns and 15 pounds of butter. To produce six more guns, Ecoland must give up 3 pounds of butter. Ecoland can produce only 26 guns and 12 pounds of butter. (29-32)

g. Ecoland can produce 34 guns and 7 pounds of butter. To see this, begin at 30 guns and 10 pounds of butter. To produce 4 more guns, 2 pounds of butter must be given up. Ecoland can produce 34 guns and 8 pounds of butter, which is more than 34 guns and 7 pounds of butter. This is an inefficient point of production. (29-32)

3. The production possibility of producing food and machinery for both Japan and the United States is shown in the graph below. The combined production possibility curve with trade is also shown. Clearly, trade shifts the production possibility curve out, showing that the two countries are better off with trade. The United States has a comparative advantage in the production of machinery. It must give up only 0.4 tons of food for each additional thousand units of machinery produced. Japan must give up 2.5 tons of food for each additional thousand units of machinery produced. A specific example is if Japan produced 12.5 tons of food and no machines while the United States produced 0 tons of food and 25 thousand units of machinery, Japan could offer the United States 2 tons of food for 3 thousand units of machinery. The United States would be at point A and Japan would be at point B. Each would be able to attain a level of production not attainable before. (29-32)

4. a. In France, the opportunity cost of producing wine is 5 pounds of butter. In Italy, the opportunity cost of producing wine is 1.6 pounds of butter. Calculate this by finding how much butter must be forgone for each bottle of wine in each country. (29-32)

b. France has the comparative advantage in producing butter because it can produce butter for a lower opportunity cost. (29-32)

c. Italy should specialize in producing wine and France should specialize in producing butter assuming one can produce only wine and the other must produce only butter. This is concluded from the principle of comparative advantage. (29-32)

ANSWERS

A BRAIN TEASER

1. a. Production possibility B. Why? Because consumer products provide for *current* satisfaction, and at B we are getting a relatively larger amount of consumer products.

b. 3 units of consumer products.

c. Point A. Producing a relatively larger amount of capital products now means workers will have more plant and equipment to work with in the future. This will increase worker's productivity and the nation's production possibilities over time. Producing more capital is an ingredient for economic growth (greater production possibilities).

ANSWERS

POTENTIAL ESSAY QUESTIONS

The following are annotated answers. They indicate the general idea behind the answer.

1. a. Although there is no debate over the existence of market failures, there is much debate over the extent to which they exist. Controversy often begins with equally reasonable and well intentioned people assessing the extent of the problem differently. (For example, consider the controversy surrounding the extent of ozone damage.) If a consensus is reached, then the same equally reasonable, equally well intentioned people will likely measure the benefits and costs associated with government involvement differently. This gives rise to debate concerning the appropriate extent of government involvement.

b. There will likely always be some degree of inefficiency in measuring the benefits and the costs associated with any problem and of any government involvement. However, greater reliance upon positive economic analysis, because it is "objective" and deals with "what is," should help everyone to avoid emotion and to see more clearly the extent of any problem. Moreover, it should help everyone to more clearly assess the benefits and costs associated with government action, or inaction, in a particular case. This is because positive economics helps us to predict or anticipate consequences. As was stated in the first chapter, "the art of economics is the application of the knowledge learned in positive economics to the achievement of the goals determined in normative economics. In the art of economics, it is difficult to be objective but it is important to try." People can argue until they are blue in the face about "what ought to be" the appropriate role for government. But that emotionally held belief, when enacted as policy, usually has little to do with the resulting real-world consequences. Too often, dismal consequences were predicted using positive economic analysis, but were ignored. This applies with equal weight to many "conservative" and "liberal" positions alike. We have experienced a rich history of real-world cases to show that sometimes government can help while at other times it only makes matters worse. That which is effective, however, may not be "politically correct" at the time.

2. Both economic systems have to answer the three central economic problems. (1) What to produce? In capitalism, firms produce what they believe people want and will make a profit. In socialism, in practice central planners decide what was produced. (2) How to produce? In capitalism firms decide how to produce efficiently, guided by their desire to make a profit. In socialism, central planners decide how to produce. (3) For whom to produce? In capitalism, distribution is decided according to ability and inherited wealth. In socialism, distribution is according to individuals' needs (as determined by central planners).

3. A decision tree is a visual description of sequential choices. It points out that decisions are made in context. See page 36.

THE CANADIAN ECONOMY IN A GLOBAL SETTING

● CHAPTER AT A GLANCE

Chapter 3 outlines how business, households and governments interact in a market economy. There are two broad categories that make up a market economy. The factor market, where households have the freedom to choose to supply the resources that they own, namely labour, and where firms employ those resources and pay households for that right. The goods market is where the firms produce goods and services demanded by households, which households purchase with the income earned in the factor market. The market economy brings firms and households together, which, with the forces of supply and demand, determine prices and allocate our scarce resources.

In essence, government has two key roles in our market economy. One is being a referee, setting rules that determine relations between business and households. This would include setting an appropriate legal system and regulations to guide behaviour. The other role is being an actor—collecting money in taxes and spending that money on their own projects such as education and defense.

The last part of the chapter discusses how economic entities such as households, business and government interact in the global economy. A large portion of goods purchased by households are produced by foreign countries. Firms are now competing internationally as well as within Canada and the role of government must include setting an environment conducive to freer trade. It is an accepted fact that engaging in international trade improves the economic well-being of our society. As result, economists have entered a variety of international trade agreements and organizations such as GATT, the WTO, the EU, and NAFTA.

This review is based upon the learning objectives that open the chapter.

1. Businesses, households and government interact in a market economy. (52)

    For a bird's-eye view of the Canadian economy, see Figure 3-1 (sometimes called the "circular flow of income model"). Be able to draw and explain it.

    Note: there are 3 basic economic institutions:

    *   *Businesses:*
        a. Supply goods in goods market
        b. Demand factors in factor market
        c. Pay taxes and receive benefits from government

    *   *Households:*
        a. Supply factors
        b. Demand goods
        c. Pay taxes and receive benefits from government

    *   *Government:*
        a. Demands goods
        b. Demands factors
        c. Collects taxes and provide services

2. The nature of business is changing with the emergence of the digital economy. E-commerce has grown enormously. Conducting business on the Internet removes the importance of geography and location for firms and reduces the costs of doing business. (55-56)

3. Households are groups of individuals living together and making joint decisions. They ultimately have great influence over government and business. Households' votes determines government policy, while decisions regarding the supply and labour and consumer preferences dictate what to produce. (56-57)

Note:
* *Do we control business and government, or do they control us?*
* *The distribution of income (rich vs. poor) determines the "for whom" question. If you're rich, you get more.*
* *Social forces affect what business and government do or don't do.*

4a. Two general roles of government are: (57-59)

* *As an actor:* Collects taxes and spends money.
* *As referee:* Sets the rules governing relations between households and businesses.

4b. For the government of Canada, the major sources of income are income taxes, consumption taxes, property taxes, and contributions to social insurance plans. The major sources of expenditures are social services, general purpose transfers, education and health care. (58)

5a. The importance of international trade to the Canadian economy is substantial. Exports as a share of GDP is 41.1%, one of the highest in the industrialized world. (60-61)

5b. The United States, the European Union and the Pacific Rim make up the largest percentage of total Canadian exports. (61)

See Figure 3-4 (a and b) on page 61 for Canadian exports and imports by region.

5c. Two ways in which *inter*national trade differs from *intra*national (domestic) trade are: (64-67)

* International trade involves potential barriers to trade; and

Free and open international trade along the lines of comparative advantage is mutually beneficial to all economies involved.

* International trade involves multiple currencies.

Foreign exchange markets exist to swap currencies.

6a. Three global trade organizations include: (67)

* The World Trade Organization (WTO),
* The General Agreement on Tariffs and Trade (GATT); and
* The North American Free Trade Agreement (NAFTA).

These are organizations that work toward lowering trade barriers among countries.

Economists generally like markets and favour trade being as free as possible.

6b. Four important international economic institutions are: (68)
* The UN
* The World Court
* The World Bank; and
* The IMF.

They are designed to enhance trade negotiations (to avoid trade wars).

Think internationally because we live in a global economy.

6c. In addition to formal institutions, there are informal meetings of various countries. (68)
* Group of Five
* Group of Ten

MATCHING THE TERMS
Match the terms to their definitions

All of these key terms are found at the end of the chapter.

____ 1. balance of trade	**a.** A free trade association of 25 western European countries.
____ 2. business	**b.** Principle that the consumer's wishes rule what's produced.
____ 3. consumer sovereignty	**c.** Corporations with substantial operations on both production and sales in more than one country.
____ 4. current account balance	
____ 5. entrepreneurship	**d.** Measures trade services.
____ 6. European Union	**e.** The difference between exports and imports of goods.
____ 7. exchange rate	**f.** Market in which one country's currency can be exchanged for another country's.
____ 8. exports	
____ 9. foreign exchange market	**g.** A U.S.-Canada-Mexico free trade zone that is phasing in reductions in tariffs.
____ 10. free trade associations	**h.** The ability to organize and get something done.
____ 11. General Agreement on Tariffs and Trade (GATT)	**i.** Measures trade in goods and services and includes the interest payments made to foreigners for the use of their savings.
____ 12. global corporations	**j.** Limitations on how much of a good can be shipped into a country.
____ 13. Group of Five	
____ 14. Group of Ten	**k.** A multinational, international financial institution concerned primarily with monetary issues.
____ 15. households	**l.** The result of a country's imports exceeding its exports.
____ 16. IMF	**m.** A tax on an imported good.
____ 17. imports	**n.** The difference between the value of goods and services Canada exports and the value of goods and services it imports.
____ 18. merchandise trade balance	
____ 19. nontariff barriers	**o.** An organization committed to getting countries to agree not to impose new tariffs or other trade restrictions except under certain limited conditions.
____ 20. NAFTA	
____ 21. profit	**p.** The Group of Ten plus Canada, Italy, Belguim, the Netherlands and Switzerland.
____ 22. quotas	**q.** Certificates of ownership in a company.
____ 23. service balance	**r.** The rate at which one currency is traded for another.
____ 24. tariffs	**s.** What is left over from total revenues after all the appropriate costs have been subtracted.
____ 25. trade deficit	
____ 26. trade surplus	**t.** The value of goods purchased abroad.
____ 27. transfer payments	**u.** Japan, Germany, Britain, France and the United States.
____ 28. World Bank	**v.** Groups of countries that have reduced or eliminated trade barriers among themselves.
____ 29. World Trade Organization (WTO)	

w. Name given to private producing units in our society.

x. When a country exports more than it imports.

y. An agreement among many subscribing countries on certain conditions of international trade.

z. The value of goods sold abroad.

z1. A multi-national, international financial institution that works with developing countries to secure low-interest loans.

z2. Group of individuals living together and making joint decisions.

z2. Indirect regulation restricting imports and exports.

● MULTIPLE CHOICE

Circle the one best answer for each of the following questions:

1. In the factor market:
    a. businesses supply goods and services to households and government.
    b. government provides income support to households unable to supply factors of production to businesses.
    c. households supply labour and other factors of production to businesses.
    d. households purchase goods and services from businesses.

2. The ability to organize and get something done generally goes under the term
    a. the corporate approach.
    b. entrepreneurship.
    c. efficiency.
    d. consumer sovereignty.

3. Initial public offerings are a way for businesses to:
    a. finance expansion of an existing privately held business.
    b. finance expansion of an existing publicly-held business.
    c. increase sales by bringing in new customers.
    d. consolidate ownership of a company among a few stockholders.

4. The largest percentage of federal government expenditures is on:
    a. education
    b. health
    c. transportation and communication
    d. social services

5. The largest revenue source of provincial and local expenditures is on:
    a. income taxes
    b. general purpose transfers
    c. investment income
    d. sale of goods and services

6. All of the following are examples of government as referee *except*:
    a. setting limitations on when someone can be fired.
    b. collecting consumption taxes from workers' paychecks.
    c. setting minimum safety regulations for the workplace.
    d. disallowing two competitors to meet to fix prices of their products.

7. Debtor nations will
    a. run trade deficits.
    b. run trade surpluses.
    c. not necessarily run a trade surplus or a trade deficit.
    d. run foreign exchange sales.

8. If a country has a trade deficit, it is:
    a. consuming more than it is producing.
    b. borrowing from foreigners.
    c. selling financial assets.
    d. selling real assets.

9. In 2002 and 2003, Canada had a:
    a. services deficit.
    b. merchandise trade surplus.
    c. current account surplus.
    d. trade deficit.

10. An important way in which international trade differs from domestic trade is:
    a. international trade involves potential barriers to the flow of inputs and outputs.
    b. the use of different communication systems.
    c. the use of different transportation systems.
    d. that money is not used in international trade.

11. A quota is
    a. taxes on imports.
    b. indirect regulatory restrictions.
    c. limitations on how much a good can be shipped into a country.
    d. taxes on exports.

12. In a foreign exchange market:
    a. imports are exchanged for exports.
    b. exports are exchanged for imports.
    c. labour services, exports, imports and currencies are exchanged.
    d. one currency is exchanged for another.

13. The general plan of NAFTA is
    a. to adjust tariffs so that they are equal across products and countries.
    b. to replace tariffs with quotas.
    c. to move towards political integration among Canada, Mexico, and the United States.
    d. to remove tariffs on most goods traded in North America within 15 years of signing.

14. The EU is an economic free trade area
    a. but not a political organization.
    b. and a loose political organization.
    c. and a federation of individual countries.
    d. and a nation-state.

15. The Group of Five consists of
    a. Japan, Germany, Britain, France and the United States.
    b. Japan, Germany, Britain, France and Italy.
    c. Italy, Japan, Germany, Britain, and the United States
    d. Canada, Japan, Germany, the United States, and France.

16. The WTO is an organization mainly committed to
    a. increasing competitive quotas and tariffs among countries
    b. legalizing international trade by getting countries to refrain from imposing new tariffs or restrictions.
    c. creating independent trade zones throughout the world
    d. increasing security alliances around the world

17. If a country is found guilty in the World Court
    a. its leaders will be put in jail.
    b. it will be forced by the UN to pay a fine.
    c. it may or may not comply with the remedy decreed by the Court, depending on whether it chooses to comply or not.
    d. its dues to finance the World Court will be doubled.

● SHORT-ANSWER QUESTIONS

1. Draw a diagram of the Canadian economy showing the three groups that comprise the Canadian economy. What is the role of each group in the economy?

2. Although businesses decide what to produce, who ultimately makes the decision what to produce?

3. Why is much of the economic decision-making done by business and government even though households have the ultimate power?

4. What are two general roles of government?

5. Which two countries are Canada's largest trading partners? With which two other areas does Canada primarily trade?

6. State two ways international trade differs from domestic trade.

7. Name 3 important free trade organizations and 4 important international economic policy organizations.

PROBLEMS AND APPLICATIONS

1. State whether the trade restriction is a quota, tariff, or nontariff barrier.
   a. The EU requires beef to be free of growth-inducing hormones in order to be traded in EU markets.

   b. Hong Kong has maintained rice import controls on quantity since 1955 in order to keep local rice importers in business and to secure a steady wartime food supply.

   c. To encourage domestic production of automobile parts, Japan limits the importation of automobile parts according to a rigid schedule of numbers.

   d. The United States charges French wineries 10% of the value of each case of French wine imported into the United States.

2. Complete the blanks in the table below.

Currency	USD equivalent	Currency per USD
British Pound	_____	0.61
German Mark (DM)	_____	1.90
Sri Lankan rupee	_____	72.50
Japanese yen	0.0095	_____
Eu euro	1.03	_____

   a. How many Sri Lankan rupees buys one Japanese yen?

   b. How many USD (U.S. dollars) are needed to buy a German Porsche at a cost of 92,000 DM?

   c. How many British pound(s) buys one euro?

A BRAIN TEASER

1. a. What are the three general types of trade barriers which a nation's government might impose on foreign producers?

b. Assuming one of these trade barriers is going to be imposed, which one do you think might be most beneficial to the government imposing the trade barrier? Why?

● POTENTIAL ESSAY QUESTIONS

You may also see essay questions similar to the "Problems & Applications" and "Brain Teasers" exercises.

1. Uglies is a brand of boxer shorts sold on the Internet. Their claim to fame is that each side of the shorts don't match. Their marketing ploy is boxer-short-of-the-month club. Suppose you were the one who came up with the idea for Uglies and wanted to start the business. What form of business would you select and why? (Thinking about where the funds to start the business will come from, who will make the shorts, and how the shorts will be sold will help you answer the question.)

2. Is it better to be a creditor nation or a debtor nation? Explain your answer.

3. Large trade deficits often inspire politicians to call for trade restrictions prohibiting imports. However, most economists oppose such restrictions because of the negative effects they may create. What are some of the problems associated with trade restrictions?

■■■■■ ANSWERS ■■■■■

MATCHING

1-n; 2-w; 3-b; 4-i; 5-h; 6-a; 7-r; 8-z; 9-f; 10-v; 11-y; 12-c; 13-u; 14-p; 15-z2; 16-k; 17-t; 18-e; 19-z3; 20-g; 21-s; 22-j; 23-d; 24-m; 25-l; 26-x; 27-q; 28-z1; 29-o.

■■■■■ ANSWERS ■■■■■

MULTIPLE CHOICE

1. c   See page 52-53.

2. b   See page 54.

3. a   An initial public offering is when a company first offers some of its stock to the general public. See pages 55.

4. d   See Figure 3-3b on page 58.

5. a   See Figure 3-2a on page 57.

6. b   Collecting consumption taxes is government as an actor. Government as referee refers to laws regulating interaction between households and businesses. See pages 57-58.

7. c   A debtor nation may currently be running a surplus if it ran deficits in the past. See p. 63-64.

8. a   If a country has a trade deficit, it is importing (consuming) more than it is exporting (producing). See page 63.

9. c   See page 64.

10. a   International trade involves potential barriers to trade. See page 64.

11. c   See page 65.

12. d   See page 67.

13. d   See page 67.

14. b   See page 67.

15. a   See page 68 for the list of the Group of Five.

16. b See page 67.

17. c The World Court has no enforcement mechanism. See page 68.

ANSWERS

SHORT-ANSWER QUESTIONS

1. As seen in the diagram below, the three groups that comprise the Canadian economy are households, business, and government. Households supply factors of production to businesses; businesses produce goods and services and sell them to households and government. The government taxes businesses and households, buys goods and services from businesses and labour services from households, and provides goods and services to each of them. (52-53)

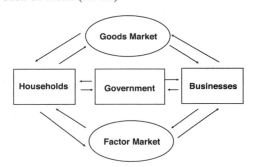

2. Although businesses decide what to produce, they are guided by consumer sovereignty. Businesses want to make a profit, so they will produce what they believe consumers will buy. That is not to say that businesses don't affect the desires of consumers through advertising. (54)

3. Business and government do much of the economic decision-making even though households retain the ultimate power. This is because in practice people have delegated much of that power to institutions and representatives – firms and the government – that are sometimes removed from the people. In the short run, households only indirectly control government and business. (56-57)

4. Two general roles of the government are as referee and actor. (56-57)

5. The United States, the European Union and the Pacific Rim make up the largest percentage of total Canadian exports. Canada also trades with the Pacific Rim. (61)

6. The two ways in which international trade differs from intranational trade are: (1) International trade involves potential barriers to trade; that is, producers' rights to sell can be limited by government-imposed quotas, tariffs, and nontariff barriers. (2) International trade involves multiple currencies that are traded in foreign exchange markets. (64-65)

7. Three important free trade organizations are the World Trade Organization (WTO), The North American Free Trade Association (NAFTA), and the General Agreement on Tariffs and Trade (GATT) the predecessor to the WTO. Four important international economic policy organizations are the United Nations (U.N.), World Bank, World Court, and the International Monetary Fund (IMF). (67-68)

ANSWERS

PROBLEMS AND APPLICATIONS

1. **a.** Nontariff barrier because this a regulation that has the final effect of reducing imports without a tax or numerical limitation. (64-65)

   b. Quota. It is a numerical restriction on the amount of rice entering the country. (64-65)

   c. Quota because it is a numerical restriction on imports. (64-65)

   d. Tariff because it is a tax on imports. (64-65)

2. The table is filled in below. (64-65)

Currency	USD equivalent	Currency per USD
British Pound	1.6393	0.61
German Mark (DM)	0.5263	1.90
Sri Lankan rupee	0.0138	72.50
Japanese yen	0.0095	105.26
Eu euro	1.03	0.97

    a. 0.6888 rupees buys one Japanese yen. Calculate this by first finding the yen per dollar (105.26) and Sri Lankan rupees per dollar (72.50). To find rupees per yen, divide rupees per dollar by Japanese yen per dollar. (64-67)

    b. $48,421.05 are needed to buy a German Porsche Carrera at a cost of 92,000 DM. To calculate this, find the German mark per U.S. dollar (1.90) and divide this into the cost of the Porsche in marks. (64-67)

    c. 0.6289 pounds are needed to buy one Euro. Calculate this by finding the British pound per USD (0.61) and euro per dollar (0.97). To find British pounds per euro, divide British pounds per dollar euro per dollar. (64-67)

■■■■■■ **ANSWERS** ■■■■■■

A BRAIN TEASER

1. **a.** The three general types of trade barriers a nation's government might impose on foreign producers are tariffs, quotas, and nontariff barriers. (64-65)

    b. Although all barriers will be costly for the host government to "police," only tariffs (a tax on an imported product) will raise revenues for the government. (64-65)

■■■■■■ **ANSWERS** ■■■■■■

POTENTIAL ESSAY QUESTIONS

The following are annotated answers. They indicate the general idea behind the answer.

1. The answer to this question will vary from person to person and will depend upon personal finances, how much risk one is able and willing to undertake, how much responsibility one wants to take on, and whether or not you want to share in any profits. Given limited financial resources, I'd find a partner I can trust who has the funds needed to launch a web site, hire a firm to carry out transactions and build inventory. With a partnership I can share the work and the risks of the venture. Since the liability associated with selling boxer shorts is not too great, unlimited liability with a partnership is not a problem. Not a corporation because establishing one is a legal hassle requiring even more money. Not a sole proprietorship because I don't have the funds to start the company on my own.

2. Whether it is better to be a creditor or debtor nation is debatable. A debtor nation is able to consume more that it produces. Countries can do this by living off foreign aid, past savings, or loans. The U.S. finances its deficits (as a debtor nation) by selling financial assets (such as stocks and bonds) and real assets (such as real estate and corporations) to foreigners. The problem with being a debtor nation is that country has to make interest payments on those bonds and has to pay profits to the foreigners who own the corporations. A creditor nation receives those interest payments and profits, but must consume less than it is producing.

3. Generally, there are two problems. First, trade restrictions reduce competition. Less competition means consumers have to pay higher prices than if the foreign competition were allowed. Second, trade restrictions often bring retaliation from other countries (they impose stricter trade restrictions as well). This reduces the amount domestic firms would otherwise be able to sell abroad.

SUPPLY AND DEMAND

● CHAPTER AT A GLANCE

Chapter 4 introduces one of the more important tools of economic analysis—the model of supply and demand. The interaction of the forces of supply and demand determine market prices in a competitive market. This is the way wheat and crude oil prices are determined in our global economy. Of course, not all prices are determined by the forces of supply and demand, however, the model does provide great insight into the behaviour of consumers and producers in a wide variety of situations.

The chapter emphasizes the law of demand and supply and the various factors influencing how much of a particular good is demanded or supplied. Demand and supply can be represented in a number of different ways—algebraically, in tabular form, or by the use of graphs. Graphing demand and supply is a very important skill that students will have to master. It will provide important insight into what happens in a market economy when external influences affect demand and supply.

Mastery of the demand and supply model will also require an understanding of specific important concepts and terms such as "demand", "quantity demanded", "supply", and " quantity supplied".

Equilibrium market prices and quantity are determined by the intersection of the demand and supply curves. Changes in demand and supply causes shifts in the demand and supply curves, which will alter the level of equilibrium price and quantity. You should become comfortable in being able to determine the resulting change in equilibrium price and quantity resulting from changes in demand and supply.

This review is based upon the learning objectives that open the chapter.

1a. The law of demand states that the quantity of a good demanded is inversely related to a good's price. When price goes up, quantity demanded goes down. When price goes down, quantity demanded goes up. (73)

Law of Demand (Inverse Relationship):
arrows move in $\uparrow P \Rightarrow \downarrow Q_d$
opposite directions $\downarrow P \uparrow \Rightarrow Q_d$

Law of Demand
expressed as a
downward-sloping
curve:

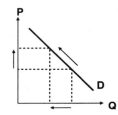

1b. Changes in quantity demanded are shown by movements along a demand curve. Shifts in demand are shown by a shift of the entire demand curve. (73-76) (Note: "Δ" means "change.")

> *Don't get this confused on the exam!*

ΔQ_d *is caused only by a*
Δ *in the P of the good*
itself.

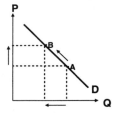

$\Delta P \Rightarrow Q_d \Rightarrow$ *movement*
along a given D
curve.

$\uparrow P \Rightarrow \downarrow Q_d$: *movement along a curve (e.g. from point A to point B).*
Δ *is caused only by Δs in the shift factors of D (not a Δ in the P of the good itself!)*
Δ *in shift factors of D = ΔD shift of a D curve*

Know what can cause an increase and decrease in demand:

↑*D*   *Rightward Shift*   ↓*D*   *Leftward Shift*

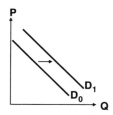

1c. To derive a demand curve from a demand table you plot each point on the demand table on a graph and connect the points. (76-77)

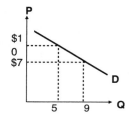

P	**Q**
$10	5
7	9

1d. Market demand curves are the horizontal sum of all individual demand curves. At each price, the quantities demanded related to the various individual demand curves are summed together. (77-78)

2a. The law of supply states that the quantity supplied of a good is directly related to the good's price. When price goes up, quantity supplied goes up. When price goes down, quantity supplied goes down. (80)

Law of Supply (Direct Relationship):
arrows move in   ↑P ↑Q_s
same direction   ↓P ↓Q_s

Law of Supply expressed as an upward-sloping curve:

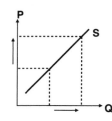

2b. Just as with demand, it is important to distinguish between a shift in supply (a shift of the entire supply curve) and a movement along a supply curve (a change in the quantity supplied due to a change in price). (80-83)

Don't get this confused on the exam!

ΔQ_s *is caused* <u>only</u> *by a* Δ *in the P of the good itself.*

ΔP ΔQ_s *movement along a given S curve.*

↑P ↑Qs: *movement along a curve (e.g. from point A to point B).*

ΔS *is caused only by* Δs *in the shift factors of S* (<u>not</u> *a* Δ *in the P of the good itself!)*
Δ *in shift factors of S* ΔS *shift of a S curve*

Know what can cause an increase and decrease in supply:

↑*S*   *Rightward Shift*   ↓*S*   *Leftward Shift*

2c. To derive a supply curve from a supply table, plot each point on the supply table on a graph and connect the points. (83-84)

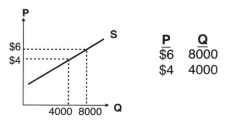

P	**Q**
$6	8000
$4	4000

2d. Market supply curves are the horizontal sum of all individual supply curves. At each price, the quantities supplied related to the various individual supply curves are summed together. (83-84)

3a. Demand and supply curves enable us to determine the equilibrium price and quantity. In addition, changes (shifts) in demand and supply curves enable us to predict the effect on the equilibrium price and quantity in a market. (87-89)

Anything other than price that affects demand or supply will shift the curves.

Know how a change in demand or supply affects the equilibrium price and quantity! Note:

$$\uparrow D \Rightarrow \uparrow P;\ \uparrow Q \qquad \uparrow D \Rightarrow \downarrow P;\ \downarrow Q$$

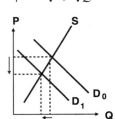

$$\uparrow S \Rightarrow \downarrow P;\ \uparrow Q \qquad \downarrow S \Rightarrow \uparrow P;\ \downarrow Q$$

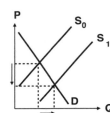

3b. Equilibrium is where quantity supplied equals quantity demanded: (84-87)
- If quantity demanded is greater than quantity supplied, prices tend to rise;
- If quantity supplied is greater than quantity demanded, prices tend to fall.
- When quantity demanded equals quantity supplied, prices have no tendency to change.

<u>*Know this!*</u>
If $Q_d > Q_s \Rightarrow$ Shortage $\Rightarrow P$ will $\uparrow$.
If $Q_s > Q_d \Rightarrow$ Surplus $\Rightarrow P$ will $\downarrow$.
If $Q_s = Q_d \Rightarrow$ Equilibrium $\Rightarrow$ no tendency for P to change (because there is neither a surplus nor a shortage).

Shortage **Surplus** **Equilibrium**
$(Q_d > Q_s)$ $(Q_s > Q_d)$ $(Q_s = Q_d)$
P is below P is above
equilibrium equilibrium

3c. Changes (shifts) in demand and supply are what cause changes in the price and the quantity traded in real-world markets. (87-93)

Shifts in both demand and supply can be tricky. But remember, simply locate the new point of intersection. When both curves shift, the effect on either price or quantity depends on the relative size of the shifts. Moreover, the effect on either price or quantity (one of them) will be certain, while the effect on the other will be uncertain. Note:

$$\uparrow D \text{ and } \uparrow S \Rightarrow ?P;\ \uparrow Q \qquad \uparrow D \text{ and } \downarrow S \Rightarrow \uparrow P;\ ?Q$$

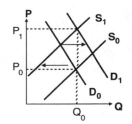

$$\uparrow D \text{ and } \uparrow S \Rightarrow ?P;\ \uparrow Q \qquad \uparrow D \text{ and } \downarrow S \Rightarrow \uparrow P;\ ?Q$$

4a. The resulting changes in equilibrium price and quantity from shifts in the demand or supply curve are very important elements of the demand-supply model. Practice shifting the curves and ensure that you get the following results: (87-93)

$$\uparrow D \Rightarrow \uparrow P \ \uparrow Q$$
$$\downarrow D \Rightarrow \downarrow P \ \downarrow Q$$
$$\uparrow S \Rightarrow \downarrow P \ \uparrow Q$$
$$\downarrow S \Rightarrow \uparrow P \ \downarrow Q$$

4b. When Qd > Qs, prices tend to rise.
When Qd < Qs, prices tend to fall. (87-89)

See also, "Appendix A: Algebraic Representation of Supply, Demand, and Equilibrium."

MATCHING THE TERMS
Match the terms to their definitions

All of these key terms are found at the end of the chapter.

___ 1. complements
___ 2. demand
___ 3. demand curve
___ 4. equilibrium
___ 5. equilibrium price
___ 6. equilibrium quantity
___ 7. excess demand
___ 8. excess supply
___ 9. inferior good
___ 10. law of demand
___ 11. law of supply
___ 12. market demand curve
___ 13. market supply curve
___ 14. movement along a demand curve
___ 15. movement along a supply curve
___ 16. normal good
___ 17. quantity demanded
___ 18. quantity supplied
___ 19. shift in demand
___ 20. shift in supply
___ 21. supply
___ 22. supply curve

a. A specific amount that will be demanded per unit of time at a specific price, other things constant.
b. Curve that tells how much of a good will be bought at various prices.
c. The effect of a change in a nonprice factor on the supply curve.
d. Curve that tells how much of a good will be offered for sale at various prices.
e. The graphic representation of the effect of a change in price on the quantity supplied.
f. Quantity demanded rises as price falls, other things constant.
g. Quantity supplied rises as price rises, other things constant.
h. A schedule of quantities of a good that will be bought per unit of time at various prices, other things constant.
i. Quantity supplied is greater than quantity demanded.
j. A concept in which opposing dynamic forces cancel each other out.
k. The effect of a change in a nonprice factor on demand.
l. The price toward which the invisible hand (economic forces) drives the market.
m. The horizontal sum of all individual demand curves.
n. Amount bought and sold at the equilibrium price.
o. Quantity demanded is greater than quantity supplied.
p. The graphical representation of the effect of a change in price on the quantity demanded.
q. A specific amount that will be offered for sale per unit of time at a specific price.
r. A schedule of quantities a seller is willing to sell per unit of time at various prices, other things constant.
s. The demand for a good decreases as income increases.
t. Goods whose demand increases with an increase in income.
u. The horizontal sum of all individual supply curves.
v. An increase in the price of one good will reduce the quantity demanded of it and the good whose price remained fixed.

● MULTIPLE CHOICE

Circle the one best answer for each of the following questions:

1. The law of demand states
    a. quantity demanded increases as price falls, other things constant.
    b. more of a good will be demanded the higher its price, other things constant.
    c. people always want more.
    d. you can't always get what you want at the price you want.

2. There are many more substitutes for good A than for good B.
    a. The demand curve for good B will likely shift out further.
    b. The demand curve for good B will likely be flatter.
    c. You can't say anything about the likely relative flatness of the demand curves.
    d. The demand curve for good A will likely be flatter.

3. If the weather gets very hot, what will most likely happen?
    a. The supply of air conditioners will increase.
    b. Quantity demanded of air conditioners will increase.
    c. Demand for air conditioners will increase.
    d. The quality demanded of air conditioners will increase.

4. If the price of air conditioners falls, there will be
    a. an increase in demand for air conditioners.
    b. an increase in the quantity demanded of air conditioners.
    c. an increase in the quantity supplied of air conditioners.
    d. a shift in the demand for air conditioners.

5. An increase in demand
    a. is reflected as a rightward (outward) shift of the demand curve.
    b. is caused by a decrease in price.
    c. means demanders are buying less at any price
    d. shifts the demand curve to the left (inward).

6. The demand curve will likely shift outward to the right if
    a. society's income falls.
    b. the price of a substitute good falls.
    c. the price of the good is expected to rise in the near future.
    d. the good goes out of style.

7. The difference between the quantity demanded and demand is
    a. the quantity demanded is associated with a whole set of prices, whereas demand is associated with a particular price.
    b. the quantity demanded is associated with a particular price, whereas demand is associated with a whole set of prices.
    c. the quantity demanded is the whole demand curve, whereas demand is a particular point along a demand curve.
    d. a change in the quantity demanded is reflected graphically as a shift of the demand curve, whereas a change in demand is reflected as movement along a given demand curve.

8. If there is a flood, what will most likely happen in the market for bottled water?
    a. Demand will increase.
    b. Demand will fall.
    c. Supply will increase.
    d. Supply will decrease.

9. The movement in the graph below from point A to point B represents

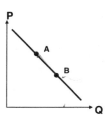

    a. an increase in demand.
    b. an increase in the quantity demanded.
    c. an increase in the quantity supplied.
    d. an increase in supply.

10. Using the standard axes, the demand curve associated with the following demand table is

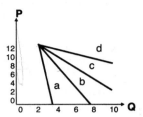

Demand Table	
P	**Q**
7	5
9	4
11	3

a. a
b. b
c. c
d. d

11. To derive a market demand curve from two individual demand curves
a. one adds the two demand curves horizontally.
b. one adds the two demand curves vertically.
c. one subtracts one demand curve from the other demand curve.
d. one adds the demand curves both horizontally and vertically.

12. The market demand curve will always
a. be unrelated to the individual demand curves and slope.
b. be steeper than the individual demand curves that make it up.
c. have the same slope as the individual demand curves that make it up.
d. be flatter than the individual demand curves that make it up.

13. The law of supply states that
a. quantity supplied increases as price increases, other things constant.
b. quantity supplied decreases as price increases, other things constant.
c. more of a good will be supplied the higher its price, other things changing proportionately.
d. less of a good will be supplied the higher its price, other things changing proportionately.

14. In the graph below, the arrow refers to

a. a shift in demand.
b. a shift in supply.
c. a change in the quantity demanded.
d. a change in the quantity supplied.

15. If there is an improvement in technology one would expect
a. a movement along the supply curve.
b. a shift upward (or to the left) of the supply curve.
c. a shift downward (or to the right) of the supply curve.
d. a movement down along the supply curve.

16. The market supply curve for the two individual supply curves S_1 and S_2 below would be

a. S_3.
b. S_4.
c. S_5.
d. S_6.

17. You're the supplier of a good and suddenly a number of your long-lost friends call you to buy your product. Your good is most likely
a. in excess supply.
b. in excess demand.
c. in equilibrium.
d. in both excess supply and demand.

18. At which point on the graph below will you expect the strongest downward pressure on prices?

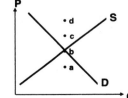

a. a.
b. b.
c. c.
d. d.

19. If at some price the quantity supplied exceeds the quantity demanded then:
  a. a surplus (excess supply) exists and the price will fall over time as sellers competitively bid down the price.
  b. a shortage (excess demand) exists and the price will rise over time as buyers competitively bid up the price.
  c. the price is below equilibrium.
  d. equilibrium will be reestablished as the demand curve shifts to the left.

20. If the price of a good
  a. rises it is a response to a surplus (excess supply).
  b. falls it is a response to a shortage (excess demand).
  c. is below equilibrium then a shortage will be observed.
  d. is below equilibrium then a surplus will be observed.

21. If the demand for a good increases you will expect
  a. price to fall and quantity to rise.
  b. price to rise and quantity to rise.
  c. price to fall and quantity to fall.
  d. price to rise and quantity to fall.

22. Compared to last year, fewer oranges are being purchased and the selling price has decreased. This could have been caused by
  a. an increase in demand.
  b. an increase in supply.
  c. a decrease in demand.
  d. a decrease in supply.

23. If demand and supply both increase, this will cause
  a. an increase in the equilibrium quantity, but an uncertain effect on the equilibrium price.
  b. an increase in the equilibrium price, but an uncertain effect on the equilibrium quantity.
  c. an increase in the equilibrium price and quantity.
  d. an decrease in the equilibrium price and quantity.

24. An increase in demand for a good will cause
  a. excess demand (a shortage) before price changes.
  b. movement down along the demand curve as price changes.
  c. movement down along the supply curve as price changes.
  d. a higher price and a smaller quantity traded in the market.

25. If a frost in Florida damages oranges, what will likely happen to the market for Florida oranges?
  a. Demand will increase.
  b. Demand will fall.
  c. Supply will increase.
  d. Supply will decrease.

26. Assume that the cost of shipping automobiles from Canada to Japan decreases. What will likely happen to the equilibrium price and quantity of cars made in Canada and sold in Japan?
  a. The price will rise, and quantity will fall.
  b. Both price and quantity will rise.
  c. The price will fall, and quantity will rise.
  d. The price will fall, what happens to quantity is not clear.

27. What will likely happen to the price and quantity of cricket bats in Trinidad as interest in cricket dwindles following the dismal performance of the national cricket team, while at the same time taxes are repealed on producing cricket bats?
  a. The price will decrease, but what happens to quantity is not clear.
  b. The price will decrease, and quantity will increase.
  c. The price will increase, but what happens to quantity is not clear.
  d. It is not clear what happens to either price or quantity.

28. If a frost hits the Florida orange orchards,
  a. demand falls causing equilibrium price and quantity to fall.
  b. demand rises causing equilibrium price and quantity to rise.
  c. supply falls causing equilibrium price to rise and quantity to fall.
  d. Supply rises causing equilibrium price to fall and quantity to rise.

● SHORT-ANSWER QUESTIONS

1. What is the law of demand?

2. What does the law of supply say that most individuals would do if their wage increased? Explain the importance of substitution in this decision.

3. Demonstrate graphically a shift in demand.

4. Demonstrate graphically a movement along a demand curve.

5. Draw a demand curve from the following demand table.

    Demand Table

P	P
50	1
40	2
30	3
20	4

6. State the law of supply.

7. Demonstrate graphically the effect on the supply of Red Hot Chili Pepper CDs of a new technology that reduces the cost of producing Red Hot Chili Pepper CDs.

8. Demonstrate graphically the effect of a rise in the price of Red Hot Chili Pepper CDs on the quantity supplied.

9. Draw a supply curve from the following supply table.

    Supply Table

Q	P
20	1
30	2
40	3
50	4

10. What are three things to note about supply and demand which help to explain how they interact to bring about equilibrium in a market?

11. Given the graph below, at what price is there no pressure on price to change? Why?

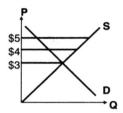

12. Demonstrate graphically what happens to the equilibrium price and quantity of M&Ms if they suddenly become more popular.

13. Demonstrate graphically what happens to the equilibrium price and quantity of oranges if a frost destroys 50 percent of the orange crop.

14. Demonstrate graphically what happens in the following situation: Income in Canada rose in the 1990s and more and more people began to buy luxury items such as caviar. However, about that same time, the dissolution of the Soviet Union threw suppliers of caviar from the Caspian Sea into a mire of bureaucracy, reducing their ability to export caviar. Market: Caviar sold in Canada.

● PROBLEMS AND APPLICATIONS

1. Draw two linear curves on the same graph from the following table, one relating P with Q_1 and the other relating P with Q_2.

P	Q_1	Q_2
$30	60	100
35	70	90
40	80	80
45	90	70

a. Label the curve that is most likely a demand curve. Explain your choice.

b. Label the curve that is most likely a supply curve. Explain your choice.

c. What is equilibrium price and quantity? Choose points above and below that price and explain why each is not the equilibrium price.

2. Correct the following statements, if needed, so that the terms "demand," "quantity demanded," "supply," and "quantity supplied" are used correctly.

   a. As the price of pizza increases, consumers demand less pizza.

   b. Whenever the price of bicycles increases, the supply of bicycles increases.

   c. The price of electricity is cheaper in the northwestern part of the United States and therefore the demand for electricity is greater in the northwest.

   d. An increase in incomes of car buyers will increase the quantity demanded for cars.

   e. An increase in the quantity demanded of lobsters means consumers are willing and able to buy more lobsters at any original price.

   f. A decrease in the supply of frog legs means suppliers will provide fewer frog legs at any original price.

3. You are given the following individual demand tables for compact discs.

Price	Juan	Philippe	Ramone
$7	3	20	50
$10	2	10	40
$13	1	7	32
$16	0	5	26
$19	0	3	20
$22	0	0	14

   a. Determine the market demand table.

   b. Graph the individual and market demand curves.

   c. If the current market price is $13, what is the total market quantity demanded? What happens to total market quantity demanded if the price rises to $19 a disc?

   d. Say that a new popular 'N Sync compact disc hits the market which increases demand for compact discs by 25%. Show with a demand table what happens to the individual and market demand curves.

   Demonstrate graphically what happens to market demand.

4. The following table depicts the market supply and demand for oranges in the United States (in thousands of bushels).

Price	Quantity supplied	Quantity demanded
$15	7000	2000
$14	5500	3000
$13	4000	4000
$12	2500	5000
$11	1000	6000

a. Graph the market supply and demand for oranges.

b. What is the equilibrium price and quantity of oranges in the market? Why?

c. Suppose the price is $14. Would we observe a surplus (excess supply) or a shortage (excess demand)? If so, by how much? What could be expected to happen to the price over time? Why?

d. Suppose the price is $12. Would we observe a surplus or a shortage? If so, by how much? What could be expected to happen to the price over time? Why?

5. Draw a hypothetical demand and supply curve for cyber cafes — coffee houses with computers hooked up to the Internet with access to daily newspapers (among other things) at each table. Show how demand or supply is affected by the following:

a. A technological breakthrough lowers the cost of computers.

b. Consumers' income rises.

c. A per-hour fee is charged to coffee houses to use the Internet.

d. The price of newspapers in print rises.

e. Possible suppliers expect Cyber cafes to become more popular.

6. Use supply and demand curves to help you determine the impact that each of the following events has on the market for surfboards in Southern California.

a. Southern California experiences unusually high temperatures, sending an unusually large number of people to its beaches.

b. Large sharks are reported feeding near the beaches of Southern California.

c. Due to the large profits earned by surfboard producers there is a significant increase in the number of producers of surfboards.

d. There is a significant increase in the price of epoxy paint used to coat surfboards.

7. Use supply and demand curves to help you determine the impact that each of the following events has on the market for beef.

a. New genetic engineering technology enables ranchers to raise healthier, heavier cattle significantly reducing costs.

b. The CBS program "60 Minutes" reports on the unsanitary conditions in poultry processing plants that may increase the chances of consumers getting sick by eating chicken.

c. In addition to developing new genetic engineering technology, we have been mistaken in the past. Highly credible new research results report that abundant consumption of fatty red meats actually prolongs average life expectancy.

d. Consumers expect the price of beef to fall in the near future.

8. Suppose you are told that the price of Cadillacs has increased from last year as well as the number bought and sold. Is this an exception to the law of demand, or has there been a change in demand or supply that could account for this?

9. The following table depicts the market supply and demand for milk in the Canada.

   a. Graph the market supply and demand for milk.

   b. What is the equilibrium market price and quantity in the market?

Price in dollars per litre	Quantity of litres supplied in 1,000	Quantity of litres demanded in 1,000
$0.70	600	800
$0.90	620	720
$1.10	640	640
$1.30	660	560
$1.50	680	440

A1. The supply and demand equations for strawberries are given by $Qs = 10 + 5P$ and $Qd = 20 - 25P$ respectively, where P is price in dollars per litres, Qs is millions of litres of strawberries supplied, and Qd is millions of litres of strawberries demanded.

   a. What is the equilibrium market price and quantity for strawberries in the market?

   b. Suppose a new preservative is introduced that prevents more strawberries from rotting on their way from the farm to the store. As a result supply of strawberries increases by 20 million litres at every price. What effect does this have on market price and quantity sold?

   c. Suppose it has been found that the spray used on cherry trees has ill effects on those who eat the cherries. As a result, the demand for strawberries increases by 10 million litres at every price. What effect does this have on market price for strawberries and quantity of strawberries sold?

A2. The supply and demand equations for roses are given by $Qs = -10 + 3P$ and $Qd = 20 - 2P$ respectively, where P is dollars per dozen roses and Q is dozens of roses in hundred thousands.

   a. What is the equilibrium market price and quantity of roses sold?

   b. Suppose the government decides to make it more affordable for individuals to be able to give roses to their significant others, and sets a price ceiling for roses at $4 a dozen. What is the likely result?

● A BRAIN TEASER

1. The invention of a self-milking cow machine allows cows to milk themselves. Not only does this reduce the need for higher-cost human assistance in milking, but it also allows the cow to milk herself three times a day instead of two, leading to both a healthier cow and increased milk production.

    a. Show the effect of this innovation on the equilibrium quantity and price of milk.

    b. Show the likely effect on equilibrium price and quantity of apple juice (a substitute for milk).

● POTENTIAL ESSAY QUESTIONS

You may also see essay questions similar to the "Problems & Applications" and "Brain Teaser" exercises.

1. Many university campuses sell parking permits to their students allowing them to park on campus in designated areas. Although most students complain about the relatively high cost of these parking permits, what annoys many students even more is that after having paid for their permits, vacant parking spaces in the designated lots are very difficult to find during much of the day. Many end up having to park off campus anyway, where permits are not required. Assuming the University is unable to build new parking facilities on campus due to insufficient funds, what recommendation might you make to remedy the problem of students with permits being unable to find places to park on campus?

2. Some products are considered to be "inferior" by most consumers. The key characteristic of inferior products is that the demand for these goods decreases as consumer incomes rise. List a few "inferior" goods.

3. Discuss how a change in demand or supply impacts a market equilibrium price and quantity.

◼◼ ANSWERS ◼◼

MATCHING

1-v; 2-h; 3-b; 4-j; 5-l; 6-n; 7-o; 8-i; 9-s; 10-f; 11-g; 12-m; 13-u; 14-p; 15-e; 16-t; 17-a; 18-q; 19-k; 20-c; 21-r; 22-a.

◼◼ ANSWERS ◼◼

MULTIPLE CHOICE

1. a   As discussed on page 73, the correct answer is a. A possible answer is d, which is a restatement of the law of demand, but since the actual law was among the choices, and is more precise, a is the correct answer.

2. d   An equal rise in price will cause individuals to switch to other goods more, the more substitutes there are. See page 73.

3. c   As discussed on pages 74-76, it is important to distinguish between a change in the quantity demanded and a change in demand. Weather is a shift factor of demand, so demand, not quantity demanded, will increase. Supply will not increase; the quantity supplied will, however. Who knows what will happen to the quality demanded? We don't.

4. b   As discussed on pages 74-76, when the price falls there is a movement along the demand curve which is expressed by saying the quantity demanded increased.

5. a   As discussed on page 74, an increase in demand is expressed as an outward (or rightward) shift of the demand curve. It is caused by something else other than the price. It means people will buy more at any price or pay a higher price for a given quantity demanded.

6. c   All of these are shift factors of demand. However, only c will increase demand and shift the demand curve to the right. See page 74.

7. b   As is discussed on pages 74-76, especially page 75, b is the only correct response.

8. a   A flood will likely bring about a significant increase in the demand for bottled water since a flood makes most other water undrinkable. A flood would be a shift factor of demand for bottled water. See pages 75-76.

9. b   The curve slopes downward, so we can surmise that it is a demand curve; and the two points are on the demand curve, so the movement represents an increase in the quantity demanded, not an increase in demand. A shift in demand would be a shift of the entire curve. (See the figures on page 76 of the text.)

10. b   This demand curve is the only demand curve that goes through all the points in the table. See page 77.

11. a   As discussed in the text on page 77 (Figure 4-4), market demand curves are determined by adding individuals' demand curves horizontally.

12. d   Since the market demand curve is arrived at by adding the individual demand curves horizontally, it will always be flatter. See page 77.

13. a   As discussed on page 80, the law of supply is stated in a. The others either have the movement in the wrong direction or are not holding all other things constant.

14. b   It is a shift in supply because the curve is upward sloping; and it's a shift of the entire curve, so it is not a movement along. See page 82 and Figure 4-6.

15. c   As discussed on pages 81-82, technology is a shift factor of supply so it must be a shift of the supply curve. Since it is an improvement, it must be a shift rightward (or downward). (See also page 82, Figure 4-6)

16. c   The market supply curve is determined by the horizontal addition of individual supply curves. See page 83, Figure 4-7.

17. b   When there is excess demand, demanders start searching for new suppliers, as discussed on page 85.

18. d The greater the extent to which the quantity supplied exceeds the quantity demanded, the greater the pressure for the price to fall. See pages 85-86.

19. a As discussed on pages 85-86, this is a surplus (excess supply) when the price is above equilibrium. A surplus will motivate sellers to reduce price to rid themselves of their excess supplies. As the price falls, the quantity demand rises and the quantity supplied rises; demand and supply curves do *not* shift.

20. c As discussed on pages 85-87 whenever the price is below equilibrium, a shortage is observed, and the price rises.

21. b Since this statement says demand increases, it is the <u>demand curve shifting</u>. There is no change in the supply curve. Assuming an upward sloping supply curve, that means that price will rise and quantity will rise. See pages 87-88.

22. c Only a decrease in demand will result in a decrease in quantity and a decrease in price. See pages 87-88.

23. a An increase in demand has a tendency to increase price and increase the quantity. An increase in supply has a tendency to *decrease* the price and increase the quantity. So, on balance, we are certain of an increase in the equilibrium quantity, but we are uncertain about the impact on the price in the market. See page 92.

24. a An increase in demand causes the quantity demanded to exceed the quantity supplied creating excess demand (a shortage). This increases the price causing movement *up* along the demand and supply curves resulting in a *greater* quantity traded in the market. See pages 87-88.

25. d A frost will reduce the quantity of oranges available for sale at every price. Supply will decrease. See pages 87-88.

26. c The supply curve will shift out, market price will fall and the quantity will rise. See pages 87-88.

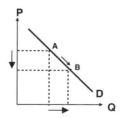

27. a Demand for cricket bats will fall, shifting the demand curve in, while the tax repeal will shift the supply curve out. Price will fall, and quantity may change depending on the relative shifts of the supply and demand curves.

28. c See P. 92

━━━ ANSWERS ━━━

SHORT-ANSWER QUESTIONS

1. The law of demand states that the quantity of a good demanded is inversely related to the good's price. When price goes up, quantity demanded goes down, other things constant. (73)

2. The law of supply states that quantity supplied rises as price rises; the quantity supplied falls as price falls. According to this law, most individuals would choose to supply a greater quantity of labour hours if their wage increased. That is, they will substitute work for leisure. (80)

3. A shift in demand is shown by a shift of the entire demand curve resulting from a change in a shift factor of demand as shown in the graph below. (76)

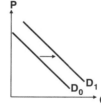

4. A movement along a demand curve is a change in quantity demanded resulting from a change in price as is shown in the graph below as a movement from *A* to *B*. (76)

5. To derive a demand curve from a demand table, you plot each point on the demand table on a graph and connect the points. This is shown on the graph below. (76-77)

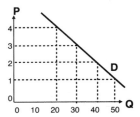

6. The law of supply states that the quantity supplied rises as price rises. Or alternatively: Quantity supplied falls as price falls. (80)

7. A new technology that reduces the cost of producing Red Hot Chili Pepper CDs will shift the entire supply curve to the right from S_0 to S_1, as shown in the graph below. (82)

8. A rise in the price of Red Hot Chili Pepper CDs from P_0 to P_1 results in a movement up along a supply curve; quantity of Red Hot Chili Pepper CDs supplied will rise from Q_0 to Q_1 as shown in the graph below. (81-82)

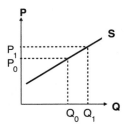

9. To derive a supply curve from a supply table, you plot each point on the supply table on a graph and connect the points. This is shown on the graph below. (84)

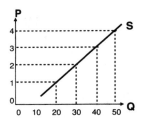

10. The first things to note is that when quantity demanded is greater than quantity supplied, prices tend to rise and when quantity supplied is greater than quantity demanded, prices tend to fall. Each case is demonstrated in the graph below. Price tends away from P_1 and P_2 and toward P_0.

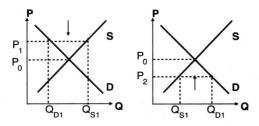

The second thing to note is that the larger the difference between quantity supplied and quantity demanded, the greater the pressure on prices to rise (if there is excess demand) or fall (if there is excess supply). This is demonstrated in the graph below. At P_2, the pressure for prices to fall toward P_0 is greater than the pressure at P_1 because excess supply is greater at P_2 compared to excess supply at P_1.

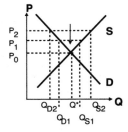

The third thing to note is that when quantity demanded equals quantity supplied, the market is in equilibrium. (85-87)

11. Because we are in equilibrium at $3 there is no pressure to change at this price. At the other prices, surpluses exist putting downward pressure on price. (96-97)

12. Increasing popularity of M&Ms means that at every price, more M&Ms are demanded. The demand curve shifts out to D1, and both equilibrium price and quantity rise to P1 and Q1 respectively. (87-88)

13. A frost damaging oranges means that at every price, suppliers are willing to supply fewer oranges. The supply curve shifts to the left to S1, and equilibrium price rises to P1, and quantity falls to Q1. (90-93)

14. The demand curve for Russian caviar shifts out; the supply shifts in; the price rises substantially. What happens to quantity depends upon the relative sizes of the shifts. (90)

ANSWERS

PROBLEMS AND APPLICATIONS

1. The linear curves are shown on the right. (77, 82)

a. As shown in the graph, the downward sloping curve is a demand curve. We deduce this from the law of demand: quantity demanded rises (falls) as the price decreases (increases). (74)

b. As shown in the graph, the upward sloping curve is a supply curve. We deduce this from the law of supply: quantity supplied rises (falls) as the price rises (falls). (80-81)

c. The equilibrium price and quantity are where the demand and supply curves intersect. This is at $P = \$40$, $Q = 80$. At a price above $40, such as $45, quantity supplied exceeds quantity demanded and there is pressure for

price to fall. At a price below $40, such as $35, quantity demanded exceeds quantity supplied and there is pressure for price to rise. (85-87)

2. a. As the price of pizza increases, the *quantity demanded* of pizza decreases. (74-76)

Note that a change in the price of an item will cause a change in the quantity demanded; not demand! A change in something else other than the price may cause a change in demand–such as a change in one of the shift factors of demand discussed in the textbook.

b. Whenever the price of bicycles increases, the *quantity supplied* also increases. (81-83)

Note that a change in the price will cause a change in the quantity supplied; not supply! A change in something else other than the price may cause a change in supply–such as a change in one of the shift factors of supply discussed in the textbook.

c. The price of electricity is cheaper in the northwestern part of the United States and therefore the *quantity demanded* of electricity is greater in the northwest. (74-76)

d. An increase in incomes of car buyers will increase the *demand* for cars. (74-76)

Notice that a change in a shift factor of demand, such as income, will change demand; not the quantity demanded!

e. An increase in the *demand* for lobsters means consumers are willing and able to buy more lobsters at any given price (whatever the current price is). (74-76)

In order for there to be an increase in the quantity demanded there would have to be a decrease in the price. Moreover, recall that an increase in demand is reflected as a rightward shift of the demand curve. Upon viewing a graph where the demand curve has shifted to the right you will see that more will be purchased at any given price.

f. This is a correct usage of the term "supply." Also note that a decrease in supply is reflected graphically as a leftward shift of the curve. Upon viewing a graph where the supply curve has shifted to the left you will see that less will be provided in the market at any given price. (81-83)

3. a. The market demand table is the summation of individual quantities demanded at each price as follows (77-79):

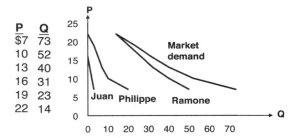

P	Q
$7	73
10	52
13	40
16	31
19	23
22	14

b. The individual and market demand curves are shown to the right of the demand table. (77-79)

c. At $13 a disc, total market quantity demanded is 40 discs. Total market quantity demanded falls to 23 when the price of discs rises to $19 per disc. (77-79)

d. Quantity demanded at each price rises by 25% for each individual and for the market as a whole. The new demand table is shown below. Graphically, both the individual and market demand curves shift to the right. The graph below shows the rightward shift in market demand. (77-79)

Price	Juan	Philippe	Ramone	Market
$7	3.75	25	62.50	91.25
$10	2.50	12.5	50	65
$13	1.25	8.75	40	50
$16	0	6.25	32.5	38.75
$19	0	3.75	20	28.75
$22	0	0	17.5	17.5

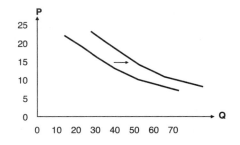

4. a. See the graph below. (77, 82)

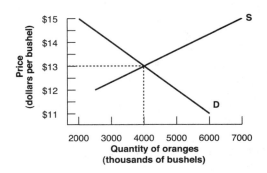

b. The equilibrium price is $13, the equilibrium quantity is 4000. This is an equilibrium because the quantity supplied equals the quantity demanded at this price. That is, there is neither a surplus (excess supply) nor a shortage (excess demand) and hence no tendency for the price to change. (85-87)

c. Because the quantity supplied exceeds the quantity demanded when the price is $14 per bushel, we would observe a surplus of 2,500 bushels (in thousands of bushels). We can expect the price of oranges per bushel to fall as sellers scramble to rid themselves of their excess supplies. (85-87)

d. Because the quantity demanded exceeds the quantity supplied at $12 per bushel, we would observe a shortage of 2,500 bushels (in thousands of bushels). We can expect the price of oranges per bushel to rise as some buyers competitively bid up the price just to get some oranges. (85-87)

5. A hypothetical market for cyber cafes shows an upward sloping supply curve, a downward sloping demand curve and an equilibrium price and quantity where the two curves intersect.

a. A technological breakthrough that lowers the cost of computers will shift the supply of cyber cafes to the right as shown in the graph below. (81-82)

b. A rise in consumers' income will shift the demand for cyber cafes to the right as shown in the graph below. (75)

Quantity of Cyber Cafes

c. If a fee is charged to coffee houses to use the Internet, the supply of cyber cafes will shift to the left as shown below. (75)

Quantity of Cyber Cafes

d. If the price of newspapers in print rises, the demand for cyber cafes will shift to the right as shown in the graph for answer (b). (75)

e. If possible suppliers expect cyber cafes to become more popular, the supply of cyber cafes will shift to the right as shown for answer (a). (81-82)

6 a. This will increase the demand for surfboards shifting the demand curve to the right. At the original price a temporary shortage would be observed putting upward pressure on price. We end up with a higher equilibrium price and a greater equilibrium quantity as illustrated in the graph below. (When dealing with a change in D or S curves, just remember to go from the initial point of intersection between the curves to the new point of intersection. The initial point of intersection will give you the initial equilibrium P and Q and the new point of intersection the new equilibrium P and Q. Then recall that if the price went up in the

market, it was a response to a temporary shortage (excess demand). If the equilibrium price went down, then it was a response to a temporary surplus (excess supply). (87-93)

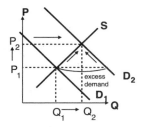

b. This would cause a decrease in the demand for surfboards shifting the demand curve to the left. At the original price a temporary surplus would be observed putting downward pressure on price. We end up with a lower equilibrium price and a lower equilibrium quantity as illustrated in the graph below. (87-93)

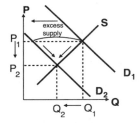

c. This would cause an increase in the supply of surfboards shifting the supply curve to the right. At the original price a temporary surplus would be observed putting downward pressure on price. We end up with a lower equilibrium price and a higher equilibrium quantity as illustrated in the graph below. (87-93)

d. This would cause a decrease in the supply of surfboards shifting the supply curve to the left. At the original price a temporary shortage would be observed putting upward pressure on price. We end up with a higher equilibrium price and a lower equilibrium quantity as illustrated in the graph below. (87-93)

7. **a.** An increase in production technology will increase the supply of beef. The temporary surplus (excess supply) of beef at the original price will cause the market price to fall. Eventually we get a lower equilibrium price of beef and a greater amount bought and sold in the market. (87-93)

   b. Chicken and beef are substitute goods–they can be used instead of each other. Therefore, this "60 Minutes" report will likely increase the demand for beef. The temporary shortage (excess demand) at the original price will cause the price to be competitively bid up. Eventually we observe a higher equilibrium price and a greater equilibrium quantity. (87-93)

   c. The new development would increase the supply of beef while the reports of the health benefits of beef would increase the demand for beef. Quantity of beef sold would rise. The impact on equilibrium price depends upon the relative sizes of the shifts. (87-93)

   d. Because people will postpone their purchases of beef until the price decreases this will reduce the demand for beef today. A decrease in demand is reflected as a leftward shift of the demand curve. The temporary excess supply (surplus) that is created at the original price puts downward pressure on the market price of beef. Eventually we get a lower equilibrium price and quantity. (87-93)

8. This is not an exception to the law of demand (there are very few exceptions). Instead, an increase in demand could account for a higher price and a greater amount bought and sold as is illustrated in the figure below. (87-93)

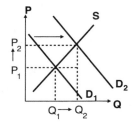

9. **a.** The market supply and demand for milk is graphed below.

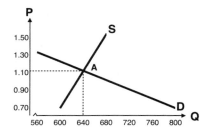

   b. The equilibrium market price is $1.10 and equilibrium quantity in the market is 640 thousand gallons of milk. This is point A on the graph above. (87-93)

A1. a. Equating Qs to Qd and then solving for equilibrium price gives us $3 per quart. Substituting $3 into the demand and supply equations, we find that equilibrium quantity is 5 million quarts. (99-101)

   b. Since supply increases by 20 million quarts, the new supply equation is $Qs = 10 + 5P$. Equating this with the demand equation, we find the new equilibrium price to be $1 per quart. Substituting into either the new supply equation or the demand equation we find that equilibrium quantity is 15 million quarts. (99-101)

   c. With demand increasing, the new demand equation is $Qd = 30 - 5P$. Setting Qs equal to Qd and solving for price we find equilibrium price to be $4 per quart. Substituting this into either the new demand or the supply equation we find equilibrium quantity to be 10 million quarts. (99-101)

A2. a. Equating Qs and Qd, then solving gives equilibrium price $6 and quantity 8 hundred thousand dozen. (99-101)

   b. If price ceiling is set at $4, Qs = 2, and Qd = 12; the resulting shortage is 10 hundred thousand dozen. (99-101)

■ **ANSWERS** ■

A BRAIN TEASER

1. a. This innovation will shift the supply curve to the right as shown in the graph on the left below. As a result, this creates excess supply and the equilibrium price falls while the equilibrium quantity rises. (81-82)

   b. The market demand and supply for apple juice is shown below on the right. As a result of the fall in milk prices, the demand for apple juice shifts to the left. This creates excess supply of apple juice. The equilibrium price will fall. The equilibrium quantity will also fall. (87-93)

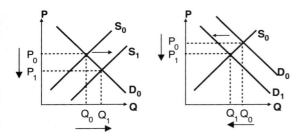

■ **ANSWERS** ■

POTENTIAL ESSAY QUESTIONS

The following are annotated answers. They indicate the general idea behind the answer.

1. The shortage of parking spaces implies that permit prices are below equilibrium. The price of a permit should be increased. At least with the purchase of a permit you could be reasonably certain that a space would be available.

2. Examples include lower grade liquor, wine, beer, "cheaper" grades of meat, and used clothes.

3. Suppose there is an increase in demand. The demand curve shifts out to the right, creating a temporary shortage (excess demand) at the original price. As a result, buyers competitively bid up the price. The quantity demanded falls (movement up along the demand curve toward the new point of intersection) and the quantity supplied rises (movement up along the supply curve toward the new point of intersection). Eventually, the price rises enough until the quantity demanded is once again equal to the quantity supplied. Because there is neither a shortage nor a surplus at this new point of intersection, the new market equilibrium price and quantity is obtained. The market equilibrium price and quantity will both increase as a result of an increase in demand. *You should be able to illustrate this graphically as well.*

ECONOMIC GROWTH, BUSINESS CYCLES, UNEMPLOYMENT, AND INFLATION

5

● CHAPTER AT A GLANCE

In analyzing macroeconomic problems and issues, economists generally consider trends as they occur in the short run and the long run. Within the short-run framework, business cycles are used to analyze the fluctuations in economic activity. There are four phases to a typical business cycle   the peak, the downturn the trough, and the upturn.

The long-run framework analyzes the trends of economic growth. Economists use real GDP as the primary measurement of growth. Real GDP is defined as the market value of all final goods and services produced in an economy in a particular year. The business cycle is a tool used to analyze the fluctuations in real GDP growth over time. Other economic indicators that are important in helping economists understand current market conditions are also discussed.

The chapter also presents detailed analysis on two very important economic problems that occur from economic instability   unemployment and inflation. Unemployment is the percentage of people in the labour force who are unemployed. There tends to be 3 different types of unemployed (frictional, structural and cyclical), each of which require specific policy intervention.

Inflation is a continual rise in the price level. It is an important issue as it can compromise competitiveness and the standard of living of a market economy. There are various measures of inflation the consumer price index and the GDP deflator. Several important terms are discussed including real and nominal output and expected and unexpected inflation.

This review is based upon the learning objectives that open the chapter.

1. The long-run framework focuses on supply. The short-run framework focuses on demand. (104-105)

    Issues of growth are considered in a long-run framework. Business cycles are generally considered in a short-run framework. Unemployment and inflation fall within both frameworks.

2a. Growth is usually measured by changes in real GDP. Canadian economic output has grown at an average annual rate of 2.5 to 3.5 percent. (105)

    Today's growth rates are within historical standards.

2b. The range in growth rates among countries is wide. (105-106)

    African economies have consistently grown at below average rates. Japan and Western Europe grew quickly in the last half of the 20th century.

2c. In the post-war era (since 1945), the average business expansion has lasted 51 months. (109)

2d. Since the late 1980s, the target rate of unemployment has been somewhere between 6% and 8%. (113)

    The target rate of unemployment has been called the "natural" rate of unemployment.

2e. Since the early 1960s, the inflation rate in Canada has almost always been positive (120)

3. The four phases of the business cycle are: the peak, the downturn, the trough, and the upturn. (109)

Note!
- There is an overall upward secular growth trend of 2.5-3.5% shown by the dotted line.
- We want to smooth out fluctuations because of the problems associated with them.
- Two problems with a downturn (recession) are (a) cyclical unemployment and (b) low economic growth rate.
- One problem with upturn (expansion) is inflation.

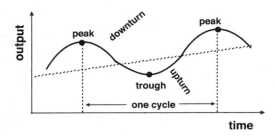

4a. The unemployment rate is measured by dividing the number of unemployed individuals by the number of people in the civilian labour force and multiplying by 100. (111, 115-116)

Unemployment measures are imperfect but are still a good gauge of the economy's performance.

4b. Some microeconomic categories of unemployment are: reason for unemployment, demographic unemployment, duration of unemployment, and unemployment by industry. (112-113)

Know the different types of unemployment — frictional, structural, and cyclical.

5. Potential output is defined as the output that will be achieved at the target rate of unemployment and the target level of capacity utilization. It is difficult to know precisely where potential output is. (118)

Recession: Actual output (income) < Potential output.

Expansion: Actual output (income) > Potential output.

Target rate of unemployment (about 7%) is the lowest rate of unemployment that policymakers believe is achievable under existing conditions (where inflation is not accelerating). It is the rate of unemployment that exists when the economy is operating at potential.

6a. Inflation is a continual rise in the price level. (119)

Price indexes are used to measure inflation; The most often used are the raw materials price index, the GDP deflator, and the Consumer Price Index (CPI).

6b. The "real" amount is the nominal amount divided by the price index. It is the nominal amount adjusted for inflation. (123)

Real means "inflation-adjusted."

$$Real\ output = \frac{nominal\ output}{price\ index} \times 100$$

7. While inflation may not make the nation poorer, it does cause income to be redistributed and it can reduce the amount of information that prices are supposed to convey. (124-125)

Inflation hurts those who cannot or do not raise their prices, but benefits those who can and do raise their prices.

See also Appendix A, "Nonmainstream Approaches to Macro"

MATCHING THE TERMS
Match the terms to their definitions

All of these key terms are found at the end of the chapter.

____ **1.** business cycle
____ **2.** Classicals
____ **3.** consumer price index
____ **4.** cyclical unemployment
____ **5.** depression
____ **6.** employment rate
____ **7.** expansion
____ **8.** expected inflation
____ **9.** final goods and services
____ **10.** frictional unemployment
____ **11.** GDP deflator
____ **12.** hyperinflation
____ **13.** inflation
____ **14.** Keynesians
____ **15.** labour force
____ **16.** labour force participation rate
____ **17.** natural rate of unemployment
____ **18.** nominal output
____ **19.** Okun's rule of thumb
____ **20.** per capita real output
____ **21.** potential output
____ **22.** price index
____ **23.** raw materials price index
____ **24.** real gross domestic product (real GDP)
____ **25.** real output
____ **26.** recession
____ **27.** structural unemployment
____ **28.** unemployment rate
____ **29.** unexpected inflation

a. A continual rise in the price level.

b. A decline in real output that persists for more than two consecutive quarters of a year.

c. A large recession.

d. A number that summarizes what happens to a weighted composite of prices of a selection of goods over time.

e. An upturn that lasts at least two consecutive quarters of a year.

f. Generally favour activist government policies.

g. Generally favour laissez-faire or non-activist policies.

h. Index of inflation measuring the prices of a fixed basket of consumer goods, weighted according to each component's share of an average consumer's expenditures.

i. Index of the price level of aggregate output, or the average price of the components in GDP, relative to a base year.

j. Inflation people expect to occur.

k. Inflation that hits triple digits (100 percent) or more per year.

l. Inflation that surprises people.

m. Measures the labour force as a percentage of the total population at least 15 years old.

n. Measures the prices of a number of important raw materials, such as steel.

o. Real GDP divided by the total population.

p. States that a 1 percentage point change in the unemployment rate will cause output to change in the opposite direction by 2 percent.

q. Goods and services produced by firms that are not used as input by other firms.

r. The market value of final goods and services produced in an economy, stated in the prices of a given period.

s. The number of people who are working as a percentage of the population aged 15 years and older.

t. The percentage of people in the economy who are willing and able to work, but who are not working.

u. The percentage of people in the labour force who are willing and able to work but who are not working.

v. The total amount of goods and services measured at current prices.

w. The total amount of goods and services produced adjusted for price-level changes.

x. The upward or downward movement of economic activity that occurs around the growth trend.

y. Those people in an economy who are willing and able to work.

z. Unemployment caused by economic restructuring making some skills obsolete.

z1. Unemployment caused by new entrants to the job market and people who have left their jobs to look for and find other jobs.

z2. Unemployment resulting from fluctuations in economic activity.

z3. The unemployment rate that coincides with a stable inflation rate.

z4. The output that would materialize at the target rate of unemployment and the target rate of capacity utilization.

● MULTIPLE CHOICE

Circle the one best answer for each of the following questions:

1. Inflation and unemployment are
   a. best studied in the long-run framework.
   b. best studied in the short-run framework.
   c. fall within both the short-and long-run frameworks.
   d. are not problems of today and therefore are not studied.

2. All of the following are long-run growth policies *except*:
   a. increasing government spending to spur consumer spending.
   b. reducing tax rates to increase incentives to work.
   c. providing funding for research.
   d. following policies to reduce interest rates and increase business investment.

3. If a country of 270 million people has a total income of $8 trillion, its per capita income is
   a. $29.63.
   b. $29,630.
   c. $33.75.
   d. $33,750.

4. The secular trend growth rate in Canada is approximately
   a. 1 to 1.5 percent per year.
   b. 2.5 to 3.5 percent per year.
   c. 5 to 5.5 percent per year.
   d. 7 to 7.5 percent per year.

5. Some people have argued that the two goals of (1) environmental protection and (2) economic growth that involves increased material consumption by individuals do not necessarily contradict each other because spending on the environment can create growth and jobs. This argument
   a. offers great hope for the future.
   b. is incorrect because environmental issues are not as important as material consumption.
   c. is correct because material consumption is not as important as the environment.
   d. is incorrect because the environmental projects will use the resources generated from growth, leaving little or nothing for increased personal consumption.

6. From 1950 to 2000, which geographic area or country had the highest per capita growth rate?
   a. China.
   b. Japan.
   c. North America.
   d. Latin America.

7. The business cycle characterized by the Great Depression occurred in the early
   a. 1900s.
   b. 1930s.
   c. 1950s.
   d. 1960s.

8. Leading indicators include
   a. manufacturing and trade sales volume.
   b. number of employees on non-agricultural payrolls.
   c. industrial production.
   d. new orders for goods and materials.

9. At what stage of the business cycle would a Classical economist be most likely to support government intervention?
   a. Peak.
   b. Trough.
   c. Depression.
   d. Upturn.

10. Under pure capitalism, the main deterrent of unemployment was
   a. pure government intervention.
   b. pure market intervention.
   c. the fear of hunger.
   d. immigration.

11. Since the late 1980s, the target rate of unemployment generally has been
   a. between 2 and 4 percent.
   b. between 3 and 5 percent.
   c. between 4 and 6 percent.
   d. between 6 and 8 percent.

12. Classical economist's view of the labour market is that
   a. labour supply creates its own labour demand.
   b. wages adjust to where the demand for labour just equals its supply.
   c. there is no involuntary unemployment, only frictional unemployment.
   d. both b and c.

13. Keynesians
   a. generally favour activist government policies.
   b. generally favour laissez-faire policies.
   c. believe that frictional unemployment does not exist.
   d. believe that all unemployment is cyclical unemployment.

14. Classicals
   a. generally favour activist government policies.
   b. generally favour laissez-faire policies.
   c. believe that frictional unemployment does not exist.
   d. believe that all unemployment is cyclical unemployment.

15. The level of output that would materialize at the target rate of unemployment and the target rate of capital utilization is called
   a. nominal output.
   b. actual output.
   c. potential output.
   d. utilized output.

16. Okun's rule of thumb states that
   a. a 1 percentage-point change in the unemployment rate will cause income to change in the same direction by 2 percent.
   b. a 1 percentage-point change in the unemployment rate will cause income to change in the opposite direction by 2 percent.
   c. a 2 percentage-point change in the unemployment rate will cause income to change in the same direction by 1 percent.
   d. a 2 percentage-point change in the unemployment rate will cause income to change in the opposite direction by 1 percent.

17. Using Okun's rule of thumb, if unemployment rises from 5 to 6 percent, one would expect total output of $5 trillion to
   a. rise by $5 billion.
   b. rise by $100 billion.
   c. fall by $100 billion.
   d. fall by $5 billion.

18. A one-time rise in the price level is
   a. inflation if that rise is above 5 percent.
   b. inflation if that rise is above 10 percent.
   c. inflation if that rise is above 15 percent.
   d. not inflation.

19. Food and beverages make up about 20 percent of total expenditure. If food and beverage prices rise by 10 percent while the other components of the price index remain constant, approximately how much will the price index rise?
   a. 1 percent.
   b. 2 percent.
   c. 20 percent.
   d. 25 percent.

20. Real output is
   a. total amount of goods and services produced.
   b. total amount of goods and services produced adjusted for price level changes.
   c. total amount of goods produced, adjusted for services that aren't real.
   d. total amount of goods and services that are really produced as opposed to ones that are resold.

21. If the price level rises by 20 percent and real output remains constant, by how much will nominal output rise?
   a. 1 percent.
   b. 5 percent.
   c. 20 percent.
   d. 40 percent.

22. A cost of inflation is that
   a. it makes everyone poorer.
   b. it makes the poor poorer but the rich richer.
   c. there are no costs of inflation because inflation does not make the society as a whole poorer.
   d. it reduces the informational content of prices.

23. Unexpected inflation
   a. makes everyone poorer.
   b. redistributes income from those who raised their prices to those who didn't.
   c. transfers income from those who didn't raise their prices to those who did.
   d. is impossible since firms always plan price increases.

● SHORT-ANSWER QUESTIONS

1. What are the two frameworks economists use to analyze unemployment, inflation, growth, and business cycles? What distinguishes the two frameworks from one another?

2. What is the average rate of real growth in output in Canada from 1870 to the present? What are the costs and the benefits of growth?

3. During the post-war period, how long has the average expansion lasted?

4. Since the late 1980s, what has been the target rate of unemployment?

5. How did the inflation rate in Canada change in this century from pre-World War II to the post-World War II period (1950 to the present)?

6. Label the four phases of the business cycle in the graph below.

7. How is the unemployment rate calculated?

8. Who in Canada does not work and is nevertheless not counted as unemployed?

9. How is the target rate of unemployment related to potential output?

10. Define inflation. If there were no inflation what would happen to the distinction between a real concept and a nominal concept?

11. Suppose the price of a Maserati in 1975 was $75,000 and the price of a Maserati in 1995 was $200,000. Your parents exclaim that the prices of Maseratis have risen by 166%! Wow! You tell them that the price of a Maserati really hasn't risen that much. They are confusing real and nominal concepts. Explain what you mean.

12. What is the difference between expected and unexpected inflation?

13. What are two important costs of inflation?

● PROBLEMS AND APPLICATIONS

1. State Okun's rule of thumb. For each of the following increases in the unemployment rate, state what will likely happen to income in the United States:

a. Unemployment rate falls 2 percentage points.

b. Unemployment rate falls 1 percentage point.

c. Unemployment rate increases 3 percentage points.

2. For each, state whether the unemployment is structural or cyclical.

a. As Canada becomes a more high-tech producer, labour-intensive factories relocate to low-wage countries. Factory workers lose their jobs and the unemployment rate rises.

b. As it becomes more acceptable for mothers to work, more women enter the labour market looking for work. The unemployment rate rises.

c. Foreign economies slow and demand fewer Canadian exports. Unemployment rate rises.

3. Calculate the following given the information about the economy in the table:

Total population	260 million
Noninstitutional population	200 million
Incapable of working	60 million
Not in the labour force	66 million
Employed	134 million
Unemployed	10 million

  a. Labour force.

  b. Unemployment rate.

4. Create a price index for Edmonton Eskimos fans using the following basket of goods with 2000 prices as the base year.

	Prices	
Quantities in 2000	**2000**	**2001**
90 lbs of cheese	$2.50/lb	$2.00/lb
12 flannel shirts	$15/shirt	$20/shirt
16 football tickets	$25/ticket	$30/ticket

  a. What is the price of the basket of goods in each year? Show how the price index is 100 in the base year 2000.

  b. Using 2000 as the base year, what is the price index in 2001? By how much have prices risen?

  c. What are some potential flaws of this price index?

5. Calculate the following given the following information about the economy in 1985, 1995, and 1999:

	1985	**1995**	**1999**
Nominal GDP (in billions of dollars)	4,213	_____	9,256.1
GDP deflator (index, 1996=100)	73.7	98.1	_____
Real GDP (in billions of 1996 dollars)	_____	7,543.8	8,848.2
Population (in millions)	238	265	275

  a. Nominal GDP in 1995.

  b. Real GDP in 1985.

  c. Rise in the price level from 1985 to 1999.

  d. Growth in real output from 1985 to 1999.

  e. Per capita real GDP in 1985, 1995, 1999. What was the growth in real output from 1985 to 1999?

6. Answer each of the following questions about nominal output, real output, and inflation:

  a. Nominal output increased from $8.8 trillion to $9.3 trillion from 1998 to 1999. The GDP deflator rose over that same year by 1.5%. By how much did real output increase?

b. Real output increased from $7.5 trillion to $7.8 trillion from 1995 to 1996. The GDP deflator rose over that same year by 2.0%. By how much did nominal output increase?

c. Real output decreased from $6.70 billion in 1990 to $6.67 billion in 1991. Nominal output rose by 3.2%. By how much did the price level rise from 1990 to 1991?

● A BRAIN TEASER

1. How could output and unemployment rise in an economy at the same time?

● POTENTIAL ESSAY QUESTIONS

You may also see essay questions similar to the "Problems & Applications" and "Brain Teasers" exercises.

1. Full employment, keeping inflation under control, and economic growth are among the major macroeconomic goals of all societies. Why is economic growth a major macroeconomic goal?

2. What is potential output and how is it related to the target rate of unemployment and the target level of capacity utilization? Which is greater: potential or actual output during a recession? During an economic boom?

3. What are some of the problems with the interpretation of unemployment statistics that can cause unemployment statistics to underestimate and to overestimate the true rate of unemployment? How do Classical and Keynesian economists differ in this regard?

━━━━━ **ANSWERS** ━━━━━

MATCHING

1-x; 2-g; 3-h; 4-z2; 5-c; 6-s; 7-e; 8-j; 9-q; 10-z1; 11-i; 12-k; 13-a; 14-f; 15-y; 16-m; 17-z3; 18-v; 19-p; 20-o; 21-z4; 22-d; 23-n; 24-r; 25-w; 26-b; 27-z; 28-t; 29. l.

━━━━━ **ANSWERS** ━━━━━

MULTIPLE CHOICE

1. c   As the text states on page 104-105, inflation and unemployment are both short- and long-run problems.

2. a   As stated on page 104-105, the long run focuses on supply issues that increase the incentive to work, create new technologies, and invest in capital.

3. b   Per capita income is calculated by dividing total income by total population as stated on page 105.

4. b   See page 105.

5. d   As more material goods made available by growth are used for antipollution equipment, less is available for personal consumption. The added material goods have already been used. See pages 106-107.

6. b   As seen in the table on page 106, Japan's per capita growth rate averaged 4.8 percent from 1950 to 2000. China's per capita growth rate was 3.4 percent.

7. b   See page 108.

8. d   The others are coincidental indicators. Even if you didn't remember this, you should be able to figure out that the change in inventory predicts what firms think will be happening in the future, whereas the others tell what is happening now. See page 111.

9. c   Almost all economists believe government should intervene during a depression. See page 110.

10. c   As discussed on page 112, the fear of hunger was the main deterrent to unemployment. A second deterrent would have been emigration, but that would not be as good an answer. Since d says immigration (the flowing in of people), not emigration, d is definitely wrong.

11. d   See page 113.

12. d   See pages 113-114.

13. a   See page 103.

14. b   See page 103.

15. c   See page 108.

16. b   See page 118.

17. c   Total output moves in the opposite direction by 2% times $5 trillion, which equals a fall of $100 billion. See page 118.

18. d   As the text points out on page 119, inflation is a continual rise in the price level, so the use of the term "one-time" should have clued you that d is the answer.

19. b   To determine the price level rise you multiply each component by its price rise. Since only 20% of the total rose, you get 10% times 20% = 2% . See pages 120-121.

20. b   See page 123. A reminder: A service is considered just as much a good and a component of real output as is a physical good.

21. c   If real output remains constant, then the nominal output must also rise by 20%, as discussed on page 123.

22. d   Inflation does not make society richer or poorer, and the distributional consequences of inflations differ, eliminating answers a and b. While the second part of c is true, that doesn't mean that there are no costs of inflation and, as discussed on pages 124-125, one of those costs is the reduction in the informational content of prices.

23. c   As discussed on pages 124-125, unexpected inflation is inflation that surprises people. Those people who didn't raise their prices are surprised. Income is redistributed from those people who didn't raise their prices to those who did.

ANSWERS

SHORT-ANSWER QUESTIONS

1. Economists use the long-run framework and the short-run framework to analyze macroeconomic problems. The long-run framework focuses on supply, while the short-run framework focuses on demand. (104-105)

2. The average rate of real growth in output in Canada from 1870 to the present is 4% per year. More recently, it has been about 2.5% to 3.5% per year. The benefits of growth are improvements in the standard of living, on average. The costs are pollution, resource exhaustion and destruction of natural habitat. (105-107)

3. The average expansion since the post-war period has lasted 51 months. (109)

4. Since the late 1980s, the target rate of unemployment has been between 6 and 8 percent. (113)

5. The inflation rate in Canada before World War II fluctuated and was sometimes positive and sometimes negative. Since World War II, the price level has nearly always risen. (120)

6. The four phases of the business cycle are: the peak, the downturn, the trough, and the upturn. They are labeled in the graph below. (109-110)

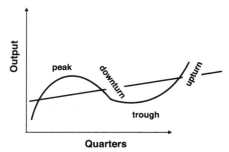

7. Unemployment is calculated by dividing the number of unemployed individuals by the number of people in the civilian labour force, and multiplying the result by 100. (115-116)

8. Those who are not in the labour force and those incapable of working are not employed and are not counted as unemployed. They include students, retirees, homemakers, those incapable of working, and those who choose not to participate in the labour force. People in the military, and residents of Indian reserves are also not included in the calculation of the labour force. (115-116)

9. Potential output is that level of output that will be achieved at the target rate of unemployment. (118)

10. Inflation is a continual rise in the price level. If there were no inflation, there would be no difference between real and nominal concepts. A real concept is the nominal concept adjusted for inflation. (119-123)

11. Nominally, Maseratis have risen by 166% from 1975 to 1995, but all other prices have risen during that time period too, including wages. You must adjust the rise in the aggregate price level to find out how much Maseratis have risen in real terms. From 1975 to 1995, the price level rose by 156%. So, the real price of the Maserati rose by only approximately 10% from 1975 to 1995. (123-124)

12. Expected inflation is the amount of inflation that people expect. Unexpected inflation is inflation that is a surprise. (124)

13. Two important costs of inflation are that it redistributes income from people who do not raise their price to people who do raise their price; and it can reduce the amount of information that prices are supposed to convey. (124-125)

━━━ ANSWERS ━━━

PROBLEMS AND APPLICATIONS

1. Okun's rule of thumb states that a 1-percentage point change in the unemployment rate will cause income in the economy to change in the opposite direction by 2 percent.
   a. Income rises 4 percent. (118)
   b. Income rises 2 percent. (118)
   c. Income falls 6 percent. (118)

2. a. Structural because this is a structural change in the economy. (111-112)
   b. Structural because this is a change in social structure. (111-112)
   c. Cyclical because this is unemployment due to a change in economic activity. (111-112)

3. a. Labour force = employed + unemployed = 144 million. (115-116)
   b. Unemployment rate = (unemployed/labour force) 100 = 6.9%. (115-116)

4. a. The price of the basket in 2000 is $805 and in 2001 is $900. Since 2000 is the base year, the index must be 100. This is calculated as (price of the basket in 2000)/(price of the basket in 2000) = $805/$805 100=100. (120-122)
   b. The price index in 2001 is (price of the basket in 2001)/(price of the basket in 2000) = $900/$805 100= 112. Prices rose by 12%. (120-122)
   c. Some potential flaws are that (1) the basket of goods is small and might not reflect the true basket of goods purchased by Edmonton Eskimos fans, (2) the basket of goods is fixed (since the price of cheese fell, fans might be buying more cheese and fewer football tickets), (3) the basket does not reflect quality improvements (since the Edmonton Eskimos won the Grey Cup in 2003, the quality of subsequent games in 2004 might improve, but the tickets are counted as if they were the same as in 2003). (120-122)

5. a. Nominal GDP in 1995 is $7,400 billion dollars. Calculate this by multiplying real GDP in 1995 by the GDP deflator and dividing by 100. (123)
   b. Real GDP in 1996 dollars in 1985 is $5,763 billion. Calculate this by dividing nominal GDP by the GDP deflator and multiplying by 100. (123)
   c. The price level rose by 42% from 1985 to 1999. Calculate this by dividing the change in the GDP price deflator by the base year deflator and multiplying by 100: (104.6 73.7)/73.7 100. (123)
   d. Real output grew by 54% from 1985 to 1999. Calculate this by dividing the change in nominal GDP from 1985 to 1999 by the base year nominal GDP and multiplying by 100: (8848.2 5763)/5763 100. (123)
   e. Per capita real GDP in 1985 was $24,214; in 1995, it was $28,467; in 1990, it was $2,175. Calculate this by dividing real GDP by the population. Per capita real GDP rose by 15% from 1985 to 1999. (124)

6. a. Nominal output increased by 5.7% from 1998 to 1999. Since the GDP deflator rose over that same year, we know that real output increased by less—specifically by 4.2% from 1998 to 1999. Subtract inflation from the change in nominal output to get the change in real output: 5.7% 1.5% = 4.2%. (123)
   b. Real output increased 4.0% from 1995 to 1996. Since the GDP deflator rose 2% over that same year, we know that nominal output increased 6.0% from 1995 to 1996. Add inflation to the change in real output to find the change in nominal output: 2% + 4% = 6%. (123)
   c. Real output fell 0.45% from 1990 to 1991. Since nominal output rose by 3.2%, we know the price level rose 3.65% from 1990 to 1991. Subtract the change in real output from the change in nominal output to find the inflation rate: 3.2% (0.45%) = 3.65%. (123)

A BRAIN TEASER

1. Usually one would expect unemployment to fall as output rises because it takes more workers to produce more output. However, an increase in productivity of workers can cause an increase in output without any reduction in unemployment. Another possibility is that the labour force participation rate could be rising so that the labour force is rising at a faster pace than the rise in employment. This would cause unemployment to rise even though output is expanding and the economy is growing. (115-117)

POTENTIAL ESSAY QUESTIONS

The following are annotated answers. They indicate the general idea behind the answer.

1. Economic growth is a major macroeconomic goal because it provides for more jobs for a growing population. If output increases more than population increases then per capita growth occurs. Assuming there is no change in the distribution of the nation's income then everybody gets a "bigger piece of the pie." In this way economic growth increases the average absolute standard of living for people. *Remember, economic growth is valued by all nations because it raises the standard of living.*

2. Potential output is the output that would materialize at the target rate of unemployment and the target level of capacity utilization. Potential output grows at the secular (long-term) trend rate of 2.5 to 3.5 percent per year. When the economy is in a recession, actual output is below potential output. When the economy is in a boom, actual output is above potential output.

3. Statistics Canada estimates the rate of unemployment. Underestimation can occur because of discouraged workers who are not counted as unemployed as well as others who may not be counted. Also, many people may be working part-time, but would like to work full-time. This "underemployment" is not reflected in unemployment statistics and suggests that it underestimates the true problem. On the other hand, some people may be counted as being unemployed when they are working in the underground economy–working for "cash under the table." The Classicals and Keynesians differ most when it comes to the number of discouraged workers. Some Keynesians argue that Statistics Canada underestimates unemployment significantly because a great number of discouraged workers are not counted as being unemployed.

NATIONAL INCOME ACCOUNTING

6

● CHAPTER AT A GLANCE

The study of macroeconomics requires the use of several tools to better understand the workings of the market economy. This chapter will introduce you to several important measures of an economy's economic performance. This body of analysis is called national income accounting.

The primary measure of an economy's domestic output is real GDP, as discussed in the previous chapter. GDP only measures the final goods and services produced for end use consumption in order to avoid double counting. There are two methods of calculating GDP — the expenditures approach and the factor incomes approach. Theoretically, both approaches will yield the same level of economic activity. Several other important terms include real GDP, nominal GDP, personal income and personal disposable income.

The last part of this chapter outlines some of the shortcomings of using the GDP concept as a measure of overall economic performance. GDP attempts to measure market activity, but cannot measure happiness or economic welfare.

This review is based upon the learning objectives that open the chapter.

1a. National income accounting is a set of rules and definitions for measuring economic activity in the aggregate economy. It enables us to measure and analyze how much a nation is producing and consuming. (130-131)

1b. Gross Domestic Product (GDP) is total market ($) value of all <u>final</u> goods and services produced in a one-year period. (131)

GDP is output produced within a country's borders; GNI is output produced by a country's citizens wherever they may be in the world.

GNI = GDP + Net foreign factor income where:

Net foreign factor income: Add the foreign income of one's citizens and subtract the income of residents who are not citizens.

1c. To avoid double counting, one must eliminate intermediate goods, either by calculating only final output (expenditures approach), or by calculating only final income (income approach) by using the value added approach. (132-135)

Know what is and is not included in calculating GDP.

<u>GDP does not include:</u>
* *intermediate goods (sold for resale or further processing);*
* *second-hand sales;*
* *government transfers, housespouse production or any other non-market activity;*
* *underground economic activity.*

2a. Gross Domestic Product:

GDP can be calculated using either the factor income or expenditures approach because of the national income identity. (136-141)

The definition of profit is key to the equality of income and expenditures. Profit is total output less payments to the factors of production.

Hint: In most "non-technical" discussions, "output" (GDP) and "income" (National Income—NI) are used interchangeably—that is, GDP is assumed to be equal to NI for purposes of simplification.

2b. GDP = C + I + G + (X − IM) is an accounting identity because it is defined as true. (136-143)

The above identity is really the expenditures approach, which states:

Total output = Total expenditures
Total output = GDP;
Total expenditures = C + I + G + (X−IM)

By substitution: GDP = C + I + G + (X−IM)

Know what C, I, G, X − IM stand for!

Also note:
$X_n = (X − IM) = Net exports.$
If X_n is positive, then X>IM Trade surplus.
If X_n is negative, then X<IM Trade deficit.
If X_n is zero, then X=IM Trade balance.

3a. GDP can be used to compare one country's production with another country's and of one year's production with another year's. (144-145)

- These comparisons can be made by looking at various countries' GDP levels or per capita GDP.

- GDP is a poor measure of relative living standards in various countries. So, economists use purchasing power parity which adjusts prices among countries.

3b. A real concept is a nominal concept adjusted for inflation. (145-146)

GDP is a price times quantity (P×Q) phenomenon. GDP can rise due to an increase in P (price level) and/or an increase in Q (real quantity of output).

Real GDP, in essence, holds prices (P) constant. Hence, real GDP is inflation (or deflation) adjusted.

3c. Using GDP to compare standards of living among countries has problems. (146-149)

GDP only measures market activity. In developing countries, individuals often produce and trade outside the market.

Market prices often vary considerably among countries making the value of the same income in terms of purchasing power different

4. Limitations of national income accounting include: (146-149)

- Measurement problems.
- GDP measures national activity, not welfare; and
- Subcategories are often interdependent.

GDP is not and was never intended to be a measure of social well-being.

See also, Appendix A: "Calculating Real GDP."

MATCHING THE TERMS
Match the terms to their definitions

All of these key terms are found at the end of the chapter.

s 1. depreciation
a 2. disposable personal income
m 3. final output
n 4. government expenditures
c 5. gross domestic product (GDP)
f 6. gross national income (GNI)
p 7. gross private investment
i 8. intermediate products
j 9. national balance sheet
d 10. national income (NI)
l 11. national income accounting
e 12. net domestic product
r 13. net exports
g 14. net foreign factor income
q 15. net private investment
b 16. nominal GDP
t 17. personal consumption expenditures
o 18. personal income
h 19. real GDP
k 20. value added

a. Personal income minus personal income taxes and other personal taxes.
b. GDP calculated at existing prices.
c. The total market value of all final goods and services produced in an economy in a one-year period.
d. Total income earned by citizens and businesses of a country.
e. GDP adjusted to take account of depreciation.
f. Aggregate final output of citizens and businesses of an economy in a one-year period.
g. Income from foreign domestic factor sources minus foreign factor incomes earned domestically.
h. Nominal GDP adjusted for inflation.
i. Products used as input in the production of some other product..
j. A balance sheet of an economy's stock of assets and liabilities.
k. The increase in value that a firm contributes to a product or service.
l. A set of rules and definitions for measuring economic activity in the aggregate economy.
m. Goods and services purchased for final use.
n. Government payments for goods and services and investment in equipment and structures.
o. National income plus net transfer payments from government minus amounts attributed but not received.
p. Business spending on equipment, structures, and inventories and household spending on new owned-occupied housing.
q. Gross private domestic investment minus depreciation.
r. Exports minus imports.
s. The decrease in an asset's value.
t. Payments by households for goods and services.

● MULTIPLE CHOICE

Circle the one best answer for each of the following questions:

1. GDP is:
    a. the total market value of all final goods and services produced in an economy in a one-year period.
    b. the total market value of all goods and services produced in an economy in a one-year period.
    c. the total market value of all final goods and services produced by a country's citizens in a one-year period.
    d. the sum of all final goods and services produced in an economy in a one-year period.

2. To move from GDP to GNI, one must:
    a. add net foreign factor income.
    b. subtract inflation.
    c. add depreciation.
    d. subtract depreciation.

3. If a firm's cost of materials is $100 and its sales are $500, its value added is:
    a. $100.
    b. $400.
    c. $500.
    d. $600.

4. If you, the owner, sell your old car for $600, how much does GDP increase?
    a. By $600.
    b. By the amount you bought it for, minus the $600.
    c. By zero.
    d. By the $600 you received and the $600 the person you sold it to paid, or $1,200.

5. There are two firms in an economy, Firm A and Firm B. Firm A produces 100 widgets and sells them for $2 apiece. Firm B produces 200 gadgets and sells them for $3 apiece. Firm A sells 30 of its widgets to Firm B and the remainder to consumers. Firm B sells 50 of its gadgets to Firm A and the remainder to consumers. What is GDP in this economy?
    a. $210.
    b. $590.
    c. $600.
    d. $800.

6. If a woman divorces her husband (who has been cleaning the house) and hires him to continue cleaning her house for $20,000 per year, GDP will:
    a. remain constant.
    b. increase by $20,000 per year.
    c. decrease by $20,000 per year.
    d. remain unchanged.

7. The national income identity shows that:
    a. the value of factor services is equal to the value of final goods plus investment.
    b. the value of factor services is equal to the value of final goods plus savings.
    c. the value of factor services is equal to the value of final goods sold.
    d. the value of consumption goods is equal to the value of factor services.

8. Which of the following correctly lists the components of total expenditures?
    a. consumption, investment, depreciation, exports minus imports.
    b. consumption, investment, government expenditures, exports minus imports.
    c. rent, profit, interest, wages.
    d. consumption, net foreign factor income, investment, government expenditures.

9. The largest component of expenditures in GDP is
    a. consumption.
    b. investment.
    c. net exports.
    d. government purchases of goods and services.

10. The largest component of national income is
    a. rents.
    b. net interest.
    c. profits.
    d. compensation to employees.

11. Gross investment differs from net investment by:
    a. net exports.
    b. net imports.
    c. depreciation.
    d. transfer payments.

12. Which of the following factors serves to equate income and expenditure?
    a. profit before taxes.
    b. depreciation.
    c. net foreign factor income.
    d. value added.

13. Switching from the exchange rate approach to the purchasing power parity approach for calculating GDP generally:
    a. does not make a significant difference for a developing country's GDP relative to a developed country's GDP.
    b. generally increases a developing country's GDP relative to a developed country's GDP.
    c. generally decreases a developing country's GDP relative to a developed country's GDP.
    d. changes the relative GDP of developing country's GDP, but not in a predictable fashion.

14. If inflation is 10 percent and nominal GDP goes up 20 percent, real GDP goes up approximately
    a. 1 percent.
    b. 10 percent.
    c. 20 percent.
    d. 30 percent.

15. Which of the following is the *best* measure available to compare changes in standards of living among countries over time?
   a. changes in nominal income.
   b. changes in nominal per capita income.
   c. changes in real income.
   d. changes in real per capita income.

16. If nominal GDP rises:
   a. welfare has definitely increased.
   b. welfare has definitely decreased.
   c. welfare may have increased or decreased.
   d. welfare most likely has increased.

17. Estimates of the importance of the underground economy in Canada indicate that it is:
   a. very small—under 1 percent of the total economy.
   b. somewhere between 1 to 5 percent all the way to 30 percent of the total economy.
   c. somewhere between 1.5 percent all the way to 60 percent of the total economy.
   d. as large as the non-underground economy.

● SHORT-ANSWER QUESTIONS

1. What is the purpose of national income accounting?

It provides a way of measuring total production in an economy as a whole. Enables us to measure an analyze how much the nation is producing or consuming.

2. What is GDP?

The total value (market) of all final goods and services produced in an economy in a one year period.

3. What is GNI? How does it differ from GDP?

Gross national Income, the whole final output of citizens and businesses of an economy in a one-year period. GDP measures economic activity within a country. Economic activity of citizens and businesses of a country is measured by GNI

4. Calculate the contribution of Chex cereal (from seeds to consumer) to GDI, using the following information:

Participants	Cost of materials	Value of Sales
Farmer	0	200
Chex factory	200	500
Distributor	500	800
Grocery store	800	1000

$1000
value added approach.

5. What are the four components of gross domestic product? What are the four components of national income?

GDP = consumption + investment + gov't expitures + net export (x−im).

6. Say the price level rises 10% from an index of 1 to an index of 1.1 and nominal GDP rises from $4 trillion to $4.6 trillion. What is nominal GDP in the second period? What is real GDP in the second period?

Nominal → 4.6 trillion
Real GDP → $\frac{4.6}{1.1}$

7. As pointed out by the quotation that begins the chapter on national income accounting, statistics can be misleading. In what way can national income statistics be misleading? Given your answer, why use them at all?

Need to know how the statistics were arrived at.

PROBLEMS AND APPLICATIONS

1. For each of the following, calculate how much the action described has added to GDP:

   a. A used car dealer buys a car for $3,000 and resells it for $3,300.

   $300

   b. A company sells 1,000 disks for $500 each. Of these, it sells 600 to other companies and 400 to individuals.

   $200000

   c. A company sells 50 computers at a retail price of $1,000 apiece and 100 software packages at a retail price of $50 apiece to consumers. The same company sells 25 computers at $800 and 50 software packages at $30 apiece to wholesalers. The wholesalers then sell the 25 computers at $1,250 apiece and the 50 software packages at $75 apiece.

   Only the amount sold to the consumer is added to the GDP!

   d. Fred purchases 100 stock certificates valued at $5 apiece and pays a 10% commission. When the price declines to $4.50 apiece, Fred decides to sell all 100 certificates, again at a 10% commission.

   Only commisions are counted in GDP 50 & 45

   e. Your uncle George receives $600 in social security each month for one year.

   gov't transfers are not related to GDP.

2. Use the following table showing the production of 500 boxes of Wheaties cereal to calculate the contribution to GDP using the value-added approach.

Participants	Cost of materials	Value of Sales
Farmer	$0	$150
Mill	$150	$250
Cereal maker	$250	$600
Wholesaler	$600	$800
Grocery store	$800	$1000

   a. Calculate the value added at each stage of production.

   b. What is the total value of sales?

c. What is the total value added?

d. What is the contribution to GDP for the production of those Wheaties?

3. There are three firms in an economy: X, Y, and Z. Firm X buys $200 worth of goods from firm Y and $300 worth of goods from firm Z, and produces 250 units of output at $4 per unit. Firm Y buys $150 worth of goods from firm X, and $250 worth of goods from firm Z, and produces 300 units of output at $6 per unit. Firm Z buys $75 worth of goods from X, and $50 worth goods from firm Y, and produces 300 units at $2 per unit. All other products are sold to consumers. Answer the following:

a. What is GDP?

b. How much government revenue would a value added tax of 10% generate?

c. How much government revenue would an income tax of 10% generate?

d. How much government revenue would a 10% sales tax on final output generate?

4. You have been hired as a research assistant and are given the following data about the economy: All figures are in billions of dollars.

Transfer payments	$70
Interest paid by consumers	5
Net exports	10
Indirect business taxes (less subsidies)	44
Net foreign factor income	3
Corporate income tax	69
Contribution for Employment Insurance (EI) and Canada Pension Plan (CPP)	37
Personal tax and non-tax payments	92
Undistributed corporate profits	49
Gross private investment	200
Government purchases	190
Personal consumption	550
Depreciation	65

You are asked to calculate the following:

a. GDP.

b. GNP. = GDP + Net foreign factor income.

c. NDP. = GDP - depreciation.

d. NI. = NDP - indirect business taxes

e. Personal income.

f. Disposable personal income. = PI - personal income tax -

5. You have been hired as a research assistant and are given the following data about another economy (profits, wages, rents, and interest are measured nationally):

Corporate income tax	$200
Non-incorporated non-farm income	225
Profits	250
Wages	800
Rents	30
Depreciation	20
Indirect business taxes (less subsidies)	110
Undistributed corporate profits	50
Net foreign factor income	−5
Interest	175
EI & CPP contribution	0
Transfer payments	0
Personal taxes	150

Calculate the following:

a. GDP.

b. GNP.

c. NDP.

d. National income.

e. Personal income.

f. Disposable personal income.

6. Use the following table to answer the questions:

	Real output in year	Nominal output billions of 1996 $	GDP deflator billions of $ (1996=100)
1995	7,543.8	7,400.5	_____
1996	7,813.2	7,813.2	100.0
1997	8,144.8	_____	101.9
1998	_____	_____	103.1
1999	_____	9,256.1	104.6

a. What is output for 1999 in 1996 dollars?

b. What is the output in nominal terms in 1997?

c. What is the GDP deflator (1996=100) in 1995?

d. Real output grew by 4.3% from 1997 to 1998. By how much did nominal output grow in 1998?

● A BRAIN TEASER

1. Why must imports be subtracted in calculating GDP?

● POTENTIAL ESSAY QUESTIONS

You may also see essay questions similar to the "Problems & Applications" and "Brain Teasers" exercises.

1. Using the circular flow model, explain why any dollar value of output must give rise to an identical amount of income (at least for all practical concerns)?

2. How might an economy experience an increase in nominal GDP, but experience negative growth at the same time?

■ ANSWERS ■

MATCHING

1-s; 2-a; 3-m; 4-n; 5-c; 6-f; 7-p; 8-i; 9-j; 10-d; 11-l; 12-e; 13-r; 14-g; 15-q; 16-b; 17-t; 18-o; 19-h; 20-k.

■ ANSWERS ■

MULTIPLE CHOICE

1. a   As the text emphasizes on page 131, GDP is the <u>market value</u> of all <u>final</u> goods and services produced <u>in</u> an economy in a one-year period.

2. a   Since GNP is total market value of production of citizens in a country, and GDP is total market value of production within a country, one must add net foreign factor income to GDP to get GNP. See page 131.

3. b   Value added equals value of sales minus cost of materials. See page 134.

4. c   As discussed on pages 134-135, sales of used goods do not contribute to GDP except to the degree that they are sold by a second hand dealer. Then the dealer's profit would be the value added.

5. b   GDP doesn't include purchases made between businesses, only final sales to consumers. To calculate the answer, calculate total sales for Firms A and B ($600 + $200 = $800) and subtract those goods sold between the firms ($60 + $150 = $210) to get final sales ($800 $210 = $590). See pages 133-134.

6. b   As discussed on pages 134-135, GDP measures market transactions. The divorce-and-hire changes the housecleaning activities from nonmarket to market and hence increases GDP.

7. c   The national income identity shows that all income (value of factor services) equals all expenditures (value of goods sold to individuals). See pages 136-141.

8. b   GDP = C + I + G + (X – IM). See page 136.

9. a   Consumption makes up the majority of expenditures. See Table 6-2, page 139.

10. d   As you can see in Table 6-3 on page 140, compensation to employees is the largest percent of national income.

11. c   Net investment equals gross investment less depreciation. See pages 137-138.

12. a   Profit is what remains after all firm's other income is paid out. Thus, profit is the key to the income/expenditures equality. See pages 141-142.

13. b   In developing countries, living expenses are generally lower than in developed countries. Thus moving towards a purchasing power parity approach generally increases GDP in a developing country. In the example of China given on pages 144-145, the switch increased China's GDP by more than 400 percent.

14. b   Subtract inflation from nominal GDP growth to find real GDP growth as a first approximation. See pages 145-146.

15. d   As discussed on pages 146-147 nominal GDP must be adjusted for price level increases before comparisons over time can be made. Dividing total real income by the population is a good indication of relative standards of living.

16. c   Nominal GDP must be adjusted by inflation to arrive at real GDP before one can even start to make welfare comparisons. And even if real GDP increases, it is not clear that welfare has increased, as discussed on pages 146-147.

17. b   On page 148 the text states that the underground economy in Canada is between 1 to 5 and 30 percent of the total economy.

ANSWERS

SHORT-ANSWER QUESTIONS

1. The purpose of national income accounting is to measure and analyze how much the nation is producing and consuming. National income accounting defines the relationship among the sub-aggregates of aggregate production. (131)

2. GDP is the total value of all final goods and services produced in an economy in a one-year period. (131)

3. GNI is aggregate final output of citizens, businesses and government of an economy in a one-year period. GDP is output produced within a country's borders, while GNI is output produced by a country's citizens. Add net foreign factor income to GDP to get GNI. (131)

4. $1,000. We could use either the value added approach or the final output approach. Summing the value added at each stage of production—the difference between cost of materials and value of sales —we get $1,000. (134)

Participants	Cost of materials	Value of Sales	Value added
Farmer	$0	$200	$200
Chex factory	200	500	300
Distributor	500	800	300
Grocery store	800	1000	200
Sum (total output)			1000

5. The four components of gross domestic product are consumption, investment, government expenditures, and net exports (X IM). The four components that comprise NI are compensation to employees, interest and miscellaneous investment income, corporate profits and farm and non-incorporated non-farm income. (136-141)

6. A real value is a nominal value adjusted for inflation. So, nominal GDP in the second period is $4.6 trillion, but real GDP is $4.6 trillion divided by the price index, 1.1, or $4.18 trillion. (145-146)

7. National income accounting statistics can be misleading. They are subject to measurement error; they are based on samples of data and assumptions about behaviour. For example, the measurement of inflation is widely believed to overestimate true inflation. Also, GDP does not include non-market activities such as housework. It measures national activity, not welfare; output could rise but welfare fall. Its subcategories are often interdependent; that is, arbitrary decisions were made when determining what goes in which subcategory. Nevertheless, national income accounting makes it possible to discuss the aggregate economy. It is important to be aware of the limitations of the data in those discussions. (146-149)

ANSWERS

PROBLEMS AND APPLICATIONS

1. **a.** $300. Only the value added by the sale would be added to GDP, which in this case is the difference between the purchase price and the sale price. (134-141)
    b. $200,000. Total output produced is 1,000 × $500 = $500,000. Of this intermediate goods valued at 600 × $500 = $300,000. So, the company's contribution to GDP is ($500,000 − $300,000) = $200,000. (134-141)
    c. Only that amount that is sold to the consumer is counted in GDP. This is 50 × 1,000 + 100 × 50 = $55,000 sold by the first company plus the sales of the wholesaler, which is 25 × $1250 + 50 × $75 = $35,000. Total contribution to GDP is $90,000. (134-141)
    d. Only the commissions of $50 and $45 are counted in GDP. Together they contribute $95. (134-141)
    e. Nothing has been added to GDP. Government transfers are not included in GDP. They are not related to the production of goods and services. (134-141)

2.

Participants	Cost of materials	Value of Sales	Value added
Farmer	$0	$150	150
Mill	$150	$250	100
Cereal maker	$250	$600	350
Wholesaler	$600	$800	200
Grocery store	$800	$1000	200

   a. The value added at each stage of production is shown in the table above. (134-141)
   b. The total value of sales is $2,800. Find this by adding the rows of the value of sales column. (134-141)
   c. The total value added is $1,000. Find this by adding the value added at each stage of production. (134-141)
   d. The contribution to GDP for the production of those Wheaties is $1,000. Value added at each stage of production is the contribution to GDP. This avoids double-counting. (134-141)

3. a. $2375: GDP is the sum of the value added by the three firms = 500 + 1,400 + 475. (134-141)
   b. $237.50: A 10% value added tax would generate = (0.10)($2,375) = $237.50 of revenue. (134-141)
   c. $237.50: A 10% income tax would generate the same revenue as a 10% value added tax. (134-141)
   d. $340: A 10% sales tax on final output would generate = $340 of revenue: (0.10) (1,000 + 1,800 + 600). (134-141)

4. a. $950: GDP = $C + I + G + (X \, IM)$ = 550 + 200 + 190 + 10 = 950. (136-141)
   b. $953: GNP = GDP + net foreign factor income = 953. (136-141)
   c. $885: NDP = GDP − depreciation = 950 − 65 = 885. (136-141)
   d. $844 : NI = NDP − indirect business taxes = 888 − 44 = 844. (136-141)
   e. $759: PI = NI + transfers from government − corporate retained earnings − corporate income taxes − contributions to EI and CPP = 844 + 70 − 49 − 69 − 37 = 759. (143)
   f. $667: DPI = PI − personal income tax = 759 − 92 = 667. (143)

5. a. $1,615: GDP = NDP + Depreciation = NNP − net foreign factor income + depreciation = NI + indirect business tax − net foreign factor income + depreciation = wages + rents + interest + profits + proprietors' income + indirect business taxes − net foreign factor income + depreciation = 800 + 30 + 175 + 475 + 110 − (−5) + 20 = 1615. (140-141)
   b. $1,610: GNP = GDP + net foreign factor income = 1615 + (−5). (140-141)
   c. $1,595: NDP = GDP − depreciation = 1615 − 20. (140-141)
   d. $1,480: NI = NDP − indirect business taxes = 1590 − 110. (140-141)
   e. $1,230: PI = NI + transfers − corporate income taxes − undistributed corporate profits − CPP and EI contributions = 1480 + 0 − 200 − 50 − 0. (143)
   f. $1,080: DPI = PI − personal taxes = 1230 − 150. (143)

6. a. $8849.0 billion 1996 dollars: Real output = (Nominal output/deflator) × 100 = 9256.1/ 104.6 × 100. (145-146)
   b. $8299.6 billion: Nominal output = (real output × deflator) / 100 = (8144.8 101.9)/100. (145-146)
   c. 98.1: Deflator = (Nominal output/real output) × 100 = (7400.5/7543.8) × 100. (176-177)
   d. Real output grew by 4.3% and inflation rose by 1.2%, so nominal output grew by 5.5%. (145-146)

ANSWERS

A BRAIN TEASER

1. Government expenditures, consumption, investment include all expenditures in those categories regardless of where the products were produced. That is, they include products produced in foreign countries. Since GDP measures domestic production, the total value of imports must be subtracted from total expenditures. (136)

━━━━━━ ANSWERS ━━━━━━

POTENTIAL ESSAY QUESTIONS

The following are annotated answers. They indicate the general idea behind the answer.

1. Whenever the business community produces some $X value of output, that dollar value reflects costs of production which were incurred in producing that output level. Those costs of production are all paid out to the resource (input) owners as their income. Hence, any dollar output level (GDP) gives rise to an identical amount of national income (NI), at least for all practical purposes.

2. The price level could have increased by a greater percentage than the decrease in the real quantity of goods and services produced. This would result in an increase in nominal GDP but a decrease in real GDP (negative growth).

GROWTH, PRODUCTIVITY AND WEALTH IN THE LONG RUN

CHAPTER AT A GLANCE

Chapter 8 expands on the discussions from the previous chapter by emphasizing the importance of economic growth to a market economy. Growth is defined as the increase in the amount of goods and services an economy produces from one period to another. Growth is important as it relates to how well an economy uses its factors of production, that is, its available labour, natural resources, capital accumulation, technology, growth-compatible institutions and entrepreneurial ability. As a result, growth has a major impact on the standard of living of an economy.

Per capita output, defined as the total output divided by the total population, is an important indicator for making international comparisons. Another important indicator of an economy's well-being is productivity. There are several different measures of productivity including labour and total factor productivity. (157-158)

This chapter also introduces you to two different theories related to growth — the Classical growth theory and the new growth theory, as well as policies that governments can implement to promote economic growth, technological innovation, basic research and development, and higher standards of living for its citizens.

This review is based upon the learning objectives that open the chapter.

1a. Growth is an increase in the amount of goods and services an economy produces. (157)

Growth can be measured either by increases in real GDP or increases in real GDP per person (per capita growth).

1b. Because growth, on average, makes more goods available for consumption, it improves physical standards of living. (157-158)

Because of compounding, small differences in growth rates can result in enormous differences in income per person.

Remember the Rule of 72: the number of years it takes for income to double equals 72 divided by the annual growth rate of income.

1c. Markets increase productivity and improve standards of living. Markets create an interdependent economy in which individuals can take advantage of the benefits of specialization and trade. (159)

1d. Even though growth is not evenly distributed within an economy, the poor benefit generally from the growth that markets foster. It depends if the poor are judged from an absolute or relative standard. (159)

1e. Per capita growth means producing more goods and services per person. It is defined as the percentage change in output less the percentage change in population. This is an important measure of standard of living because even though many economies may have grown fast, their populations have increased faster, so per capita output growth has been lower. (160-161)

2. Markets create specialization and division of labour and have been empirically highly correlated with growth. The growth rate has increased as the importance of markets has increased. Five important sources of growth are: (161-165)

• Capital accumulation–investment in productive capacity;

Can be: (1) Privately owned by business, (2) publicly owned and provided by government–our infrastructure, (3) human capital–investment in people, (4) social capital–institutions and conventions.

- Available resources;

  Technological advances can help overcome any lack of resources.

- Institutions with incentives compatible with growth;

  Government policy can help or hinder growth. Regulations have both costs and benefits, but too much regulation definitely hinders growth.

- Technological development;

  Technology not only causes growth, it changes the entire social and political dimensions of society.

- Entrepreneurship.

  This is the ability to get things done. It involves creativity, vision, and an ability to translate that vision into reality.

3a. The Classical growth model focuses on the role of capital accumulation in the growth process. Increases in capital lead to growth. (166-167)

The Classical growth model predicts that the rise in output per worker will eventually slow as additional amounts of capital are less productive. It also predicts that as economies add capital, capital-poor countries will grow faster than capital-rich countries.

The graph below depicts early economists' view of the effects of diminishing marginal productivity of labour. Increases in the population beyond N* leads to starvation. Below N*, the population grows because of the surplus output.

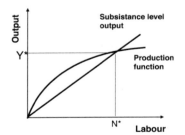

3b. The new growth theory emphasizes the role of technology in the growth process. Positive externalities and learning by doing mean that increasing returns may predominate and that growth rates can accelerate over time. (170-171)

Technological advance is not necessarily the result of investment.

Technology often has positive externalities that can result in an acceleration in growth.

3c. Most growth theories centre around the production function: Output = A·f(labour, capital, land). (165-166)

- *Returns to scale describes what happens to output when all inputs are increased.*

- *Constant returns to scale: output rises by same proportion as the increase in all inputs. (An example: ↑ all inputs 10% ⇒ ↑ output by 10%)*

- *Increasing returns to scale: output rises by a greater proportion than the increase in all inputs. (An example: ↑ all inputs 10% ⇒ ↑ output by 15%)*

- *Decreasing returns to scale: output rises by a smaller proportion than the increase in all inputs. (An example: ↑ all inputs 10% ⇒ ↑ output by 5%)*

- *Diminishing marginal productivity involves increasing one, not all, inputs. In general, economists assume diminishing marginal productivity—the increase in output falls as more of one input is added.*

4. Seven government policies to promote growth are: (173-179)

- Policies to improve incentives to work

  The use of tax cuts, or implementing supply-side economics, can improve the incentive to work and thereby raise output.

- Policies to encourage saving and investment;

  Even though new growth theorists downplay the role of capital, they agree that capital and investment is still important.

  Tax laws impact saving and consequently investment.

- Policies to control population growth;

  Providing enough capital and education for a large population that is growing is difficult.

  Perhaps a country needs to grow first. Then the residents will choose to have fewer children and the population growth will slow.

- Policies to increase the level of education;

  Education increases the productivity of workers. Basic education is important to economic growth.

- Policies to create institutions that encourage technological innovation;

  This means having institutions that provide incentives to innovate such as patents. Patents, however, also reduce the positive externalities associated with innovation.

  Corporations and financial institutions reduce the risk of innovating.

- Policies to provide funding for basic research;

  Canada's spending on research and development lags behind many industrialized countries. The Canadian government funds the lion's share of basic research in Canada.

- Policies to increase the economy's openness to trade.

  Trade allows specialization, which leads to increases in productivity and innovation.

MATCHING THE TERMS
Match the terms to their definitions

____ 1. Classical growth model	**a.** Output rises by a greater proportionate increase than all inputs.
____ 2. constant returns to scale	**b.** Producing more goods and services per person.
____ 3. decreasing returns to scale	**c.** Legal ownership of a technological innovation that gives the owner of the patent sole rights to its use and distribution for a limited time.
____ 4. division of labour	
____ 5. growth	**d.** An increase in the amount of goods and services an economy produces.
____ 6. human capital	**e.** The habitual way of doing things that guides people in how they approach production.
____ 7. increasing returns to scale	
____ 8. law of diminishing marginal productivity	**f.** The way we make goods and supply services.
	g. Output will rise by the same proportionate increase as all inputs.
____ 9. learning by doing	**h.** Model of growth that focuses on the role of capital accumulation in the growth process.
____ 10. new growth theory	
____ 11. patents	**i.** Output per unit of input.
____ 12. per capita growth	**j.** Rule in which you divide 72 by the annual growth rate of income (or any variable) to get the number of years over which income (or any variable) will double.
____ 13. positive externality	
____ 14. production function	
____ 15. productivity	**k.** Output rises by a smaller proportionate increase than all inputs.
____ 16. Rule of 72	**l.** Positive effects on others not taken into account by the decision-maker.
____ 17. Say's Law	
____ 18. social capital	**m.** The skills that are embodied in workers through work experience, education and on-the-job training.
____ 19. specialization	
____ 20. technology	**n.** Theory that emphasize the role of technology rather than capital in the growth process.
____ 21. total factor productivity	
	o. Increasing one input, keeping all others constant, will lead to smaller and smaller gains in output.
	p. The concentration of individuals in certain aspects of production.
	q. Supply creates its own demand.
	r. Improving the methods of production through experience.
	s. The splitting up of a task to allow for specialization of production.
	t. The relationship between the quantity of inputs used in production and the quantity of output resulting from production.
	u. Weighted average of real GDP per worker and real GDP per $1,000 of capital stock.

MULTIPLE CHOICE

Circle the one best answer for each of the following questions:

1. Long-run growth analysis focuses
   a. on demand.
   b. on supply.
   c. on both supply and demand.
   d. on the distribution of output.

2. According to Say's Law
   a. aggregate supply will exceed aggregate demand.
   b. aggregate demand will exceed aggregate supply.
   c. there will be no relation between aggregate supply and demand.
   d. aggregate demand will equal aggregate supply.

3. If the growth rate is 6%, how many years will it take for output to double?
   a. 4.
   b. 8.
   c. 12.
   d. 16.

4. The average worker today
   a. earns about the same as a worker in 1919 when earnings are adjusted for inflation
   b. earns less than a worker in 1919 when earnings are adjusted for inflation.
   c. earns more than a worker in 1919 when earnings are adjusted for inflation.
   d. is better off than a worker in 1919.

5. Suppose output grew at 4% in China and 2% in the United States.
   a. Per capita income grew faster in China
   b. Per capita income grew faster in the U.S.
   c. We cannot say in which country per capita income grew faster.
   d. Per capita output grew faster in China.

6. If the Canadian economy's output grew by 4%, but the population grew by 2%, per capita growth would be
   a. 8
   b. 0.5
   c. 2
   d. -2

7. If people have incomes of $20,000, $30,000, and $70,000, the mean and median incomes are
   a. $30,000 and $0,000, respectively.
   b. $20,000 and $120,000, respectively.
   c. $40,000 and $30,000, respectively.
   d. cannot be determined with the information provided.

8. In 1996, the top 20% of income earners in Canada earned what percentage of total income?
   a. 15%
   b. 5%
   c. 38.2%
   d. 40.6%

9. Investment is:
   a. the same thing as capital.
   b. the decrease in capital over time.
   c. the increase in capital over time.
   d. unrelated to capital.

10. Types of capital discussed in the book do *not* include:
    a. human capital.
    b. social capital.
    c. physical capital.
    d. investment capital.

11. Available resources:
    a. must always decrease.
    b. are always constant because of the entropy law.
    c. must always increase.
    d. may increase or decrease.

12. Total factor productivity deals with
    a. labour productivity.
    b. capital productivity.
    c. technology productivity.
    d. labour and capital productivity.

13. In terms of productivity growth, Canada has historically
    a. lead all industrialized countries.
    b. been behind the U.S.
    c. has lagged behind most industrialized countries.
    d. been higher than that of the U.S.

14. A production function:
    a. shows the relationship between inputs and outputs.
    b. is a type of technological manufacturing.
    c. is a type of manufacturing technology.
    d. is an important source of growth.

15. If there are increasing returns to scale:
    a. as inputs rise, outputs fall.
    b. as inputs rise, output rises by a smaller percentage.
    c. as inputs rise, output rises by a larger percentage.
    d. as one input rises, output rises by a larger percentage.

16. The law of diminishing marginal productivity states that:
    a. as inputs increase by equal percentages, output will increase by less than that percentage.
    b. as inputs increase by equal percentages output will eventually increase by less than that percentage.
    c. as one input increases by a certain percentage output will increase by less than that percentage
    d. as one input increases output will increase by decreasing percentages.

17. The Classical growth model focuses on:
    a. technology.
    b. saving and investment.
    c. entrepreneurship.
    d. available resources.

18. Early predictions of the Classical model of growth were that:
    a. the economy would grow without limit.
    b. the economy will end because of pollution.
    c. wages would be driven to subsistence because of diminishing marginal productivity.
    d. wages would be driven to subsistence because of decreasing returns to scale.

19. Which of the following is *not* an explanation for why the growth rates of rich and poor countries have not converged?
    a. Human capital has increased.
    b. Technology has increased.
    c. The law of diminishing marginal productivity is wrong.
    d. Both human capital and technology have increased.

20. In empirically explaining per capita growth an increase in:
    a. physical capital is the most important element.
    b. human capital is the most important element.
    c. technology is the most important element.
    d. the quantity of labour is the most important element.

21. The new growth theory is a theory that emphasizes:
    a. technology.
    b. human capital.
    c. physical capital.
    d. entrepreneurship.

22. In the new growth theory which of the following may be true?
    a. The law of increasing marginal productivity overwhelms the law of diminishing marginal productivity.
    b. Learning by doing overwhelms the law of diminishing marginal productivity.
    c. The law of technology overwhelms the law of diminishing marginal productivity.
    d. The law of QWERTY overwhelms the law of diminishing marginal productivity.

23. QWERTY is a metaphor for:
    a. the invisible hand.
    b. technological lock-in.
    c. the law of diminishing marginal productivity.
    d. the pollution caused by positive spillovers.

24. In the borrowing circle case study:
    a. loans were made to large firms.
    b. loans were made to an entire circle of firms.
    c. guarantees of friends replaced traditional collateral.
    d. individuals were given collateral so they could get loans.

25. The Laffer curve shows
    a. the effect of population growth on productivity
    b. the effect of savings and investment on foreign capital flows.
    c. the effect on tax collections on changing tax rates.
    d. the effect of the level of education on per capita output growth.

26. Growth usually leads to decreased birth rates because when there is growth because:
    a. men and women are too tired to have kids.
    b. the opportunity cost of having children rises.
    c. pollution reduces the fertility of the population.
    d. immigration crowds out endogenous population growth.

27. Patents create:
    a. incentives to innovate and hence are a good thing.
    b. barriers to entry and hence are a bad thing.
    c. both barriers to entry and incentives to innovate and hence are both a bad and good thing.
    d. common knowledge and hence are a good thing.

28. Canada's spending on research and development
    a. leads all industrialized countries.
    b. has been less than the U.S.
    c. has lagged behind many industrialized countries.
    d. has been higher than that of the U.S.

29. Which of the following policies will likely *slow* an economy's growth rate?
    a. Increased trade restrictions.
    b. Increase the level of education.
    c. Increasing saving.
    d. Protecting property rights.

SHORT-ANSWER QUESTIONS

1. What assumption do economists make that allows them to focus only on supply in the long run?

2. What are the two ways to measure growth?

3. What is the difference between mean income and median income?

4. You've been called in by a political think tank to develop a strategy to improve growth in Canada. What are five things that would you recommend they concentrate on that would contribute positively to economic growth?

5. Write a production function. Use the production function to explain the difference between diminishing marginal returns from decreasing returns to scale.

6. Why did the early Classical model predict that output would gravitate toward a subsistence level?

7. What is the focus of new growth theory?

8. How do the predictions of the Classical growth theory differ from the predictions of the new growth theory?

9. What is supply-side economics?

10. What are seven policies to promote growth?

PROBLEMS AND APPLICATIONS

1. According to the Classical growth model, how will each of the following events affect a country's growth rate?

    a. An increase in the percent change in population.

b. An increase in the saving rate.

c. An improvement in technology.

d. The government passes a law extending the time frame in which the holder of a patent has sole ownership of a technological innovation.

2. State the Rule of 72. Answer each of the following questions:

    a. How many years will it take for income to double if a country's total income grows at 2 percent? 4 percent? 6 percent?

    b. If a country's income doubles in 16 years, at what rate is its income growing?

    c. In 2001, per capita output in Canada was about $35,000. If real income per capita is growing at a 2% annual rate, what will per capita output be in 36 years? In 72 years?

d. If real income is rising at an annual rate of 4% per year and the population is growing at a rate of 1% per year, how many years will it take for per capita income to double?

3. Calculate per capita income for each of the following countries:

	GDP (in millions of dollars)	Population (in millions)
Brazil	773,400	164
Ghana	6,600	18
Croatia	20,700	4
France	1,526,000	59

4. The inputs to an economy are labour and capital only. In each of the following state whether the production function exhibits (a) increasing returns to scale, (b) decreasing returns to scale, (c) constant returns to scale, or (d) diminishing marginal productivity.

a. Output rises by 16% when both labour and capital rise by 16%.

b. Output rises by 10% when both labour and capital rise by 16%.

c. Output rises by 10% when labour rises by 16%.

5. What prediction did Thomas Malthus make about growth?

a. Draw a graph that demonstrates his predictions and explain the predictions using the graph.

b. What law are those predictions based upon?

c. According to Classical economists, why didn't his predictions come true?

6. Country A has per capita income of $10,000 while Country B has per capita income of $20,000.

    a. According to the Classical growth theory, which country is predicted to grow more quickly? Why?

    b. According to the new growth theory, which country is predicted to grow more quickly? Why?

● A BRAIN TEASER

1. How can two countries with equal population sizes have different levels of output?

● POTENTIAL ESSAY QUESTIONS

You may also see essay questions similar to the "Problems & Applications" and "Brain Teasers" exercises.

1. What does the Classical model predict about the growth rates of poor countries relative to rich countries? What accounts for that prediction?

2. How does human capital differ from physical capital?

3. How can patents be both a deterrent and a reason for growth?

ANSWERS

MATCHING

1-h; 2-g; 3-k; 4-s; 5-d; 6-m; 7-a; 8-o; 9-r; 10-n; 11-c; 12-b; 13-l; 14-t; 15-i; 16-j; 17-q; 18-e; 19-p; 20-f; 21-u.

ANSWERS

MULTIPLE CHOICE

1. b   On page 157 it states that in the short run economists analysis focuses on demand; in the long run it focuses on supply.

2. d   Say's law states that supply creates its own demand. See page 157.

3. c   According to the rule of 72 on page 158, divide 72 by the growth rate to determine the number of years in which output will double.

4. c   As discussed in Figure 7-1 on page 160 the average worker's wages buy many more goods now than in 1919. Whether that makes them better off is debatable, but they definitely earn more.

5. c   Per capita income (output) growth equals output growth less population growth. Without knowing population growth, we do not know for which country per capita income (output) growth is greater. See pages 160-161.

6. c   As defined on page 161, per capita growth is the percentage change in output less the percentage change in population.

7. c   The mean income is the average income, while the median income is the middle income with one income level above and one below. (161)

8. d   The largest share of income earned by the top 20 percent of income earners is 40.6% (161-162)

9. c   As defined in the text on pages 162-163 investment is the increase in capital over time.

10. d   Investment is the change in capital; it is not a description of capital. See pages 162-163.

11. d   Available resources depend on technology. That is why they can increase or decrease. See page 163.

12. d   See page 165

13. c   See page 165.

14. a   The definition given in the text on page 165 is the relationship between inputs and outputs.

15. c   As discussed in the text on page 166 increasing returns to scale refers to the relation between all inputs and outputs. Increasing returns to scale exist when output increases by a greater percentage than the increase in all inputs.

16. d   The law of diminishing marginal productivity refers to one input, not all, and to what will happen to output as that input is continually increases, keeping other inputs constant. See page 166.

17. b   The Classical growth focuses on increases in capital and hence on saving and investment. See pages 166-167.

18. c   In the early Classical model, fixed land and diminishing marginal productivity meant that wages would be driven to subsistence. See pages 166-167.

19. c   Economists continue to believe in the law of diminishing marginal productivity because there are many other explanations for the lack of convergence. See page 168.

20. c   Although increases in technology and increases in the quantity of labour are of almost equal importance in explaining total growth, per capita growth decreases the importance of the quantity of labour. See page 168.

21. a   The growth theorie centers its explanation of growth on technology. See pages 170-171.

22. b   The only law mentioned in the book is the law of diminishing marginal productivity. The others are not laws and can't overwhelm anything. See page 171.

23. b   Qwerty stands for the upper left keys on a keyboard. Placing them there is not especially efficient, but once they were placed there, they were locked in. See page 172.

24. c   The essence of the borrowing circle was guarantees of friends. The loans were small loans to individuals, not to firms. See pages 173-174.

25. c   The Laffer curve suggests that reduced tax rates will increase tax revenue for the government as individuals respond to higher after-tax income by working more.

26. b   In industrialized countries, people have chosen to have fewer children because the benefits of having children (such as being supported by them in your old age) is reduced. See page 175.

27. c   Patents have both good and bad aspects; the policy debate is about what the optimal length of the patent should be. See pages 177-178.

28. c   See page 178. Spending on research and development as a percentage of GDP, particularly business-sector research and development, is very small for Canada. (178-179)

29. a   Economists generally believe that trade increases growth, so increasing trade restrictions would decrease growth. See page 179.

ANSWERS

SHORT-ANSWER QUESTIONS

1. Economists assume that demand is sufficient to buy whatever is supplied. This assumption is called Say's law—supply creates its own demand. According to Say's law, aggregate demand will always equal aggregate supply. This way, one can focus only on aggregate supply. (157)

2. Growth can be measured either as increases in the amount of goods and services an economy produces (real GDP), or as increases in the amount of goods and services an economy produces per person (per capita real GDP). Increases in per capita output is a better measure of improvements in the standard of living because it tells you how much income the average person has. (157-161)

3. Mean income is average income, while median income is the income level that divides the population in equal halves. (161)

4. I would tell them: (1) To promote institutions with incentives compatible with growth. Institutions that encourage hard work will lead to growth. (2) To promote institutions that foster creative thinking and lead to technological development; (3) To be creative in recognizing available resources. Growth requires resources and although it may seem that the resources are limited, available resources depend upon existing technology. New technology is a way of overcoming lack of resources. (4) To invest in capital. This would include not only buildings and machines, but also human and social capital. (5) To encourage entrepreneurship. An economy deficient in the other four areas can still grow if its population can translate vision into reality. Each of these will contribute to growth. (161-165)

5. A typical production function is: Output = A f(labour, capital, land), where labour, capital and land are the only inputs. A is a factor that is used to capture changes in technology. Decreasing returns to scale describes the situation where output rises by a smaller percentage than the increase in all inputs. For example, if labour, capital and land all increase by 20%, but output increases by only 10%, the production function exhibits decreasing returns to scale. Diminishing marginal productivity describes what happens to output when only one input is changed—output rises by a percentage that is smaller than the percentage increase in one input (while all other inputs remain the same). (165-166)

6. The early Classical model predicted that output would gravitate toward a subsistence level because they focused on the law of diminishing marginal productivity of labour. As long as an additional worker could produce more than enough for him or herself, the population would grow. But land was relatively fixed. As more and more workers were added to a fixed amount of land, eventually, additional workers would not be able to produce enough additional output to survive. Workers would starve to death and the population would shrink. The equilibrium number of workers was where output was just enough to survive—no more and no less. (166-169)

7. New growth theory focuses on the role of technology rather than capital in the growth process. New growth theory considers the possibility that there are positive externalities associated with technological advance so that growth rates can accelerate. It also focuses on learning by doing. Just the process of producing results in lower costs and technological innovation. (170-172)

8. Classical growth theory predicts that the growth rates of poor countries will be higher than the growth rates of rich countries because the law of diminishing marginal productivity of capital is stronger in rich countries. Eventually the incomes of rich and poor countries will converge. New growth theory, because of the positive externalities associated with technological advance, is consistent with the possibility that rich countries may grow faster than poor countries because they have more technology. Classical growth theory also predicts that growth rates will slow over time whereas the new growth theory is consistent with an acceleration in growth rates. (196-200)

9. Supply-side economics is a body of economics which considers how the use of income tax cuts could stimulate increased labour supply. Greater incentives to work due to high after-tax wages leads to greater labour supply, which leads to higher output and more tax revenue for the government. (174-175)

10. Seven policies to promote growth are (1) policies to encourage saving and investment; (2) policies to improve incentives to work; (3) policies to control population growth; (4) policies to increase the level of education; (5) policies to create institutions that encourage technological innovation; (6) provide funding for basic research; and (7) policies to increase the economy's openness to trade. (173-179)

━━━━━ ANSWERS ━━━━━

PROBLEMS AND APPLICATIONS

1. **a.** An increase in the percent change in population will lead to a reduction in the growth rate per capita because each worker will have less capital to produce with. (166-169)
   b. An increase in the saving rate will lead to an increase in the growth rate per capita because saving results in increased investment and more capital for each worker. Eventually, however, the law of diminishing marginal productivity of capital would set in and per capita income would cease to grow. (166-169)
   c. An improvement in technology will increase the growth rate per capita because each worker will be more productive. This will increase per capita output at the time of the technological improvement, but would not result in a lasting increase in the growth rate per capita. (166-169)
   d. Technological innovation is outside the model. Thus government policies to affect technological innovation would not affect the growth rate of an economy. (166-169)

2. The Rule of 72 is that the number of years that it takes income (or any variable) to double equals 72 divided by the annual growth rate of income (or that variable).
   a. 36 years if income grows at 2 percent per year; 18 years if income grows at 4 percent per year; 12 years if income grows at 6 percent per year. (158)
   b. Its income is growing at 4.5 percent per year. Divide 72 by 16 to find the answer. (158)

   c. If real income per capita is growing at 2 percent per year, per capita output will double in 36 years. So, real per capita output will be $70,000 in 36 years and $140,000 in 72 years. (158)
   d. Per capita real income is rising at an annual rate of 3% per year (4% - 1%). At 3% per year, real per capital income will double in 24 years (72/3 = 24). (158)

3. Divide GDP by the population to find per capita income:
   a. Brazil $4,716
   b. Ghana $367
   c. Croatia $5,175
   d. France $25,864 (See pages 160-161)

4. **a.** Since output is rising by the same percentage as the increase in all inputs, the production function exhibits constant returns to scale. (165-166)
   b. Since output is rising by a smaller percentage as the increase in all inputs, the production function exhibits decreasing returns to scale. (165-166)
   c. Since capital is fixed, the correct description involves marginal productivity. Since output rises by less than the percentage increase in labour only, the production function exhibits diminishing marginal productivity. (165-166)

5. Thomas Malthus predicted that since land was relatively fixed, as the population grew, diminishing marginal productivity would set in. The growth in output would not keep pace with the growth in the population and eventually people would starve.
   a. The graph below demonstrates Malthus' predictions. The production function is dd because of diminishing marginal productivity. Each additional worker adds less output than the individual before. At population levels below N*, there is surplus output (because output per worker exceeds the subsistence level of output). Because there is surplus output, people have more children and the population grows. Once the population grows beyond N*, per capita output is not sufficient to feed the

population (output per worker is less than the subsistence level of output) and people starve to death. The population declines to N*. (167-168)

b. The predictions of Thomas Malthus are based upon the law of diminishing marginal productivity. (167-168)

c. According to Classical economists, his predictions didn't come true because some output produced is used to increase the amount of capital that workers have to work with. As capital increases, even if land is fixed, output can also increase. The economy could still grow if capital increased at the same rate that labour increased. (166)

6. a. According to the Classical growth theory, Country A is expected to grow more quickly because increases in capital per worker in country A are more productive than in country B due to the law of diminishing marginal productivity. (166)

b. According to the new growth theory, income doesn't need to converge. In fact, new growth theory stresses the possibility that countries with higher output will grow faster than poor countries because of positive externalities associated with technology and learning by doing. Increases in technology have significant positive externalities that can accelerate the growth rate. Further, as output increases, the benefits from learning by doing also increase. Therefore, greater output can lead to faster growth rates. (170-172)

ANSWERS

A BRAIN TEASER

1. Total output in the long run depends upon capital, labour, and land. It could be that the two countries have different levels of capital or natural resources (captured in land). For instance, Canada has many natural resources, but Japan does not. Japan overcomes its lack of natural resources by investing heavily in capital and importing natural resources. If two countries had equal amounts of capital, land and labour, however, their outputs could still differ if they had different amounts of human capital (the skills that are embodied in workers through experience, education, and on-the-job training) and social capital (the habitual way of doing things that guides people in how they approach production). (161-165)

ANSWERS

POTENTIAL ESSAY QUESTIONS

The following are annotated answers. They indicate the general idea behind the answer.

1. The Classical model predicts that poor countries with little capital will grow at faster rates than rich countries with a lot of capital. The reason for this prediction is the law of diminishing marginal productivity. Capital that is added in poor countries will be much more productive because the law of diminishing marginal productivity is weaker compared to that in rich countries.

2. Physical capital are the buildings and machines available for production while human capital are the skills that are embodied in workers through experience, education, and on-the-job training. Both are considered important to growth, but the connection between investment and each type of capital differs. Expenditures on plant and equipment (investment) clearly increase physical capital. Human capital can increase without direct investment—one example is just

experience. Investment in human capital can also be unproductive and not lead to increases in human capital—an example would be providing education in areas that do not increase the productivity of its workers.

3.   Patents provide an incentive for people to innovate because the holder of a patent has the right to be the sole provider of the innovation. As a sole provider, the holder can charge more for its use by others. Based upon the law of supply, a greater incentive will result in a greater quantity of innovations supplied. On the other hand, patents, because they are privately held will be lower than if they could be used by all. Since the innovation is priced high, less of the innovation will be demanded and the innovation will have less of an impact on growth. Further, it is the common knowledge aspect of a technology that leads to positive externalities. Patents limit the common knowledge aspect of a technology and thus limit its impact on growth. Policymakers face a dilemma. Before the innovation is developed, the best strategy is to offer patents. Once the innovation is developed, the best strategy is to make it free to everyone.

THE GOODS MARKET AND THE AGGREGATE EXPENDITURES MODEL

8

● CHAPTER AT A GLANCE

Another important model for analyzing economic performance is the Aggregate Expenditures (AE) model. This model is designed to explain how changes in various macroeconomic variables determine changes in total spending in the economy and how this affects total production (real GDP). There are essentially two parts to the AE model – aggregate production, which is the total amount of goods and services produced in every industry in an economy, and aggregate expenditures which consists of consumption, investment, spending by government, and net foreign spending on Canadian goods. When both of these concepts are plotted together an a graph, it allows economists to determine the equilibrium level of output when there are changes in expenditures.

The equilibrium level of output in this model is that output whereby the production of that output creates an equivalent level of aggregate expenditures sufficient to purchase that output. As expenditures change, so does the equilibrium level of output. The multiplier is used to determine how much output will change in response to a change in expenditures. The multiplier effect reflects the ripple effect through the economy that a spending change creates. The chapter also looks at some limitations of the AE model and introduces a new expanded AE model which is a more comprehensive representation of the economy.

This review is based upon the learning objectives that open the chapter.

1a. The Aggregate Expenditures (AE) model attempts to explain how various macroeconomic variables determine changes in total spending in the economy and alter income and GDP. (184)

The macroeconomic model is a framework which allows economists to simplify the real world. A lot of assumptions are developed to express the relationship between different macroeconomic variables in equation form. Solving these equations yields information about variables of particular interest, such as real GDP. It also allows for analysis to be conducted on how changes in economic variables influences the level of real GDP.

1b. Autonomous expenditures are expenditures unrelated to income; induced expenditures are directly related to income or output. (189-190)

Autonomous expenditures include consumption, investment, government spending, and net exports. When these autonomous expenditures change, the AE curve shifts.

Note: AE = C + I + G + (X−IM).

1c. The marginal propensity to consume is the ratio of a change in consumption to a change in income. (191)

1d. Anything that lowers (raises) autonomous spending will shift the AE curve down (up) by the amount of the change in autonomous expenditures. (202)

2a. To determine income graphically in the AE model, you find the income level at which aggregate expenditures equal aggregate production. (194-195)

2b. To determine income using the multiplier equation, determine the multiplier and multiply it by the level of autonomous expenditures (196)

multiplier = 1/(1 mpc)

Y = (multiplier)(Autonomous expenditures)

ΔY = (multiplier)(ΔAutonomous expenditures)

2c. The multiplier process works because when expenditures don't equal production, businesspeople change planned production, which changes income, which changes expenditures, which.... (197-198)

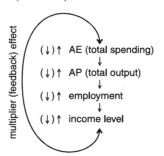

This is the income adjustment process—the multiplier effect on income given a change in spending.

2d. The circular flow model essentially shows that when all individuals spend all of their income earned from production, the aggregate economy is in equilibrium. For the economy, this translates into aggregate income = aggregate output. Typically, however, income does not equal expenditures. Therefore, any changes in expenditures will have an amplified effect on income. This is the multiplier process. (198-199)

3a. The multiplier can be expressed as either 1/MPS or 1/1-MPC. The multiplier can be used to determine the resulting change in equilibrium income from a change in spending. Assuming an MPC of 0.8, the multiplier is 5. Assuming a change in autonomous expenditures of $20 and given Y = multiplier * autonomous expenditures, the change in autonomous income is 5 * 20 = 100 (five times as large as the initial income of $20). (199-201)

3b. The change in equilibrium income can also be derived using $\Delta y = \Delta AE/(1-mpc)$. (201)

3c. The AE model can be applied to real world situations, particularly to explain events of the past. Changes in autonomous expenditures causes the AE curve to shift, which through the multiplier process, causes a magnified change in output/income. (202)

4a. The AE model is not a complete model of the economy. (203-206)

- Values for autonomous expenditures are determined by economic variables not made explicit in the model.
- The AE model is only a model of aggregate demand. Changes in output can also be due to changes in factors affecting aggregate supply.
- The AE model assumes prices are fixed. This may be true in the very short run, but in some markets, such as stock markets, prices can adjust very quickly.
- The AE model does not explicitly include expectations of consumers, firms, and government. Individual decisions are forward looking.

5a. The simple AE model can be expanded to include the budget balance and the trade sector. If T > G, there is a budget surplus and if T < G, there is a budget deficit. If X > M, there is a trade surplus and if X < M, there is a trade deficit. (207-208)

5b. If tax collections increase as income rises, the spending multiplier will decrease, so the increase in equilibrium income is not as large as in the simple AE model. If import spending increases as income rises, the spending multiplier will decrease, so the increase in equilibrium income is not as large as in the simple AE model. (206-208)

MATCHING THE TERMS
Match the terms to their definitions

All of these key terms are found at the end of the chapter.

_f_ **1.** aggregate expenditures

_k_ **2.** aggregate (AE) expenditures curve

_g_ **3.** aggregate production curve

_i_ **4.** autonomous expenditures

_m_ **5.** equilibrium income

_j_ **6.** expenditures function

_b_ **7.** induced expenditures

_h_ **8.** marginal propensity to consume

_n_ **9.** marginal propensity to import

_l_ **10.** marginal propensity to save

_e_ **11.** multiplier

_d_ **12.** multiplier equation

_a_ **13.** potential income

_c_ **14.** real business cycle theory

a. The level of income that the economy technically is capable of producing without generating accelerating inflation.

b. Expenditures that change as income changes.

c. The theory where changes in aggregate supply are the principal means by which changes in real income occur.

d. Equation that tells us that income equals the multiplier times autonomous expenditures.

e. A number that tells us how much income will change in response to a change in autonomous expenditures.

f. $AE = C + I + G + (X - IM)$.

g. The total amount of goods and services produced in every industry in an economy.

h. The ratio of a change in consumption to a change in income.

i. Expenditures that are independent of income.

j. Representation of the relationship between expenditures and income as a mathematical function ($AE = AE_0 + mpcY$, where AE = aggregate expenditures, AE_0 = autonomous expenditures, mpc = marginal propensity to consume, Y = income).

k. Graphical representation of the expenditures function.

l. The percentage of income flow that is withdrawn from the income/expenditure flow of the economy in each round.

m. The level of income toward which the economy gravitates in the short run because of the cumulative cycles of declining or increasing production.

n. The increase in spending on imported goods and services from an additional dollar of after-tax income.

MULTIPLE CHOICE

Circle the one best answer for each of the following questions:

1. Classical economists are generally associated with:
   a. laissez faire.
   b. QWERTY.
   c. an activist policy.
   d. their support of low unemployment.

2. Keynesian economics focuses on
   a. the long run.
   b. the short run.
   c. both the long run and the short run.
   d. neither the long run nor the short run.

3. In Keynesian economics equilibrium income:
   a. will be equal to potential income.
   b. will be below potential income.
   c. will be above potential income.
   d. may be different than potential income.

4. In the AE model,
   a. production is assumed to be fixed.
   b. planned expenditures are assumed to equal actual production.
   c. the price level is assumed to be fixed.
   d. the price level is assumed to be flexible.

5. Autonomous expenditures are expenditures that:
   a. are automatically created by income.
   b. are unrelated to income.
   c. change as income changes.
   d. automatically change as income changes.

6. The marginal propensity to consume is:
   a. the change in consumption expenditures times the change income.
   b. the change in consumption expenditures divided by the change in income.
   c. the change in consumption expenditures divided by income.
   d. consumption expenditures divided by the change in income.

7. *Mpc* plus *mps* equals
   a. zero.
   b. one.
   c. ten.
   d. unknown (cannot be determined).

8. If the mpc is 0.8, what is the size of the multiplier in the multiplier model?
   a. −0.5.
   b. 5.
   c. 1.
   d. 10.

9. As the *mpc* rises, the multiplier
   a. increases.
   b. decreases.
   c. remains the same.
   d. sometimes rises and sometimes falls.

10. Changes in autonomous consumption expenditures are due to changes in all factors except,
    a. interest rates.
    b. household wealth.
    c. expectations of future economic conditions.
    d. imports

11. The level of Canadian exports is determined by
    a. interest rates.
    b. economic prospects abroad.
    c. economic prospects in the domestic economy.
    d. government spending.

12. Which of the following expenditures function is depicted in the graph below?

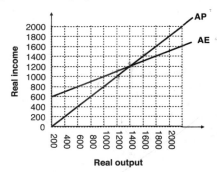

    a. AE = $600 + 0.5Y.
    b. AE = 0.5Y.
    c. AE = $600.
    d. AE = $600Y/0.5.

13. Refer to the graph for Question #12. Planned expenditures exceed production at:
    a. income levels above $1,200.
    b. income levels below $1,200.
    c. income level of $1,200.
    d. no income level since planned expenditures equals production.

14. If consumer confidence suddenly falls, you would expect:
    a. the aggregate production curve to shift down.
    b. the aggregate expenditures curve to rotate to the right and equilibrium income to fall.
    c. the aggregate expenditures curve to shift up and equilibrium income to rise.
    d. the aggregate expenditures curve to shift down and equilibrium income to fall.

15. In the AE model, if autonomous expenditures are $5,000 and the *mpc* equals 0.9, what is the level of income in the economy?
    a. $5,000.
    b. $10,000.
    c. $20,000.
    d. $50,000.

16. In the AE model if autonomous exports falls by 40 and the *mpc* is 0.5, what happens to the income?
    a. Income rises by 20.
    b. Income falls by 20.
    c. Income rises by 80.
    d. Income falls by 80.

17. In the AE model if autonomous consumption increases by 100 and the AE curve is upward sloping, income:
    a. will rise by 100.
    b. will rise by more than 100.
    c. will fall by 100.
    d. may rise or fall. We cannot tell without more information.

18. In the AE model if autonomous consumption increases by 10 and the *mpc* is 0.8, what happens to the income?
    a. Income rises by 8.
    b. Income falls by 8.
    c. Income rises by 50.
    d. Income falls by 50.

19. In the AE model if autonomous exports fall by 40 and government spending increases by 20, and the *mpc* is 0.8, what happens to the income?
    a. Income rises by 300.
    b. Income falls by 300.
    c. Income rises by 100.
    d. Income falls by 100.

20. In the AE model, if people begin to save more of their income:
    a. leakages out of the circular flow will rise and equilibrium income will fall.
    b. because leakages from the circular flow will still equal injections from the circular flow, equilibrium income will not change.
    c. injections into the circular flow will rise and equilibrium income will rise.
    d. the flow of income and expenditures will no longer be circular.

21. The following are all limitations of the AE model except
    a. It is not a complete model.
    b. It is only a model of aggregate supply.
    c. It assumes prices are fixed.
    d. It does not explicitly include expectations.

22. The AE model
    a. determines equilibrium from scratch.
    b. determines the direction the economy might take in response to changes in the economy.
    c. is best applied to an economy with rapidly rising prices.
    d. reflect the complicated adjustment process that results from people's forward-looking expectations.

23. If there is some price level flexibility
    a. the AE model is no longer relevant.
    b. the results of the AE model will be reversed.
    c. the results of the AE model will be modified but the central point will remain the same.
    d. the AE model will turn into a Classical model.

24. In the real-business-cycle theory, business cycles occur because of:
    a. changes in the real price level.
    b. changes in real income.
    c. technological and other natural shocks.
    d. changes in the money supply.

25. If the marginal tax rate increases, what would happen to the general expenditures multiplier?
    a. It would increase.
    b. It would decrease.
    c. It would remain the same.
    d. One cannot say.

26. Assuming the marginal propensity to import is 0.1, the tax rate is 0.2, and the marginal propensity to consume is 0.6, the multiplier will be approximately
    a. 0.
    b. 1.2.
    c. 1.7.
    d. 2.6.

27. Assume the marginal propensity to import is 0.1, the tax rate is 0.25, the marginal propensity to consume is 0.8, and that the government wants to increase income by 100. In the multiplier model you would suggest increasing government spending by
    a. 10.
    b. 35.7.
    c. 47.4.
    d. 100.

● SHORT-ANSWER QUESTIONS

1. What is the difference between induced and autonomous expenditures?

Induced → expenditures that change as income changes.

autonomous → expenditures that are independent of income.

2. Draw an AP and AE curve and show how the level of income is graphically determined in the multiplier model. Describe the forces that are set in motion when income levels are above and below equilibrium?

3. In the AE model, if autonomous expenditures were $200 and the *mpc* were 0.75, what is equilibrium income?

$$\frac{1}{1-0.75} = 4$$

$$\frac{200}{1-0.75} = 800$$

4. Explain the process by which the economy reaches a new equilibrium income if autonomous expenditures increase by $100. The marginal propensity to consume is 0.5.

$$AE = AC_0 + mpc \cdot Y$$

$$Y = \frac{AE_0}{1-mpc} \qquad \frac{100}{0.5} = 200$$

5. True or false: The AE model is a complete model of the economy. Explain your answer.

It has its limitations
- assumes price level is

6. How does the Keynesian explanation of the Great Depression differ from the Classical explanation?

Classical focused on wages
Keys focused on insufficient aggregate expenditures!

● PROBLEMS AND APPLICATIONS

1. Answer the following questions about the aggregate production curve.

  a. Draw an aggregate production curve. Label all axes.

  b. What is the slope of the aggregate production function?

c. Why is the slope as you have drawn it?

2. You are given the following information about the economy:

Income	Expenditures
0	100
500	500
1000	900
2000	1700
3000	2500

a. What is the level of autonomous expenditures?

b. What is the marginal propensity to consume? Explain why it is important.

c. What expenditures function (an equation) corresponds to the table?

d. What is the *mps*?

3. Putting expenditures and production together:

a. Graph the expenditures function from question 2 on the aggregate production curve from question 1.

b. What is the slope of the expenditures function?

4. Given the following equation, answer the questions: $AE = C_0 + .6Y + I + G + (X\,IM)$ where $C_0 = 1000$, $I = 500$, $G = 300$, $X = 300$, $IM = 400$.

a. Draw the aggregate expenditures curve.

b. What is the slope of the curve?

c. What is the vertical axis intercept?

d. Add the aggregate production curve on the graph.

e. What is the multiplier?

f. What is equilibrium income? Label that point A on the graph.

g. What is the effect of an increase in autonomous consumption of $200 on equilibrium income? Demonstrate your answer graphically.

h. What is the effect on equilibrium income of a change in the *mpc* from 0.6 to 0.8? Demonstrate your answer graphically. How does your answer to (g) change with the new *mpc*?

5. Calculate the multiplier in each case.

a. *mpc* = 0.7

b. *mps* = 0.4

6. For each of the following, state what will happen to equilibrium income.

a. The *mpc* is 0.9 and autonomous government expenditures just rose $200 billion. Graph your analysis.

b. The *mpc* is 0.65 and autonomous investment just fell $70 billion. Graph your analysis.

7. You've just been appointed chairman of the Council of Economic Advisers in Textland. The *mpc* is 0.8, and all nonconsumption expenditures and taxes are exogenous.

a. How can the government increase output by $400 through a change in expenditures?

b. Oops! There's been a mistake. Your research assistant tells you that taxes are actually not exogenous, and that there is a marginal tax rate of 0.1. How can the government change expenditures to increase income by $400?

c. There's more new news which your research assistant just found out. She tells you that not only is there a marginal tax rate of 0.1; there's also a marginal propensity to import of 0.2. You have to change your solutions now. How can the government change expenditures to increase income by $400?

8. What happens to output in the AE model if there is perfect price-level flexibility when the AE curve shifts up due to a shift in autonomous expenditures?

● A BRAIN TEASER

1. We have all heard about the extent to which local communities go to in attracting and recruiting new businesses, conventions, trade shows, professional meetings, etc. into their area. Sometimes they seem to "give away the farm." They may offer a commitment not to impose property taxes for so many years or offer land at no charge if a company will build a production facility in the area, and so forth. Why do local governments offer lucrative tax incentives, etc., to attract new businesses into their area–especially considering that there are relatively only a few number of modestly higher paying jobs created?

● POTENTIAL ESSAY QUESTIONS

You may also see essay questions similar to the "Problems & Applications" and "Brain Teasers" exercises.

1. In the AE model, can macroeconomic equilibrium exist below full employment? Why, or why not?

2. Why does the multiplier process exist? What does the multiplier do to the income level given any change in aggregate expenditures?

3. What is meant by "the paradox of thrift" and how did it help perpetuate the Great Depression?

4. What was the Keynesian's main argument against the Classical view that the economy will get itself out of the Depression?

━━━ ANSWERS ━━━

MATCHING

1-f; 2-k; 3-g; 4-i; 5-m; 6-j; 7-b; 8-h; 9-n; 10-l; 11-e; 12-d; 13-a; 14-c.

━━━ ANSWERS ━━━

MULTIPLE CHOICE

1. a   Laissez faire is the non-activist policy that Classical economists generally support. See page 185.

2. b   The essence of Keynesian economics was its focus on the short run. See page 186.

3. d   Because of coordination problems equilibrium income could be different than potential income in Keynesian economics; it could be higher, lower or equal to it. See pages 186-187.

4. c   The AE model assumes that the price level remains constant and asks how much aggregate equilibrium income will change when aggregate expenditures change. During the adjustment to equilibrium, planned expenditures will not equal actual production. See page 188.

5. b   Autonomous expenditures are expenditures that exist even when income is zero. They do not change as income changes. See page 189.

6. b   The marginal propensity to consume is the fraction of additional income that is consumed. It can be calculated by dividing the change in consumption expenditures by the change income. See page 191.

7. b   This is true by definition. Income that is not spent is saved. See page 198.

8. b   The multiplier equals $1/(1-0.8) = 1/0.2 = 5$. See page 196.

9. a   You can determine this by substituting into the formula. See page 196.

10. d   Changes in imports does not affect the level of consumer spending. (192)

11. b   The economic conditions within the economies of Canada's trading partners influences the level of Canadian goods and services purchased. (193)

12. a   The graph shows that the y-axis intercept is $600 and the slope is 0.5. Calculate the slope as rise over run. For example, beginning at the y-intercept, increasing expenditures by 600 means income rises by 1200 (600/1200 = 0.5). Substitute these values in the equation for a straight line: y = (slope)x + (intercept). See pages 194-195.

13. b   Planned expenditures exceed production where the AE curve is above the AP curve. This occurs at income levels below $1,200. See pages 194-195.

14. d   A drop in consumer confidence would be expected to reduce consumption expenditures. This shifts the AE curve down and leads to a reduction in equilibrium income (output). See pages 192-193, 200.

15. d   The multiplier is 10 so the answer is 10 times $5,000. See page 196.

16. d   The multiplier is 2 so the answer is 2 times 40. See pages 199-203.

17. b   In the multiplier model, as long as the mpc is greater than zero, a change in autonomous expenditures will lead to a change in income in the same direction that is a multiple of the change in expenditures. See pages 199-203.

18. c   The multiplier is 5 so the answer is 5 times 10. See pages 199-203.

19. d   The multiplier is 5 so the answer is 5 times $(-40 + 20)$ or minus 100. See pages 199-203.

20. a   If people save more of their income, the mps will rise. Because more income leaks from the circular flow, less returns in the form of expenditures and equilibrium income falls. See pages 198-199.

21. c   One limitation of the AE model is that it is a model of aggregate demand, and not aggregate supply. (203)

22. b   The AE model is best used as a historical model that suggests the direction an economy might take given a shock. See page 187.

23. c   The AE model assumes that the price level is constant. If, however, the price level is not constant, the multiplier model is modified. The central point, however, that an increase in expenditures has a multiplied effect on equilibrium output is still relevant. See pages 204-205.

24. c   Real business cycle theory suggests that fluctuations in output are the result of shifting aggregate supply resulting from changes in technology. See page 204.

25. b   This is a hard question since it requires some deduction. The marginal tax rate is one of the components of the marginal propensity to consume. It is a leakage from the circular flow, so it makes the multiplier smaller. See pages 206.

26. c   The multiplier for the full model is $1/(1-t)(mpc-mpi) = 1/1(1-0.2)(0.6-0.1)$ $= 1/(`-0.4) = 1.67$. See page 210.

27. c   First you determine the multiplier. The multiplier for the full model is $1/1-(1-t)(mpc-mpi) = 1/1-(1-0.25)$ $(0.8-0.1) = 1/0.475 = 2.11$. Dividing 200 by 2.11 gives an increase of government spending of 47.4. See page 210 .

■■■ ANSWERS ■■■

SHORT-ANSWER QUESTIONS

1.   Induced expenditures depend upon the level of income. Autonomous expenditures are independent of income. (189-190)

2.   The *AP* curve is a 45-degree line through the origin. At all points on the *AP* curve, output equals income. The *AE* curve is an upward-sloping line with a slope less than one that intersects the expenditures axis at the level of autonomous expenditures. These curves are shown in the graph below. Equilibrium income is where the two curves intersect (where *AE* = *AP*). At points to the left, aggregate expenditures exceed aggregate production and businesses find their inventories are being depleted. They increase production, which increases income and expenditures, moving income toward equilibrium. At points to the right, aggregate expenditures are less than aggregate production and businesses see their inventories accumulating. They cut production, which reduces income and expenditures, moving income toward equilibrium. (191-192)

3.   To determine equilibrium income, multiply the sum of all autonomous expenditures by the multiplier. In this case the multiplier is 1/(1 .75) = 4, so equilibrium income is $800. (196)

4.   The initial shock is $100. This increase in expenditures causes aggregate production to increase also by $100, which creates an additional $100 in income. Consumers spend $50 of this additional income on additional goods. Once again aggregate production rises by the same amount as the $50 increase in aggregate expenditures. Subsequent increases in aggregate expenditures and aggregate production are determined in a similar fashion, each time getting smaller and smaller. Equilibrium income is $200 higher at the end of this multiplier process. This is determined by calculating the multiplier, 1/(1 *mpc*) = 2 and multiplying it by the initial rise in aggregate expenditures of $100. (199-200)

5. The AE model is not a complete model of the economy. While it provides a method of determining equilibrium income using values for autonomous expenditures, it does tell us where the spending comes from. The values for the autonomous expenditure components are determined by other economic variables not explicitly presented in the model. (203)

6. Classical economists focused on the real wage. They explained that unemployment would decline if the real wage were allowed to decline. Political and social forces were keeping the real wage too high. Keynesians focused on insufficient aggregate expenditures that resulted in a downward spiral. The economy was at a below-potential-income equilibrium. (185)

ANSWERS

PROBLEMS AND APPLICATIONS

1. **a.** The aggregate production curve is a 45-degree line as shown below. Production is on the vertical axis and real income is on the horizontal axis. (189)

    b. The slope is 1. (189-190)
    c. The slope is one because the aggregate production curve represents the identity that aggregate production must equal aggregate income. That can only be represented by a straight line through the origin with a slope of one. (189-190)

2. **a.** Autonomous expenditures are $100. It is that amount that is independent of income. (189)
    b. The marginal propensity to consume is 0.8: This is calculated as the change in expenditures/change in disposable income = 400/500. It is important because it tells us how much of any additional income is respent as

the economy expands. It is because of the mpc that income changes by a multiple of a change in autonomous expenditures. (191)
    c. The expenditures function that corresponds to the table is $AE = 100 + .8Y$. The 100 comes from the level of expenditures when income is zero and the .8 is the *mpc*. (181-191)
    d. The *mps* is 0.2. The *mps* $= 1$ *mpc*. (198)

3. **a.** The graph of the expenditure function from question 2 and the aggregate production from question 1 are shown together on the graph below. (197)

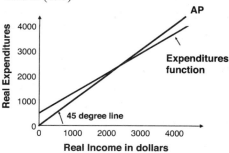

    b. The slope of the expenditure function is the *mpc,* or 0.8. (191)

4. **a.** The aggregate expenditures curve is drawn below. The slope of the *AE* curve is the *mpc* and the vertical intercept is autonomous expenditures. (191)
    b. The slope of the curve is 0.6. It is the *mpc*. (191)
    c. The vertical axis intercept is $1000+500+300+(300 \quad 400) = 1700$. The vertical axis intercept is the level of autonomous expenditures. (196-198)
    d. The aggregate production curve is shown in the graph below. It is a 45-degree line through the origin. (194)
    e. The multiplier is 2.5. It is $1/(1-mpc)$. (196)
    f. Equilibrium income is $4,250: autonomous expenditures $\times$ multiplier, $1,700/(1 \quad 0.6)$. This is shown as point A on the graph below. (194-196)

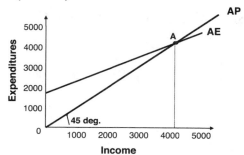

g. An increase in autonomous expenditures of $200 will increase equilibrium income by $500. This is calculated by multiplying $200 by the multiplier, 2.5. The new equilibrium income is $4,750. This is shown below as an upward shift in the AE curve by 200. The new equilibrium income is point B on the graph below. (194-196, 201)

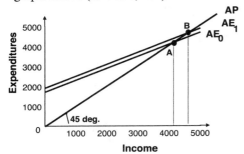

h. The *AE* curve becomes steeper with a slope of 0.8. The multiplier is now 5 and equilibrium income is now $8,500. This is shown as point C in the graph below. Equilibrium income is calculated by multiplying autonomous expenditures, $1,700, by the multiplier. Since the multiplier is larger, an increase of $200 in autonomous expenditures now increases equilibrium income by $1,000, up to $9,500. (201)

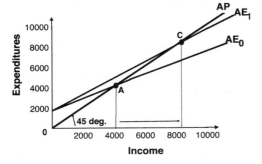

5. a. The multiplier is 3.33: $1/(1-0.7)$. (196)
b. The multiplier is 2.5: $1/(0.4)$. (196)

6. a. Income rises by $2 trillion: $200/(1-0.9)$. In this case, the aggregate expenditures curve has a slope of 0.9 as shown in the graph below. The increase in government expenditures shifts the *AE* curve up from AE_0 to AE_1 and income increases by a multiple of that amount, in this case by a multiple of 10. (199-202)

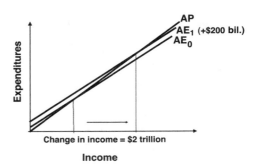

b. Income falls by $200 billion: $70/0.35$. In this case the aggregate expenditures curve has a slope of 0.65 as shown in the graph below. The decrease in investment shifts the *AE* curve down from AE_0 to AE_1 and income decreases by a multiple of that amount, in this case by a multiple of 2.86. (199-201)

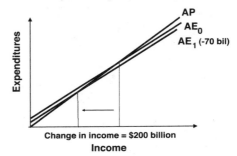

7. Given an *mpc* of .8:
a. Increase expenditures by $80. The multiplier is $1/(1-mpc) = 1/(1-0.8) = 5$. Therefore, to increase GDP by $400, government spending has to increase $80. (191, 196)
b. Increase expenditures by $112. The multiplier is $1/(1-mpc + t-mpc) = 1/(1 - 0.8+0.1-0.8) = 3.57$. Therefore, to increase GDP by $400, government spending has to increase by $112. (191, 196)
c. Increase expenditures by $193. The multiplier is $1/(1 - mpc + t\ mpc + mpm) = 1/(1 - 0.8+0.1\times0.8+0.2) = 2.08$. Therefore, to increase GDP by $400, government spending has to increase by $192. (191, 196)

8. In the AE model, a change in autonomous expenditures will be offset entirely by a change in the price level that shifts the AE curve in a direction opposite to the initial shift. If the initial shift causes the AE curve to shift up, prices will rise sufficiently to shift the AE curve back to its initial position. (204-205)

━━━━ ANSWERS ━━━━

A BRAIN TEASER

1. It may appear that the benefits do not outweigh the costs to the community of "giving away the farm"–especially when one considers that the tax breaks offered new businesses will likely result in higher property tax rates imposed on other members of the community if the same quantity and quality of local government services are to be provided. However, even though a relatively few number of modestly higher paying jobs are created, because of the multiplier effect, this *can* translate into still more jobs and even more income, etc.–creating "significant growth and opportunities within the community." Next time you read a headline indicating the amount of jobs (or income) created in the city by having the "Pigs are Beautiful" convention in town you'll know what they mean. (197-199)

━━━━ ANSWERS ━━━━

POTENTIAL ESSAY QUESTIONS

The following are annotated answers. They indicate the general idea behind the answer.

1. Yes, because equilibrium exists *wherever* AE = AP. That is, planned expenditures need not equal production at full employment. If there is inadequate spending, then the income adjustment process moves the economy to an equilibrium below full employment.

2. Because a change in spending changes people's incomes, which changes their spending, which changes people's incomes... Because of the induced effects within the income adjustment process, the multiplier magnifies any changes in spending into much larger changes in income. However, given an increase in expenditures, real income increases by a smaller amount when prices are flexible.

3. The paradox of thrift indicates that when people decide to save more this may end up causing people to save less. The increased savings (reduced spending) due to the panic

following the stock market crash of 1929 did help perpetuate the Great Depression. This is because when people decided to save more (spend less) businesses responded by cutting back on production and laying off workers. (Businesses were also doing their share of causing a reduction in aggregate expenditures. They were cutting back on investment spending because they were pessimistic about the future as well.) The lower aggregate expenditures in the economy contributed to a multiple decline in income well below full employment. At the lower income levels during the Great Depression savings was much lower than before–hence, the paradox of thrift.

4. The Classical prescription for the Great Depression was to do nothing (except remove the obstacles which they argued kept wages and prices artificially high) and wait for the market (the downward movement in wages and prices) to work its magic over time (in the long run). But, Keynes was concerned that "in the long run, we're all dead!"

    Keynes believed that equilibrium income was not the same as potential income. He disagreed with Say's law. He argued that supply does not create its own demand. That is, there is no guaranteed equality between savings and investment. This is because households or banks may hoard funds. If they do then savings will exceed investment, aggregate expenditures will be insufficient to clear total output off the market, inventories will rise, and output, employment, and incomes would fall creating a further decline in total spending, etc... Note also that Keynes doubted whether falling prices could stop this downward spiral. So, we get stuck in a rut.

    The policy implications are that insufficient total spending in the economy could result in an equilibrium level of output, employment, and income below the potential full employment output level. Therefore, the Keynesian recommendation for a recession: activist expansionary macro policy. That is, increase government spending, reduce taxes (fiscal policy), and increase the money supply (monetary policy) to stimulate aggregate expenditures. (This would shift the AD curve to the right and increase real output, employment and income.)

THE AGGREGATE DEMAND–
AGGREGATE SUPPLY (AD-AS) MODEL

● CHAPTER AT A GLANCE

The previous chapters discussed the calculation of economic output and the fluctuations of real GDP growth throughout the business cycle and, in the last chapter, we developed a model to predict how changes in autonomous expenditures determine changes in real equilibrium income through the multiplier effect. But, so far, there has been little discussion as to how the level of output is actually determined. That is the goal of this chapter. This chapter addresses some of the limitations of the AE model, namely, the lack of aggregate supply and the assumption of a fixed price level.

Aggregate demand (AD) illustrates the total amount of goods and services that are demanded within an economy at each price level. The AD curve is downward sloping to reflect the fact that less is demanded at higher price levels. Aggregate supply (AS) illustrates the total amount of goods and services supplied at each price level.

There are two types of aggregate supply curves a short run aggregate supply (SAS) curve and a long run aggregate supply (LAS) curve. The SAS curve is upward sloping to reflect that fact that more is supplied as the price level rises. The LAS curve shows the output that an economy can produce when all resources are fully employed. The LAS is vertical because, at potential output, only price levels can change.

The intersection of the AD and SAS curves delivers the equilibrium level of output at an equilibrium price level. Depending on where the equilibrium output is in relation to potential output (or the LAS curve), various policies can be implemented to move the actual output to the potential output level. Usually, this will take the form of fiscal and monetary policies.

This review is based upon the learning objectives that open the chapter.

1a. The AD curve can be derived from the AE model. The AE model determines the initial level of equilibrium income. If the price level is assumed to fall, more autonomous spending is generated which shifts the AE curve upward and increases the level of equilibrium income. Real GDP also rises, thereby forming a downward sloping AD curve, reflecting an inverse relationship between the price level and real income/GDP. (215-216)

1b. The AD curve is downward sloping due to the wealth effect, the interest rate effect, the international effect, and repercussions of these effects. (216-217)

As the aggregate price level of the economy falls, the cash people hold is worth more, making people richer, so they buy more (wealth effect). Also, as the price level falls, the value of money rises, inducing people to lend more money, which reduces the interest rate and increases investment expenditures (interest rate effect). Also, as the price level in Canada falls (assuming the exchange rate does not change), the price of Canadian goods relative to foreign goods goes down. Canadian exports increase and Canadian imports decrease. That is, the quantity of Canadian goods demanded rises (the international effect). Repercussions of these effects are called multiplier effects (and make the AD curve flatter than otherwise).

1c. Five important initial shift factors of the AD curve are: (219-221)

• Changes in foreign income.

A rise in foreign income leads to an increase in Canadian exports and an increase (outward shift to the right) of the Canadian AD curve.

- Changes in expectations.

  Positive (optimistic) expectations about the future state of the economy could cause an outward (rightward) shift of the AD curve

- Changes in exchange rates.

  A decrease in the value of the dollar relative to other currencies shifts the AD curve outward to the right.

- Changes in the distribution of income.

  Typically, as the real wage increases, the AD curve increases (shifts out to the right).

- Changes in government aggregate demand policy.

  Expansionary macro policy (an increase in government spending and/or a decrease in taxes—fiscal policy; or an increase in the money supply—monetary policy) increases the AD curve, shifting it outward to the right.

  Note: Anything that affects autonomous components of aggregate expenditures (AE or "total spending") is a shift factor of AD (aggregate demand). (Recall that $AE = C + I + G + X - IM$). These components are autonomous consumption (C), investment (I), government spending (G), and net exports (X−IM). Any change in these components of total spending is multiplied by the multiplier effect shifting the AD curve by a multiple of the original change in spending.

2a. In the short run, the SAS curve is upward sloping and is called the short run aggregate supply (SAS). (221)

  The SAS curve shows the fact that the price level will change in response to changes in AD. Firms adjust each price and quantity in response to changes in AD.

2b. The SAS curve shifts in response to changes in the prices of the factors of production. (222)

  % change in the price level = % change in input prices − % change in productivity.

  If productivity is constant, increases (decreases) in input prices shift the SAS curve up (down).

  If input prices are constant, increases (decreases) in productivity shift the SAS curve down (up).

  What makes input prices change? Whether there is a shortage or surplus in the market for factors of production.

  What makes productivity change? Many things: increases in capital, learning by doing, etc.

3. The long-run aggregate supply curve is vertical at potential output. (223)

  The potential output curve is vertical because an increase in the price level will not change potential output. At potential output, all resources are fully utilized.

4a. Equilibrium in the short run is determined by the intersection of the SAS curve and the AD curve. (224)

  Increases (decreases) in aggregate demand increase (decrease) output and the price level.

  To find the effect of a shift in aggregate demand, start at some point of intersection between the AD curve and the SAS curve. Given a shift of either the AD curve or SAS curve, simply find the new point of intersection. This is the new short-run equilibrium. However, note that any initial change in the AD curve is magnified because of the multiplier effect.

4b. Equilibrium in the long run is determined by the intersection of the long run aggregate supply curve and the AD curve. (224-225)

If the economy begins at a long-run equilibrium, increases in aggregate demand will lead to changes in the price level only.

If an economy is in short-run equilibrium, but not long-run equilibrium, the SAS curve will shift up or down.

If short-run equilibrium output is below long-run equilibrium output, the economy is in a recessionary gap. The price level will fall and the SAS curve will shift down. (See the figure below.)

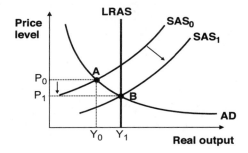

If short-run equilibrium output is above long-run equilibrium output, the economy is in an inflationary gap. The price level will rise and the SAS curve will shift up. (See the figure below)

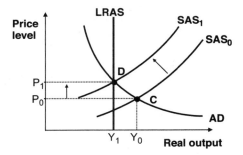

4c. If the economy is in a recessionary gap, the government could implement epansionary fiscal policy (raise government spending and/or lower taxes) or expansionary monetary policy (lower interest rates). (225-229)

5a. There are three policy ranges in the AD/AS model
- The Keynesian range, where prices are fixed.
- The Classical range, where prices are flexible.
- The intermediate range, where prices are somewhat flexible. (230)

6. Knowing where potential output is is just one reason why macro policy is more complicated than the model makes it look. (230-232)

Knowing potential output is important to knowing whether changes in aggregate demand will affect output or the price level. Economists have divided the economy into three ranges: the Keynesian range (the economy is far below potential and the price level is fairly fixed), the intermediate range (between low and high potential output where the price level is somewhat flexible), and the Classical range (above high potential output where the price level is very flexible). We have no way of precisely determining for sure what range the economy is in, or precisely where the correct target level of potential output is, and, therefore, of precisely knowing by how much we should shift the AD curve (with the use of macro—fiscal and monetary—policy).

MATCHING THE TERMS
Match the terms to their definitions

All of these key terms are found at the end of the chapter.

___1.   aggregate demand curve
___2.   short-run aggregate sup-
        ply curve
___3.   inflationary gap
___4.   interest rate effect
___5.   international effect
___6.   multiplier effect
___7.   long-run aggregate sup-
        ply curve
___8.   quantity-adjusting and
        price-adjusting markets
___9.   recessionary gap
___10. wealth effect

a.   As the price level falls, the interest rate falls, which leads to greater
     investment expenditures.
b.   A curve that shows the amount of goods and services an economy
     can produce when both labour and capital are fully employed.
c.   A curve that gives combinations of price levels and real income that
     correspond to equilibrium in the market for goods and services.
d.   Markets in which firms respond to changes in demand by modify-
     ing both their outputs and their prices.
e.   A curve that shows how firms adjust the quantity of real output
     they will supply when the price level changes, holding all input
     prices fixed.
f.   Amount by which equilibrium output is below potential output.
g.   As the price level falls, people are richer, so they buy more.
h.   As the price level in a country falls, the quantity of that country's
     goods demanded by foreigners and residents will increase.
i.   Amplification of initial changes in expenditures.
j.   Amount by which equilibrium output is above potential output.
k.   The level of income toward which the economy gravitates in the
     short run.
l.   The level of income that the economy technically is capable of
     producing without inflation generating accelerating.

MULTIPLE CHOICE

Circle the one best answer for each of the following questions:

1.   In the AD/AS model,
     a. price of a good is on the horizontal axis.
     b. price level is on the horizontal axis.
     c. price of a good is on the vertical axis.
     d. price level is on the vertical axis.

2.   Which of the following is *not* an explanation of
     the downward slope of the AD curve?
     a. the wealth effect.
     b. the interest rate effect.
     c. the consumption effect.
     d. the international effect.

3.   If the exchange rate becomes flexible so that
     changes in the price level have little effect on
     exports and imports:
     a. the AD curve will become steeper.
     b. the AD curve will become flatter.
     c. the AD curve will become unaffected.
     d. the AS curve will become steeper.

4.   If the multiplier effect is 2 rather than 3,
     a. the AD curve will be steeper.
     b. the AD curve will be flatter.
     c. the AD curve will be unaffected.
     d. the AS curve will be steeper.

5.   If there is a rise in foreign income the AD curve
     will likely:
     a. shift in to the left.
     b. shift out to the right.
     c. become steeper.
     d. become flatter.

6.   If there is a rise in a country's exchange rate, the
     AD curve will likely:
     a. shift in to the left.
     b. shift out to the right.
     c. become steeper.
     d. become flatter.

7. Expansionary monetary policy will likely:
   a. shift the AD curve in to the left.
   b. shift the AD curve out to the right.
   c. make the AD curve steeper.
   d. make the AD curve flatter.

8. If government spending increases by 40, the AD curve will shift to the
   a. right by 40.
   b. left by 40.
   c. right by more than 40.
   d. right by less than 40.

9. The slope of the SAS curve is determined by:
   a. opportunity cost
   b. the law of diminishing marginal returns.
   c. institutional realities.
   d. the wealth effect, the international effect and the interest rate effect.

10. If productivity rises by 2% and wages rise by 6%, the SAS curve will
   a. likely shift up.
   b. likely shift down.
   c. become flatter.
   d. become steeper.

11. The LAS curve is:
   a. another name for the AD curve.
   b. another name for the AS curve.
   c. a vertical line.
   d. a horizontal line.

12. Refer to the graph below. The graph demonstrates the expected short-run result if:

   a. productivity increases by less than wages.
   b. the government increases the money supply.
   c. the exchange rate value of a country's currency falls.
   d. there are suddenly expectations of a rising price level.

13. The graph below demonstrates the expected short-run result if:

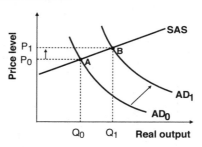

   a. productivity increases by less than wages
   b. the government increases the money supply
   c. a country's exchange rate appreciates (gains value).
   d. wages rise by less than the increase in productivity.

14. The graph below demonstrates the expected short-run result if:

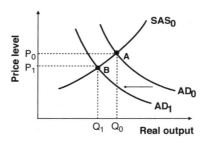

   a. productivity increases by less than wages
   b. the government increases the money supply
   c. a country's exchange rate appreciates (gains value).
   d. wages rise by less than the increase in productivity.

15. Assume the economy is initially at potential B. The graph below correctly demonstrates an economy moving to point C if:

a. productivity increases by less than the increase in wages.
b. the government increases the money supply.
c. a country's exchange rate appreciates (gains value).
d. wages rise by less than the increase in productivity.

16. Assume the economy is initially at point B. The graph below correctly demonstrates an economy moving to point C if:

a. productivity increases by less than the increase in wages.
b. the government decreases the money supply.
c. a country's exchange rate appreciates (gains value).
d. wages rise by less than the increase in productivity.

17. Which of the following distances in the graph below is the inflationary gap?

a. A.
b. B.
c. C.
d. D.

18. In the Keynesian range the price level is:
a. flexible.
b. somewhat flexible.
c. indeterminate.
d. fixed.

19. The Classical range is shown by range:

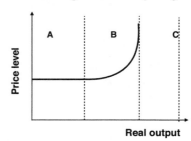

a. A.
b. B.
c. C.
d. The Classical range is not shown.

20. If the target rate of unemployment falls, potential income will:
a. first decrease, then increase.
b. increase.
c. decrease.
d. first increase, then decrease.

SHORT-ANSWER QUESTIONS

1. What effects determine the slope of the AD curve?

2. List some of the important shift factors of the AD curve.

3. What is the slope of the SAS curve? Why does it have this shape?

4. What will shift the SAS curve up or down?

5. What is the slope of the potential output curve? Why does it have this shape?

6. Show graphically the effect of increased government expenditure on real output when (a) the economy is far below potential output and (b) the economy is at potential output.

7. Why is the AD/AS model more complicated than it looks?

● PROBLEMS AND APPLICATIONS

1. What will likely happen to the shape or position of the *AD* curve in the following circumstances?

   a. A rise in the price level does not make people feel poorer.

   b. Income is redistributed from poor people to rich people.

   c. The country's currency depreciates.

   d. The exchange rate changes from fixed to flexible.

   e. Expectations of future rises in the price level develop without any current change in the price level.

2. State what range of the price/output path you think the economy is in, given the following information:

   a. The economy is significantly below potential. Downward shifts in aggregate demand do not result in falls in the price level.

   b. Increases in aggregate demand result in little change in real output and large increases in the price level.

   c. Increases in aggregate demand seem to be split roughly equally between increases in real output and increases in the price level.

3. What will happen to the position of the *SAS curve* in the following circumstances?

   a. Productivity rises by 3 percent and input prices rise by 3 percent.

   b. Productivity rises by 3 percent and input prices rise by 5 percent.

   c. Productivity rises by 3 percent and input prices rise by 1 percent.

4. Graphically demonstrate the effect of each of the following on either the SAS curve or the long-run aggregate supply curve. Be sure to label all axes.

    a. Businesses find that they are able to produce more output without having to pay more wages nor increase their costs of capital.

    b. A severe snow storm paralyzes most of the United States.

    c. The country's currency appreciates dramatically.

5. The government of Germany wants to expand its economy through increased spending. Show the likely effects of an activist policy in the short run and in the long run in the following three cases.

    a. The economy is far below potential output.

    b. The economy is close to, but still below, potential output.

    c. The economy is at potential output.

6. Demonstrate the following two cases using the AD/AS model. What will happen in the long run if the government does nothing?

    a. Inflationary gap.

    b. Recessionary gap.

    c. What could government do (a) and (b) to keep the price level constant?

● A BRAIN TEASER

1. Suppose the economy has been experiencing a recession for a couple of years with no apparent relief in sight. Currently, the unemployment rate is 10%. In response to political pressure "to put Canada back to work," government policy makers have recently reduced taxes significantly and have dramatically increased government spending on public works projects to rebuild the nation's crumbling infrastructure (roads, bridges, airports, etc.). During a recent press conference the Prime Minister of Canada remarked that the new government policy of tax cuts and spending programs will be successful in reducing unemployment and there should be no reason to fear inflation either. As a student in an economics course one of your friends has asked you to evaluate the likely success of these recent policy moves. How would you respond?

● POTENTIAL ESSAY QUESTIONS

You may also see essay questions similar to the "Problems & Applications" and "Brain Teasers" exercises.

1. Why is the AD/AS model more complicated than the model makes it look?

2. What is the paradox of thrift and how does it relate to the AD/AS model?

━━━━ ANSWERS ━━━━

MATCHING

1-c; 2-e; 3-j; 4-a; 5-h; 6-i; 7-b; 8-d; 9-f; 10-g.

━━━━ ANSWERS ━━━━

MULTIPLE CHOICE

1.   d   The AD/AS model is different than the micro supply/demand model. It has price *level* on the vertical axis and *total* output on the horizontal axis. See pages 215-216.

2.   c   No consumption effect is discussed in the book. See page 217.

3.   a   This question refers to the international effect; if the international effect is reduced, the change in the price level will have less effect on AD and the AD curve will be steeper. See page 218.

4.   a   The multiplier effect increases the effect of the other effects and hence a smaller multiplier makes the AD curve steeper. See page 218.

5.   b   The rise in foreign income will increase demand for exports shifting the AD curve to the right. See page 219.

6.   a   The rise in the country's exchange rate will decrease demand for its exports shifting the AD curve in to the left. See page 219.

7.   b   Expansionary monetary policy will increase aggregate demand, shifting the AD curve out to the right. See page 220.

8.   c   The multiplier effect would increase the effect, so the rightward shift would by more than 40. See pages 220-221.

9.   c   The SAS curve is not a derived curve; it is an empirical curve determined by institutional realities. See pages 221-222.

10.   a   Because wages are rising by more than productivity costs, the SAS curve will shift up. Since it is flat it cannot become flatter or steeper. See pages 222-223.

11.   c   The LAS curve shows the amount of goods and services an economy can produce when both labour and capital are fully employed. It is a vertical line since price level does not affect potential output. See page 223.

12.   a   The aggregate supply curve shifts upward when wages rise by more than increases in productivity. Real output will decline and the price level will rise. See pages 222-223 and 226-227.

13.   b   An increase in the money supply and the resulting lower interest rates will shift the AD curve to the right. In the short run, real output and the price level will rise. See pages 226-227.

14.   c   Demand for domestic goods will decline if one's currency appreciates because foreign goods will be less expensive compared to domestic goods. Real output will decline with the price level in the short run. (226-227)

15.   d   Since at point B, the economy is below potential, there will be downward pressure on wages. Or at least wages will rise by less than the increase in productivity. The SAS curve will shift down until the economy reaches point C. See pages 226-227.

16.   a   Since at point B, the economy is above potential, there will be upward pressure on wages. Wages will rise by more than the increase in productivity. The SAS curve will shift up until the economy reaches point C. See pages 226-227.

17.   a   The inflationary gap occurs when the price level is such that the quantity of aggregate demand exceeds the quantity of potential income. See page 227.

18.   d   Fixed prices are the key characteristic of the Keynesian range. See page 230.

19. c   The Classical range is where increases in aggregate demand result only in increases in the price level and no increase in aggregate output. This is where the price/output path is vertical. See page 230.

20. b   Potential income varies inversely with unemployment. See pages 230-231.

ANSWERS

SHORT-ANSWER QUESTIONS

1.   The wealth effect, the interest rate effect, international effect, and the repercussions these effects cause, i.e., the multiplier effect, determine the slope of the AD curve. (217-218)

2.   Five important initial shift factors of the AD curve are: 1. Changes in the foreign income. 2. Changes in exchange rates. 3. Changes in expectations. 4. Changes in the distribution of income. 5. Changes in government aggregate demand policy. (219-220)

3.   The SAS curve specifies how a shift in the aggregate demand curve affects the price level and real output. A standard SAS curve is upward sloping. That is, increase in aggregate demand lead to increases in both output and the price level. Institutional realities about how firms set prices determines the shape of the SAS curve. Differences between the actual price level and its expected value causes firms to misinterpret changes in the price level to be changes in relative prices leading them to adjust output. (221-222)

4.   The SAS curve will shift up or down when input prices rise or fall or if productivity rises or falls. The change in the SAS curve is determined by the following: % change in price level = % change in input prices − % change in productivity. (222-223)

5.   The Long Run Aggregate Supply (LAS) curve is vertical. It has this shape because potential output is output when all inputs are fully employed. Changes in the price level do not affect potential output. (223-224)

6.   If the economy begins at point A, increased government expenditures shifts the AD out to the right from AD_0 to AD_1. If the economy begins below potential output, the price level would rise from P_0 to P_1, and real output would increase from Y_0 to Y_1. I've drawn it so that the AD curve shifts out enough so that the economy is in both long-run and short run equilibrium at potential output at point B. (225-227)

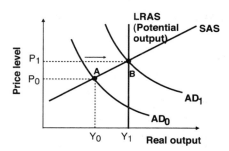

Now suppose the economy begins at point C in both short run and long-run equilibrium. In the short run, when the aggregate demand curve shifts from AD_0 to AD_1, real output rises from Y_1 and Y_2. Since the economy is now above potential output, however, input prices begin to rise and the SAS curve shifts up. The SAS curve continues to shift up to SAS_1 where the economy returns to a long-run equilibrium at a higher price level, P_1, but the same output level as before, Y_1. (225-227)

8.   The AD/AS model is more complicated than it looks because we do not know the level of potential output, which is the key to knowing whether an increase in aggregate demand will lead to an increase in output, the price level, or a combination of the two. Economists have no sure way of estimating potential output. One method is to estimate the unemployment rate where inflation begins to rise. Unfortunately, this is also difficult to predict. Another way is to add a historical growth factor of 3% to previous levels of real output. This can be problematic if the economy is moving to a lower or higher growth rate. (228-230)

ANSWERS

PROBLEMS AND APPLICATIONS

1. **a.** This would cause the wealth effect to become inoperative and the AD curve will become steeper. (216-217)

   b. Assuming the marginal propensity to consume of rich people is less than that of poor people, the AD curve will shift to the left. (216-217)

   c. As the exchange rate depreciates, exports will rise and imports will fall. This shifts the AD curve out. (216-217)

   d. If the exchange rate was originally fixed and became flexible, increases in the price level will be offset by changes in the exchange rate and the international effect becomes inoperative. The *AD* curve will be steeper. (216-217)

   e. Expectations of future price increases without changes in the current price level will tend to cause the *AD* curve to shift to the right. (216-217)

2. **a.** Keynesian range. (230)
   b. Classical range. (230)
   c. Intermediate range. (230)

3. **a.** The SAS doesn't shift at all because rises in input prices are completely offset by increases in productivity. (222-223)

   b. The SAS curve shifts up because the rise in input prices exceed the rise in productivity. (222-223)

   c. The SAS curve shifts down because the rise in input prices are less than the rise in productivity. (222-223)

4. **a.** The LAS curve shifts to the right as shown below because businesspeople are finding that their productive capacity is larger than they had thought. (223-224)

   b. The LAS curve shifts to the left as shown below because bad weather will hinder production. Because the storm is temporary, however, the shift in the LAS curve is also temporary. (223-224)

   c. The aggregate supply curve shown below shifts down from SAS_0 to SAS_1, because businesses will benefit from the declining import prices to the extent that imports are used in production. The fall in input prices is passed through to the goods market. (226-227)

5. a. The economy is far below potential output at point A in the graph below. As the AD curve shifts out, the economy moves to point B—the price level rises from P_0 to P_1, and output increases to Y_1. Government activism in this range is very effective. As I have drawn it, Y_1 is potential output, and point B is both a short-run and a long-run equilibrium. (225-227)

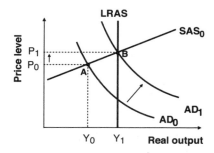

b. The economy is close to potential output at point A in the graph below. The AD curve shifts to AD_1 and real output rises to Y_1, beyond potential.   Point B is a short-run equilibrium. Since output is above potential, input prices begin to rise which shifts the SAS curve up. As the AS curve shifts up, real output declines and the price level rises. The SAS curve will continue to shift up until the economy is at potential output Y_2 and a new price level P_1—point C. Expansionary fiscal policy will increase both real output and the price level when the economy begins at close to potential. Real output rises by less than in (a) and the economy experiences some inflation. (225-227)

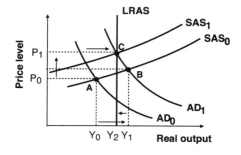

c. The economy is at potential output at point A in the graph below. As the AD curve shifts out, real output rises to Y_1 in the short run where the price level is fixed at P_0—point B. Since the economy is above potential however, eventually input prices will rise and the SAS curve will shift up. The SAS curve shifts up until real output falls back to potential output—Y_0—but the price level is now at P_1. In the long run, real output remains unchanged at Y_0 and only the price level increases from P_0 to P_1. Government activism in this range is ineffective in the long run. (225-227)

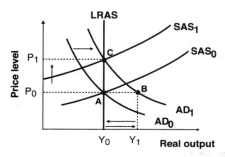

6. a. The graph below demonstrates an inflationary gap—short-run equilibrium output is above potential at existing prices—point A. If government does nothing, eventually wages will be bid up as firms try to hire more workers. This will shift the SAS curve up to SAS_1. Real output will fall to potential and the price level will rise—to point B. (225-227)

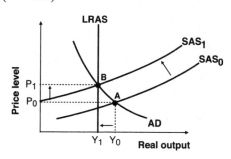

b. The graph below demonstrates a recessionary gap—short-run equilibrium output is below potential at existing prices—point A. Given the excess supply in the labour market firms will be able to offer workers lower wages. Input prices will fall and the SAS curve will shift down to SAS_1. Real output will rise to potential and the price level will fall—to point B. Generally, government intervenes to increase expenditures (shifting the AD curve) before the price level declines. (225-227)

ANSWERS

A BRAIN TEASER

1. My response depends on where I believe the economy is along the price/output path. If we are in the Keynesian range, then the Prime Minister is right—the policy moves will increase the AD curve and the real output (employment) level will rise without creating any inflation. However, if we are in the intermediate range, then wages will rise pushing the AD curve up and the price level may rise some—the extent to which is difficult to predict. Moreover, it is also very difficult to determine which of the two ranges we would currently find ourselves in. (We know we are not in the Classical range because we are not at full employment—the potential output level.) (229-232)

ANSWERS

POTENTIAL ESSAY QUESTIONS

The following are annotated answers. They indicate the general idea behind the answer.

1. Knowing where potential output is why macro policy is more complicated than the model makes it look. That is, we have no way of precisely determining for sure what range the economy is in, or precisely where the correct target level of potential output is, and therefore of precisely knowing by how much we should shift the AD curve (with the use of macro—fiscal and monetary—policy). However, most economists see the economy in the intermediate range.

2. The paradox of thrift is that when people collectively decide to save more and consume less, consumption expenditures fall. If that saving is not immediately transferred into investment, total expenditures falls. Faced with excess supply, firms cut production and income falls. As people's income falls, consumption and saving both fall. It is the paradox of thrift that leads to the multiplier effect. This multiplier effect makes the AD curve flatter than it otherwise would have been and accounts for the multiplied effect of shift factors of aggregate demand.

THE AD-AS MODEL AND FISCAL POLICY

10

CHAPTER AT A GLANCE

Chapter 10 draws upon everything we have learned so far regarding business cycles, the AD/AS model, and the AE model, to analyze an important tool at the government's disposal to alter economic activity. Fiscal policy is the government's use of spending and taxation powers to achieve a specific level of economic activity and price stability.

Fiscal policy can take two forms. Countercyclical fiscal policy is the deliberate actions by government to alter spending and taxation in order to achieve a specific economic goal — usually dealing with a recession or inflation. A built-in policy or an automatic stabilizer is where the fluctuations of the business cycle are dampened without any explicit government action. Automatic stabilizers include welfare payments, employment insurance and the income tax system.

Fiscal policy is not without problems. The last part of the chapter highlights several of them including the lack of knowledge of what policy is called for, government's inability to respond quickly enough, and conflicting goals.

This review is based upon the learning objectives that open the chapter.

1a. Expansionary fiscal policy involves decreasing taxes or increasing government spending. Contractionary fiscal policy involves increasing taxes or decreasing government spending. (237)

> *Use expansionary fiscal policy to combat cyclical unemployment and slow growth during a recession (a downturn in the business cycle).*
> *Use contractionary fiscal policy to combat inflation during an upturn in the business cycle.*

1b. Expansionary fiscal policy shifts the aggregate demand curve to the right. The effect on prices and output depends upon how close the economy is to potential output. (237-239)

If the multiplier is 5 and there is a recessionary gap of $250, government must increase expenditures by $50 (since $50 × multiplier of 5 = $250) to arrive at potential income. If the recessionary gap was less than $250, the effect of the shift in the AD curve (and the multiplier effect) would be split between increases in real output and increases in the price level.

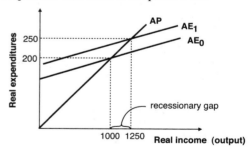

Here is the story using the AP/AE model: In the graph above, initial autonomous AE is $200 and the mpc is 0.8. The multiplier is $1/(1-0.8) = 5$. Equilibrium income is $1000. Since there is a recessionary gap of $250, government increases expenditures by $50 (since $50 × multiplier of 5 = $250). This depends upon the price level being fixed.

1c. Contractionary fiscal policy shifts the AD curve leftward. (239-240)

1d. Countercyclical fiscal policy is designed to always keep the economy at its target or potential level of income. This is sometimes called "fine tuning" (240-241)

2a. Three alternatives to fiscal policy are directed investment policies, trade policies, and autonomous consumption policies. (241-245)

Anything which government can do to alter components of AE (C, I, G, and X−IM) will have a multiple impact on Y (the income-output level in the macro economy) because of the multiplier. For example, rosy scenarios, bank guarantees, reduction in interest rates, export-led growth policies, and increases in consumer credit availability could increase AE and stimulate the economy.

2b. Governments can enhance AD by creating a climate conducive to investment spending and business confidence by not creating uncertainty and surprises, particularly in the financial markets. This can be done by implementing regular, honest and accurate policy announcements. (242)

Another way would be to protect the financial system to prevent bank and financial institution failures.

2c. Governments can influence AD through exchange rate policies. A low value of a currency relative to foreign currencies encourages exports and discourages imports. A high value of currency relative to foreign currency encourages imports and discourages exports. (244)

2d. Governments can alter AD by autonomous consumption policy. One way would be by increasing the availability of consumer credit. (244-245)

3a. During the Depression of the 1930s, the economy was far below potential. World War II spending increased aggregate expenditures and output. (245)

The economy exceeded its potential output during World War II, but price controls kept inflation low.

3b. In the late 1990s, the Canadian deficit turned into a surplus. (246)

The surplus was the result of a booming economy driven by consumer and investment spending. The surplus helped to keep the economy from inflation.

4a. Six assumptions of the model that could lead to problems with fiscal policy are: (246-251)

1. Financing the deficit doesn't have any offsetting effects.
   In reality, it often does (e.g., the crowding-out effect).

2. The government knows what the situation is.
   In reality, the government must estimate what the situation is.

3. The government knows the economy's potential income.
   In reality, the government may not know what this level is.

4. The government has flexibility in terms of spending and taxes.
   In reality, the government cannot change them quickly.

5. The size of the government debt doesn't matter.
   In reality, the size of the debt often does matter.

6. Fiscal policy doesn't negatively affect other government goals.
   In reality, it often does.

4b. Crowding out is the offsetting effect on private expenditures caused by the government's sale of bonds to finance expansionary fiscal policy. (247-249)

Increases in the deficit financed by borrowing (selling bonds) leads to increases in interest rates (which increases the cost of borrowing). This leads to lower investment (business spending on capital) which offsets the rise in government spending.

So, increased deficit spending may be partially or totally offset by decreases in other spending components.

The size of the crowding-out effect is debatable.

5a. When the price level is flexible, the multiplier effect is smaller than when the price level is fixed. This is because an increase in spending leads to higher prices, which partly offsets the increase in desired spending in the economy. The crowding out effect of fiscal policy also results in the increase in the level of real output to be smaller than it would be under fixed prices. (252-253)

5b. Expansionary fiscal policy under flexible prices results in increased government spending and/or lower taxes, which raises aggregate demand and real output. To finance this spending, the government issues bonds which contain higher interest rates in order to make them attractive to investors. This pushes up the interest rates in the economy and raises the cost of borrowing for private business. Investment spending in the private sector falls, thereby reducing aggregate demand and real output.

The end result of expansionary fiscal policy is still higher real output, but not by as much as under a fixed price system. The level of real GDP depends on the multiplier effect and the crowding out effect. (252-253)

6. An automatic stabilizer is any government program or policy that will counteract the business cycle without any new government action. (254-255)

Automatic stabilizers include:
- Welfare payments
- Employment insurance, and
- Income tax system.

Assume a recession that is caused by too little total spending. Government expenditures automatically rise (because of increased welfare payments and unemployment claims). Taxes automatically decrease (because fewer people are earning income). The budget deficit increases and AE (total spending) increases. The opposite occurs during an upturn in the business cycle. <u>Automatic stabilizers help smooth out the business cycle.</u>

MATCHING THE TERMS
Match the terms to their definitions

All of these key terms are found at the end of the chapter.

___ **1.** aggregate demand management	**a.** Policies designed to stimulate Canadian exports and increase aggregate expenditures on Canadian goods.
___ **2.** automatic stabilizer	**b.** Any government program or policy that will counteract the business cycle without any new government action.
___ **3.** contractionary fiscal policy	**c.** Countercyclical fiscal policy designed to keep the economy always at its target or potential level of income.
___ **4.** crowding out	**d.** Deliberate change in either government spending or taxes to stimulate or slow down the economy.
___ **5.** exchange rate policy	**e.** Deliberately affecting a country's exchange rate to affects its trade balance.
___ **6.** expansionary fiscal policy	**f.** The offsetting effect of a change in government expenditures by a change in private expenditures in the opposite direction.
___ **7.** export-led growth policies	**g.** Governments attempt to control the aggregate level of spending in the economy.
___ **8.** fine tuning	**h.** Increase taxes or decrease government spending.
___ **9.** fiscal policy	**i.** Decrease taxes or increase government spending.
___ **10.** countercyclical fiscal policy	**j.** Fiscal policy in which the government offsets any change in aggregate expenditures that would create a business cycle.

MULTIPLE CHOICE

Circle the one best answer for each of the following questions:

1. Expansionary fiscal policy involves
   a. increasing taxes.
   b. increasing the money supply.
   c. increasing government spending.
   d. changing the exchange rate.

2. According to the AE model, government has a role in getting an economy out of recession because
   a. individuals collectively don't have the spending power to make a difference.
   b. government spending will increase income and induce individuals to spend more.
   c. the economy could never be expected to return to potential output on its own.
   d. only the government knows when the economy is in a recession.

3. The macro policy that follows from the multiplier and AD/AS model is generally called
   a. aggregate supply management.
   b. aggregate demand management.
   c. price-level policy.
   d. exchange rate policy.

4. In the graph below, actual income is below potential income. The government is planning to use expansionary fiscal policy. This will:

   a. shift the *AP* curve up.
   b. shift the *AE* curve up.
   c. shift the *AP* curve down.
   d. shift the *AE* curve down.

5. In the graph below, autonomous imports have just increased. In the short run, this will cause:

   a. the aggregate supply curve to shift down.
   b. the aggregate supply curve to shift up.
   c. the aggregate demand curve to shift out to the right.
   d. the aggregate demand curve to shift in to the left

6. The economy has a fixed price level, an *mpc* of 0.5, and a recessionary gap of 240. Using the AE *model*, an economist would advise government to
   a. increase autonomous expenditures by 120.
   b. increase autonomous expenditures by 240.
   c. increase autonomous expenditures by 480.
   d. increase autonomous expenditures by 620.

7. The economy is in the Keynesian range, has an *mpc* of 0.8, and is in a recessionary gap of 600. Using the AE model, an economist would advise government to
   a. increase autonomous expenditures by 120
   b. increase autonomous expenditures by 480.
   c. increase autonomous expenditures by 600.
   d. increase autonomous expenditures by 3000.

8. The economy has a fixed price level, an *mpc* of 0.66, and a recessionary gap of 900. Using the AE model, an economist would advise government to increase autonomous expenditures by about:
   a. 30.
   b. 300.
   c. 600.
   d. 2700.

9. The economy has an inflationary gap, the government should use fiscal policy to shift:
   a. the *SAS* curve up.
   b. the *SAS* curve down.
   c. the *AD* curve out to the right.
   d. the *AD* curve in to the left.

10. If an economy has an inflationary gap and the government does nothing, the AE model predicts that:
    a. the *SAS* curve will shift up as input prices increase, and output will decline.
    b. the *SAS* curve will shift down as input prices decline, and output will rise.
    c. the AD curve will shift out to the right as individuals collectively decide to increase expenditures, and output will rise.
    d. the AD curve will shift in to the left as individuals collectively decide to reduce expenditures, and output will decline.

11. Which of the following is true today?
    a. Keynesian economists support fine tuning.
    b. Classical economists support fine tuning.
    c. Both Keynesian and Classical economists generally support fine tuning.
    d. Both Keynesian and Classical economists generally oppose fine tuning.

12. Expansionary aggregate demand policy includes all of the following except
    a. increasing government spending.
    b. increasing autonomous expenditures.
    c. increasing imports.
    d. decreasing taxes.

13. Contractionary aggregate demand policy includes all of the following except
    a. decreasing autonomous investment.
    b. lowering the value of one's currency by buying foreign currencies.
    c. increasing the value of one's currency by selling foreign currencies.
    d. decreasing government spending.

14. During World War II,
    a. expansionary fiscal policy pushed the economy beyond potential and the price level rose tremendously.
    b. expansionary fiscal policy pushed the economy beyond potential, but the price level was controlled by legislation.
    c. contractionary monetary policy pushed the economy into a depression.
    d. increased taxes to finance the war pushed the economy into recession.

15. Exchange rate policy is
    a. increasing the size of the government deficit.
    b. deliberately affecting the country's exchange rate in order to affect its trade balance.
    c. deliberately affecting the country's money supply in order to affect its trade balance.
    d. deliberately affecting the country's tax rate in order to affect its trade balance.

16. The economy in the late 1990s:
    a. expanded because government spending on Employment Insurance rose tremendously.
    b. was definitely beyond potential, creating inflationary pressures.
    c. expanded as consumption and investment expenditures rose, but inflation did not rise.
    d. slowed from its rapid pace in the mid-1990s because of a growing budget surplus.

17. Crowding out occurs when
    a. the government runs a deficit and sells bonds to finance that deficit.
    b. the government prints money.
    c. the government runs a surplus and sells bonds and the people who buy those bonds sell their older bonds to the government.
    d. the tendency for new workers to replace more expensive older workers is a factor.

18. If potential output is 2 percent higher than forecasted, the target rate of unemployment is probably:
    a. 1 percentage point lower than expected.
    b. 1 percentage point higher than expected.
    c. 2 percentage points lower than expected.
    d. 2 percentage points higher than expected.

19. Automatic stabilizers:
    a. are government programs to employ workers during recessions.
    b. create government budget surpluses during economic recessions.
    c. are designed to reduce the price level directly.
    d. counteract both recessions and expansions through changes in spending without government action.

● SHORT-ANSWER QUESTIONS

1. The initial policy proposal by U.S. Keynesian economists was to introduce public works programs. How did that proposal work and what was added to that policy by subsequent Keynesian policymakers?

2. Suppose you are the featured speaker at a primer for the first-year economics students. You have been asked to speak about fiscal policy. An MP asks what fiscal policy tools the federal government has to affect the economy, and what effect they have on the level of output. You tell her.

3. What are contractionary and expansionary fiscal policies?

4. How does fiscal policy affect the economy? Demonstrate an expansionary fiscal policy graphically using the AD/AS model.

5. The first-year economics students are worried about your answer to question 2. They feel they are politically unable to implement those policies. What three alternatives to fiscal policy can you offer?

6. How do the six problems of fiscal policy limit its use?

7. You are speaking at the business conference. An economics student wonders whether financing deficit spending will change the direct effect of fiscal policy. You tell her that it might and explain how.

8. Some economists argue that crowding out totally undermines the activist view of fiscal policy. Explain their argument.

9. A country has just removed its employment insurance program and is experiencing a recession. How will this recession differ from earlier recessions?

PROBLEMS AND APPLICATIONS

1. You are hired by the Prime Minister who believes that the economy is operating at a level $300 billion beyond potential output. You are told that the marginal propensity to consume is 0.5.

    a. The Prime Minister wants to use taxes to close the gap. What do you advise? Show your answer using the AP/AE model.

    b. The Prime Minister wants to compare your plan in (a) to a plan using spending to close the inflationary gap. What do you advise? Show your answer graphically using the AD/AS model.

    c. Advisers realize that the marginal propensity to consume is 0.75. Recalculate your answer to (b) and show using the AD/AS model.

2. You are called by the Prime Minister to raise equilibrium income by $1,000. You are told that the mpc is 0.

    a. You estimate that the economy has a recessionary gap of $1000. Make a proposal to increase short-run equilibrium income as desired by the president. What will happen to the economy in the long run?

    b. You've re-estimated potential output. The economy has a recessionary gap of only $500. The Prime Minister still wants to raise equilibrium income by $1,000. Make a proposal to increase short-run equilibrium income as desired by the Prime Minister. What will happen to the economy in the long run?

3. Suppose the government wants to increase income by $250 billion. The *mpc* is 0.6.

    a. Assuming the economy is far below potential output, by how much must government increase spending to reach its goal? Show the effect of this action, using the AD/AS model.

    b. Suppose government finances this increase in spending with the sale of bonds. As a result, interest rates increase. How does this affect the analysis? Demonstrate using the multiplier model.

4. Congratulations. You have just been appointed economic adviser to Dreamland. For each of the following, advise the president.

   a. The Prime Minister wants to reduce unemployment from 8 to 6 percent. Income is $40,000 and the *mpc* is 0.4. What spending policy would you advise? (Hint: Use Okun's rule of thumb from a previous chapter.)

   b. The Prime Minister wants to reduce unemployment from 8 to 6 percent. Income is $50,000 and the *mpc* is 0.75. What fiscal spending policy would you advise?

5. In 2001, national income was $9 trillion and unemployment was 4%.

   a. Suppose that a private sector research organization believed that the natural rate of unemployment was 4% while the Governor of the Bank of Canada believed that natural rate was 5%. Calculate the difference in the underlying estimates of potential income.

   b. What spending policy would each recommend to close the recessionary gap, assuming the *mpc* is 0.5?

● A BRAIN TEASER

1. Do the problems associated with implementing activist fiscal policy in practice mean that the multiplier model is wrong? Or, that fiscal policy ought to be eliminated?

● POTENTIAL ESSAY QUESTIONS

You may also see essay questions similar to the "Problems & Applications" and "Brain Teasers" exercises.

1. According to the multiplier model, what is appropriate fiscal policy over the course of the business cycle?

2. How do the automatic stabilizers add stability to the business cycle? Are there any time lag (delay) problems associated with the use of the automatic stabilizers?

3. What is the crowding-out effect? What impact does this have on the effectiveness of fiscal policy in stimulating the economy during a recession? How large is the crowding-out effect according to the Keynesians? The Classicals? What does the empirical evidence suggest about the size of the crowding-out effect?

━━━━ ANSWERS ━━━━

MATCHING

1-g; 2-b; 3-h; 4-f; 5-e; 6-i; 7-a; 8-c; 9-d; 10-j.

━━━━ ANSWERS ━━━━

MULTIPLE CHOICE

1. c   Expansionary fiscal policy is the deliberate change in either government spending or taxes to stimulate the economy. Increasing government spending will increase expenditures and increase income. Changing the money supply is monetary policy, not fiscal policy. See page 237.

2. b   With fiscal policy, government provides the needed increased spending that increases individuals' incomes, inducing them to spend more. The multiplier takes over and income increases by more than the government stimulus. Individuals collectively do have the spending power to get an economy out of recession, but do not act collectively because individuals do not take into account the effect of their spending on aggregate income. See pages 237-241.

3. b   Aggregate demand management is government's attempt to control the aggregate level of spending in the economy. See page 237.

4. b   Expansionary fiscal policy increase aggregate expenditures which is shown by a shift up in the AE curve. See Figure 11-1 on pages 237-239.

5. d   See Figure 10-1 on page 238. Also remember from earlier chapters that an increase in imports is a decrease in autonomous expenditures.

6. a   To determine how much to increase expenditures in the *AE model* to reach potential income, you divide the recessionary gap of 240 by the multiplier of 2. See pages 237-239.

7. a   To determine how much to increase expenditures in the AD/AS model when the AS curve is flat, divide the recessionary gap, 600, by the multiplier, 5. See pages 237-239.

8. b   To determine how much to increase expenditures in the Keynesian *AE model* to reach potential income, you divide the recessionary gap of 900 by the multiplier of 3. See pages 237-239.

9. d   Aggregate demand management policies do not affect SAS, so a and b are out. With an inflationary gap you want to decrease output, so the answer is d. See Figure 10-2 on page 240.

10. a   Inflation results in higher input prices which shifts the SAS curve up. See page 239.

11. d   As discussed on page 241, while earlier Keynesian economists supported fine tuning, modern Keynesian economists do not.

12. c   Increasing imports is contractionary. See pages 239-241.

13. b   Decreasing imports and increasing exports is expansionary. See pages 239-241.

14. b   During World War II, taxes rose, but spending rose even more so that the net result was expansionary. Although the economy exceeded potential, inflation was avoided by price controls. See page 245.

15. b   By changing the value of one's currency, government can affect the level of exports and imports and thus affect aggregate output. See page 244.

16. c   In the 1990s, the economy expanded beyond the potential forecasted by economists, but did not result in accelerating inflation. The expansion was led by consumption and investment expenditures. See page 246.

17. a   As discussed on page 247 crowding out is the offsetting of a change in government expenditures by a change in private expenditures in the opposite direction. Answer c, if you could follow it, is nonsensical.

18. a   Okun's law says that a 1 percentage point fall in the unemployment rate is associated with a 2 percent rise in income. An economist who underpredicts potential output by 2 percent is overpredicting the target rate of unemployment rate by 1 percentage point. See pages 249-250.

19. d   Automatic stabilizers are welfare payments, unemployment insurance and taxes that raise income during recessions and lower income during expansions. See page 254.

ANSWERS

SHORT-ANSWER QUESTIONS

1. Keynesian economists' policy proposals worked by starting the multiplier process that got the economy in a low-income equilibrium to work in reverse. It increases aggregate expenditures. Businesses produce more to meet the additional demand, which creates additional income. The additional income results in a further increase in expenditures. The process continues until a new, higher equilibrium level of income is reached. Later Keynesians added to that policy: (1) another way to stimulate the economy by reducing taxes, (2) a way to slow down the economy when called for by decreasing spending or increasing taxes, (3) policies to change the money supply as a way of controlling the economy, and (4) general policies to influence components of aggregate expenditures. (237-241)

2. The tools of fiscal policy are changing taxes and changing government spending. Increasing taxes and lowering spending contract the economy; decreasing taxes and expanding spending expand the economy. (237)

3. Contractionary fiscal policies involve increasing taxes or decreasing government spending. Expansionary fiscal policies involve decreasing taxes or increasing government spending. (237)

4. Fiscal policy affects the economy by changing aggregate expenditures, which changes people's incomes, which increases people's spending even more. Expansionary fiscal policy shifts the aggregate demand curve to the right by a multiple of the increase in government spending, as shown in the diagram below. The change in income equals the multiplier times the change in government expenditures. (237-241)

5. Three alternatives to fiscal policy are directed investment policies, trade policies, and autonomous consumption policies. Directed investment policies include talking up the economy so that businesses will invest in expectation of better days and protecting the financial system by guarantees. Trade policies would include government assistance to promote exports. Autonomous consumption policies would include creating institutions conducive to easy credit. (241-245)

6. The six problems with fiscal policy limit its use in the following ways: (1) Financing the deficit might have offsetting effects, reducing the net effect. (2) The government doesn't always know the current state of the economy and where it is headed, meaning these must be forecast; if you don't know the state of the economy you don't know what fiscal policy to use. (3) The government doesn't know what potential income is, meaning it must be estimated; if you estimated it wrong, you get the wrong fiscal policy. (4) The government cannot implement policy easily; if you can't implement it you can't use it. (5) The size of the debt might matter and since deficits create debt, you might not want to use it. Finally, (6) fiscal policy often negatively affects other government goals; if it does, you might not use the policy even though it would change the economy in the direction you want. The bottom line is: In extreme cases, the appropriate fiscal policy is clear, but in most cases, the situation is not extreme. (246-251)

7. This first-year economics student is sharp! What she has described is crowding out. Crowding out is the offsetting effect on private expenditures caused by the government's sale of bonds to finance expansionary fiscal policy. If the government finances expansionary fiscal policy through the sale of bonds, interest rates will tend to rise. This will cause investment to decline, offsetting the initial stimulus. (247-248)

8. If crowding out is so strong that the reduced investment totally offsets the expansionary effect of fiscal spending, the net effect of fiscal policy can be zero. (247-248)

9. Employment insurance is an automatic stabilizer, a government program that counteracts the business cycle without any new government action. If income falls, automatic stabilizers will increase aggregate expenditures to counteract that decline. Likewise with increases in income: when income increases, automatic stabilizers decrease the size of the deficit. Eliminating employment insurance will eliminate this stabilization aspect of the policy and will contribute to making the recession more severe than it otherwise would have been. However, it would also make people more likely to accept lower wages and search harder for a job, thereby reducing the amount of unemployment. As usual, the answer depends. (254)

═══ **ANSWERS** ═══

PROBLEMS AND APPLICATIONS

1. **a.** The spending multiplier is 2, $1/(1-0.5)$, but only a fraction of the increase in taxes reduces spending. Taxes must be increased by $300 billion to reduce income by $300 billion. We calculate this by solving the following for change in taxes: change in taxes $\times mpc \times 1/(1-mpc)) = \$300$ billion. (237-241)

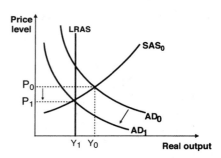

b. The spending multiplier is 2. Spending must be decreased by $150 billion to reduce income by $300 billion. We calculate this by solving the following for change in government spending: change in government spending $\times (1/(1-mpc)) = -300$ billion. This is shown in the graph below. (237-241)

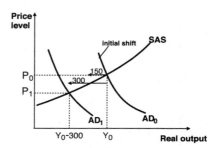

c. The spending multiplier is now 4, $1/(1-0.75)$. Government spending must be decreased by $75 billion to reduce income by $300 billion. We calculate this by solving the following for change in government spending: change in government spending $\times 4 = -300$ billion. This is shown in the graph below. Notice that the initial shift in the AD curve is smaller than in (b). If (b) and (c) had been shown using the multiplier model, the *AE* curve in (c) would be steeper than the AD curve for (b). (237-241)

2. **a.** To close the recessionary gap, government expenditures need to rise by the full amount of the gap because the multiplier is 1. This is shown as a shifting from AD_0 to AD_1. In the short run, output rises by $1,000 and the price level rises. This is also a long-run equilibrium since short-run equilibrium output equals potential output. (237-239)

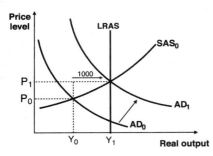

b. An increase in expenditures of $1,000 shifts the AD curve to the right by $1,000. In the short run, output rises by $1,000 and the price level remains constant. This time, however, short-run equilibrium output exceeds potential output. As long as output exceeds potential, wages will continue to rise, the SAS curve will continue to shift up. In the long run, the SAS curve will shift up to SAS_1 and real output will decline by $500 to potential output. (237-239)

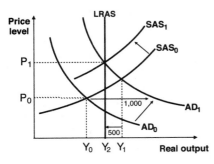

3. The spending multiplier is 2.5 $(1/(1-0.4))$. (237-239)

a. Assuming the economy is far below potential output, the government must increase spending on goods and services by $100 billion to increase income by $250 billion. This is shown below as a rightward shift in the AD curve of $100 billion from AD_0 to AD_1. Income increases by a multiple of that amount, by $2.5 \times 100 = \$250$ billion. (237-239)

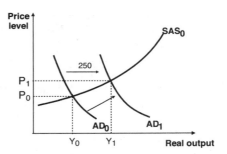

b. Since interest rates have risen, investment declines and the *AE* curve shifts down, partially offsetting the initial increase in aggregate expenditures. The net effect of the spending increase is smaller than $250 billion. This is shown by a shift down in the *AE* curve from AE_1 to AE_2, resulting in income Y_2, lower than Y_1. (247)

4. **a.** Increase spending by $1,200. According to Okun's Law, to decrease unemployment by 2 percent income must rise 4 percent, which, in this case, is $1,600 ($40000\times0.04$). With an *mpc* of .4 and, thus, a multiplier of 1.67, the government needs to increase spending by $1,600/1.67 or $960 (249-250)

b. Increase spending $500. According to Okun's Law, to decrease unemployment by 2 percent income must rise 4 percent, which is $2,000. With an *mpc* of 0.75 and, thus, a multiplier of 4, the government needs to increase spending by $2,000/4 or $500. (249-250)

5. **a.** A 1 percent increase in the unemployment rate means a decrease in income of 2%, or, in 2001, $180 billion. The private sector research organization believed potential income was $9 trillion, while the Governor of the Bank of Canada believed potential income was $8.820 trillion. (249-250)

b. The spending multiplier is $(1/(1-mpc)) = 2$. The private sector research organization would suggest no change in spending since the economy is at potential, while the Governor of the Bank of Canada would suggest a decrease in spending of $180/2 = 90$ billion. (249-250)

━━━━━━ ANSWERS ━━━━━━

A BRAIN TEASER

1. Although a number of important problems arise, which makes the actual practice of fiscal policy difficult, these problems don't mean that the model is wrong; they simply mean that for fiscal policy to work, the policy conclusions drawn from the model must be modified to reflect the real world problems. Unless, of course, you are a committed ("hard-core") Classical economist. (246-251)

━━━━━━ ANSWERS ━━━━━━

POTENTIAL ESSAY QUESTIONS

The following are annotated answers. They indicate the general idea behind the answer.

1. Recall that a downturn in the business cycle is caused by a decline in aggregate expenditures (AE–or, total spending). So, government needs to stimulate AE. Therefore, it should use expansionary fiscal policy to combat a recession. Use contractionary fiscal policy to combat the inflation during the expansionary phase of the business cycle. Note that it is appropriate for government to run a deficit during a recession but to move in the direction of a surplus when the economy is expanding.

2. When the economy is in a recession and total spending is too low then government spending automatically rises while tax collections automatically fall (the government automatically incurs a deficit). This helps to stimulate total spending and cushion the downturn in the economy. The opposite is true when the economy is expanding. Note that these changes take place while the income level falls and expands. Therefore, there are no time lag problems accompanying the automatic stabilizers.

3. The crowding-out effect states that deficit spending financed by borrowing will increase interest rates and, therefore, crowd out private spending. Any "crowding out" associated with deficit spending renders fiscal policy less effective in stimulating total spending and therefore the economy during a recession. The Keynesians argue that the crowding out effect is relatively small. Committed Classicals argue that there is a total crowding out effect, which renders fiscal policy impotent in stimulating total spending. Some Classicals have argued that the effect of deficit spending may even be negative on the economy if private spending is more productive than government spending. The empirical evidence on the size of the crowding-out effect is mixed and has not resolved the debate. However, everyone agrees that the closer the economy comes to its potential income level, the greater is the crowding-out effect.

POLITICS, SURPLUSES, DEFICITS, AND DEBT

● CHAPTER AT A GLANCE

Historically, the federal government has run budgetary deficits and surpluses. Since 1969, Canada has run deficits up until 1997-98, when Canada has since run surpluses. The accumulation of all deficits and surpluses, called the debt, now totals $502 billion. In a long run framework, surpluses and deficits both have desirable and undesirable effects on the economy

When analyzing the fiscal position of an economy, economists consider different definitions of the deficit – the nominal deficit which is the published deficit and the real deficit, which is the nominal deficit adjusted for inflation. As well, economists consider structural and passive surpluses and deficits. A structural deficit or surplus is the deficit or surplus that remains when the cyclical elements created by fluctuations in the business cycle have been removed. The passive deficit or surplus is that deficit or surplus caused by the cyclical fluctuations of the business cycle.

Canada's debt situations have been caused by a number of factors including recessions, which caused the federal government to spend more on provincial transfers, automatic stabilizers kicking in to reduce tax revenues and the lack of political will to take appropriate measures to pay down the debt. In the last few years, the surplus has been brought about by fiscal restraint, strong growth in the economy and low and stable inflation.

Economists use indicators such as deficits- and debt relative to GDP to measure a country's ability to pay off a deficit and service its debt.

This review is based upon the learning objectives that open the chapter.

1a. A surplus is an excess of revenues over payments. A deficit is a shortfall of revenues under payments. (Surpluses are negative deficits and vice versa.) Debt is accumulated deficits minus accumulated surpluses. (262, 265-266)

Surpluses and deficits are flow concepts; all deficits must be financed.

1b. Surpluses and deficits are simply summary measures of the financial health of the economy. To understand that summary you must understand the methods that were used to calculate it. (263)

Different accounting procedures yield different figures for surpluses and deficits.

2. The real deficit is the nominal deficit adjusted for inflation.

Real deficit = Nominal deficit (Inflation Total debt.) (263-264)

Inflation wipes out debt. Inflation also causes the real deficit to be less than the nominal deficit. However, inflation means a higher percentage of the deficit (or spending) will be devoted to debt service (paying interest on the debt). Moreover, creditors who do not anticipate the inflation pay the cost of eliminating the debt through inflation.

3. A structural deficit or surplus is that part of a budget deficit or surplus that would exist even if the economy were at its potential level of income. A passive (also called cyclical) surplus or deficit is that part that exists because the economy is operating below or above its potential income. (265)

Passive (cyclical) deficits or surpluses are largely due to the automatic stabilizers.

4a. Debt is accumulated deficits minus accumulated surpluses. It is a <u>stock</u> concept. (265-266)

Debt is a summary measure of a country's financial situation.
GDP serves the same function for government as income does for an individual. The greater the GDP (income), the greater the ability to handle debt. However, government debt is different than an individual's debt. Government is ongoing; government can pay off the debt by printing money; and much of the government debt is internal—owed to its citizens.

4b. Since, in a growing economy, a continual deficit is consistent with a constant ratio of debt to GDP, and GDP serves as a measure of the government's ability to pay off the debt, a country can run a continual deficit. (268-270)

The more you earn, the more debt you can handle.

4c. There are three reasons why government debt is different from individual debt: (268)

- The government lives forever; people don't.
- The government can print money to pay its debt; people don't.
- Government owes much of its debt to itself – to its own citizens.

5a. From WWII until the early 1970s, Canada ran small surpluses and deficits. From the mid 1970s to 1977, Canada ran continual deficits. Since 1997, Canada has experienced surpluses. (268)

5b. When an economy experiences real growth, the ability of the government to incur debt is increased; the economy becomes richer and, being richer, can handle more debt. (269)

5c. Compared to many countries, Canada has a low debt-to-GDP ratio. At 52% of Canadian GDP, Canada's debt ratio lies below the debt ratios of Italy, Japan, Germany and France. (270)

But, we still have debt.

6a. The surpluses of the late 1900s were brought about by the unexpected growth of the economy, fiscal restraint, and a low and stable rate of inflation. (272-273)

6b. At a time when the federal government is experiencing surplus, the provinces and municipalities have run deficits, causing net provincial and territorial debt to rise significantly during the 1990s. (273-274)

6c. There are two ways that public debt causes crowding out: (273-275
- Higher levels of government spending raises interest rates, which, in turn, reduces the level of private investment.
- The higher interest rates causes the domestic currency to appreciate, causing exports to fall.

6d. A good measure of the stance of fiscal policy is the structural deficit – the deficit adjusted for the business cycle. (275-276).

7. Ricardian equivalence states that government spending financed through current taxes and government spending financed by selling bonds are equivalent. It is an important theory to determining the effectiveness of fiscal policy. (277-278)

MATCHING THE TERMS
Match the terms to their definitions

All of these key terms are found at the end of the chapter.

____ **1.** crowded out
____ **2.** debt
____ **3.** debt service
____ **4.** deficit
____ **5.** external debt
____ **6.** internal debt
____ **7.** nominal deficit
____ **8.** passive deficit or surplus
____ **9.** real deficit
____ **10.** Retirement Income System
____ **11.** Ricardian equivalence
____ **12.** structural deficit or surplus
____ **13.** surplus

a. Social insurance programs that provide financial benefits to the elderly and disabled and to their eligible dependents and/or survivors.

b. Higher levels of government spending raises interest rates which, in turn, reduces the level of private investment.

c. A shortfall of revenue under payments.

d. Accumulated deficits minus accumulated surpluses.

e. An excess of revenues over payments

f. Government debt owed to individuals in foreign countries.

g. The interest rate on debt times the total debt.

h. That portion of the surplus or deficit that exists because the economy is operating below or above its potential level of output.

i. The deficit or surplus determined by looking at the difference between expenditures and receipts.

j. Government debt owed to its own citizens.

k. The part of a budget deficit or surplus that would exist even if the economy were at its potential level of income.

l. The nominal deficit adjusted for inflation.

m. Government spending financed through current taxes and government spending financed by selling bonds are equivalent.

● MULTIPLE CHOICE

Circle the one best answer for each of the following questions:

1. A deficit is:
   a. the total amount of money that a country owes.
   b. the shortfall of payments under revenues in a particular time period.
   c. the shortfall of revenues under payments in a particular time period.
   d. accumulated debt.

2. If the Canadian government raised the retirement age to 72 starting in 2010, the current budget deficit would be:
   a. reduced.
   b. increased.
   c. unaffected.
   d. eliminated.

3. The nominal deficit is $100 billion; inflation is 4 percent; total debt is $2 trillion. The real deficit is:
   a. zero.
   b. $20 billion.
   c. $80 billion.
   d. $100 billion.

4. If the nominal surplus is $200 billion, inflation is 10 percent, and total debt is $2 trillion,
   a. the real surplus is zero.
   b. the real deficit is $100 billion
   c. the real surplus is $400 billion.
   d. the real surplus is $2.2 trillion.

5. The real deficit is $100 billion; inflation is 4 percent; total debt is $2 trillion. The nominal deficit is
   a. zero.
   b. $120 billion.
   c. $180 billion.
   d. $200 billion.

6. If creditors are able to forecast inflation perfectly and there are no institutional constraints on interest rates,
   a. the government will not have to make interest payments.
   b. interest payments will rise by the amount that the real debt declines.
   c. the real deficit will equal the nominal deficit.
   d. the government will be unable to finance the debt.

7. Country A has a debt of $10 trillion. Country B has a debt of $5 trillion.
   a. Country A is in a better position than Country B.
   b. Country B is in a better position than Country A.
   c. One cannot say what relative position the countries are in.
   d. Countries A and B are in equal positions.

8. As a percentage of GDP, since World War II,
   a. debt in Canada has been rising.
   b. debt in Canada has been falling.
   c. debt in Canada has been sometimes rising and sometimes falling.
   d. the Canadian government has had no debt.

9. The portion of the budget deficit or surplus that would exist even if the economy were at its potential level of income is called the:
   a. structural deficit or surplus.
   b. passive deficit or surplus.
   c. primary deficit or surplus.
   d. secondary deficit or surplus.

10. If an economy is $100 billion below potential, the tax rate is 20 percent, and the deficit is $180 billion, the passive deficit is:
    a. $20 billion.
    b. $160 billion.
    c. $180 billion.
    d. $200 billion.

11. Government debt is different from individual debt because:
    a. government does not pay interest on its debt.
    b. government never really needs to pay back its debt.
    c. all government debt is owed to other government agencies or to its own citizens.
    d. the ability of a government to pay off is debt is unrelated to income.

12. If there is growth and a country with a debt of $1 trillion has decided it wants to keep its ratio of debt-to-GDP ratio constant:
    a. it should run a deficit.
    b. it should run a surplus.
    c. it should run a balanced budget.
    d. the deficit has no effect on debt.

13. Crowding out occurs when
    a. higher economic growth does not permit further expansions to take place.
    b. higher levels of private investment leaves no room for government spending.
    c. higher levels of government spending raise interest rates which, in turn, reduces the level of private investment.
    d. higher levels of government spending reduces interest rates which, in turn, reduces the level of private investment.

14. A good measure of the stance of fiscal policy is
    a. the debt
    b. the deficit
    c. the passive deficit
    d. the structure deficit

15. If the budget deficit rises, we can conclude that
    a. fiscal policy has been more expansionary
    b. government spending and taxation have changed
    c. there was a shift in an autonomous component of demand
    d. income is rising

16. The Ricardian equivalence suggests that
    a. the effect of monetary and fiscal policy are equivalent.
    b. expansionary monetary policy and expansionary fiscal policy give the same results to the price level and real output.
    c. the effects of inflation and unemployment are equivalent.
    d. government spending financed through current taxes and government spending financed through selling bonds are equivalent.

A1. Which of the following statements is true?
    a. If there is zero expected inflation, the nominal interest rates equals the real interest rate.
    b. The nominal interest rate equals the real interest rate plus the expected inflation rate.

c. Borrowers will not permit lenders to raise the nominal interest rate if all expect that the inflation rate will rise.

d. The nominal interest rate equals the real interest rate minus the expected inflation rate.

A2. If the nominal interest rate is 7% and the inflation rate is 3%, the real interest rate is

a. 4%

b. 7%

c. 10%

d. 21%

● SHORT-ANSWER QUESTIONS

1. How much importance do most economists give to the budget deficit or surplus?

2. If the nominal interest rate is 6%, the inflation rate is 4%, the nominal deficit is $100 billion, and the debt of the country is $2 trillion, what is the real deficit?

3. If the nominal interest rate is 5%, the inflation rate is 5%, the real deficit is $100 billion, and the debt of the country is $1 trillion, what is the nominal deficit?

4. If the Canadian economy is below potential and the surplus is $40 billion, is the structural surplus greater or less than $40 billion?

5. In an expanding economy, a government should run a continual deficit. True or false? Why?

6. If a politician presents you with a plan that will reduce the nominal budget deficit by $40 billion, but will not hurt anyone, how would you in your capacity as an economist likely respond?

7. Can the Canadian government take credit for the budget surpluses in the late 1990s? How would you likely respond?

PROBLEMS AND APPLICATIONS

1. Calculate the debt and deficit in each of the following:

   a. Your income has been $30,000 per year for the last five years. Your expenditures, including interest payments, have been $35,000 per year for the last five years.

   b. Your income is $50,000 per year; $15,000 of your $65,000 expenditures are for the purchase of the rights to an invention.

   c. Your wage income is $20,000 per year. You have a bond valued at $100,000, which pays $10,000 per year. The market value of that bond rises to $110,000. Expenses are $35,000 per year. Use the opportunity cost approach in your calculations.

2. For each of the following calculate the real deficit:

   a. Inflation is 5%. Debt is $2 trillion. Nominal deficit is $100 billion.

   b. Inflation is -3%. Debt is $500 billion. Nominal deficit is $20 billion.

   c. Inflation is 10%. Debt is $3 trillion. Nominal deficit is $100 billion.

   d. Inflation is 8%. Debt is $20 billion. Nominal deficit is $5 billion.

3. Assume a country's nominal GDP is $7 trillion, government expenditures less debt service are $1.5 trillion, and revenue is $1.3 trillion. The nominal debt is $4.9 trillion. Inflation is 2% and real interest rates are 5%. Expected inflation is fully adjusted.

   a. Calculate debt service payments.

   b. Calculate the nominal deficit.

   c. Calculate the real deficit.

   d. Suppose inflation rose to 4%. Again, expected inflation is fully adjusted. Recalculate (a) - (c).

4. Potential income is $8 billion. The income in the economy is $7.2 billion. Revenues do not vary with income, but taxes do; they increase by 20% of the change in income. The current deficit is $400 million.

a. What is the economy's structural deficit?

b. What is the economy's passive deficit?

A BRAIN TEASER

1. How could deficit spending actually reduce the debt burden of future generations?

POTENTIAL ESSAY QUESTIONS

You may also see essay questions similar to the "Problems & Applications" and "Brain Teasers" exercises.

1. What are three reasons why government debt is different from individual debt?

2. How can a growing economy reduce the concern over deficits and the debt?

MATCHING

1-b; 2-d; 3-g; 4-c; 5-f; 6-j; 7-i; 8-h; 9-l; 10-a; 11-m; 12-k;13-e.

MULTIPLE CHOICE

1. c A country has a budget deficit if it does not collect sufficient revenue to cover expenditures during the year. See page 262.

2. c Canada uses a cash flow accounting method, so changes affecting the future are not seen in the current budget. See pages 262-263.

3. b Real deficit = nominal deficit (inflation total debt). See page 263.

4. c Real surplus = nominal surplus + (inflation total debt). See page 263.

5. c Real deficit = nominal deficit (inflation total debt). See page 263.

6. b If creditors can forecast inflation perfectly, the interest rate will rise when inflation rises and the subsequent increase in interest payments will match the decline in the real debt due to higher inflation. See pages 263-264.

7. c Debt must be judged relative to assets and to total GDP. See pages 265-267.

8. c See Figure 11-2 on page 269 and page 268.

9. a The passive deficit or surplus is the deficit or surplus that exists because the economy is below potential. The structural deficit or surplus is the deficit or surplus that exists because the economy is at potential. The text doesn't define primary or secondary deficits or surpluses. See page 265.

10. a   The passive deficit is the deficit that exists because the economy is below potential. The government would collect $20 billion more in revenue if the economy were at potential, so the passive deficit is $20 billion. See page 265.

11. b   Because government goes on forever it doesn't ever need to pay back its debt. Only about 75 percent of government debt is owed to other government agencies or to its own citizens. The other government debt is owed to foreign individuals. Government is better able to pay off debt when income rises. Both government and individuals pay interest on debt. See page 268.

12. a   Real growth will reduce the ratio of existing debt to GDP so to hold the ratio constant a continual deficit is necessary. See page 269.

13. c.   As governments attempt to finance their deficits, they need to borrow at higher interest rates which makes it difficult for the private sector to raise capital at these higher interest rates. See pages 273-274.

14. d.   The structural deficit is that part of the budget deficit or surplus that would exist even if the economy were at its potential level of income. See pages 275-276.

15. c.   A change in an aggregate demand component such as investment will change income, tax revenues and the deficit. See pages 275-276.

16. d   See pages 277-278.

A1. a   See page 281.

A2. a   The Fisher condition states that nominal interest rates is equal to the real interest rate plus the expected rate of inflation. (281)

ANSWERS

SHORT-ANSWER QUESTIONS

1.   While there are differences of opinion, most economists are hesitant to attach too much importance to a deficit or a surplus. The reason why is that the deficit and surplus depends on the accounting procedures used, and these can vary widely. Only with much more additional information will an economist attribute importance to a surplus or deficit. It is financial health—by which is meant the ability to cover costs over the long term—of the economy that most economists are concerned with. (262-263)

2.   To calculate the real deficit you multiply inflation times the total debt (4% $2 trillion), giving $80 billion; then subtract that from the nominal deficit of $100 billion. So in this example the real deficit equals $20 billion. The interest rate does not enter into the calculations. (263-264)

3.   To calculate the nominal deficit you multiply inflation times the total debt (5% $1 trillion), giving $50 billion, and add that to the real deficit of $100 billion. So in this example the nominal deficit equals $150 billion. The interest rate does not enter into the calculation. (263-264)

4.   Since the economy is below potential, the structural surplus is larger than the nominal surplus. (265)

5.   It depends. In an expanding economy with no deficits, the ratio of debt to GDP will be falling; if the government wants to hold the debt-to-GDP constant, it will need to run a continual deficit. If it wants to reduce that ratio, then it need not run a continual deficit. (268-269)

6.   TANSTAAFL. I would check to see what accounting gimmick the politician was proposing and what the plan would do to the long-run financial health of the country. (262-263)

7.   The budget surplus came about because the Canadian economy grew at a much faster rate than economists had thought possible. It also came about because of the federal government's fiscal restraint and the low and stable rate

of inflation. To the degree that the federal government played a role in these, the federal government deserves credit, but none of the government's policy initiatives can be seen as the cause of the budget surplus. (272-273)

ANSWERS

PROBLEMS AND APPLICATIONS

1. **a.** Deficit is $5,000 per year; Debt is $25,000. On page 627, deficit is defined as income less expenditures and debt is defined as accumulated deficits minus accumulated surpluses. For each of the past 5 years, you have incurred an annual deficit of $5,000. Total debt is $5,000 times five years, or $25,000. (263-265)

b. Deficit is $15,000; Debt is $15,000. Page 287 tells you that what is included as expenses is ambiguous. If you count the purchase of the rights to the invention as a current expenditure, the deficit is $15,000. If you had no previous debt, debt is also $15,000. If, however, you count the purchase of the invention as an investment and include it in your capital budget, then your expenses are only $50,000 and your current account will be in balance. (263-265)

c. Surplus of $5,000. Using an opportunity cost approach, a person holding bonds should count the rise in the bonds' market value as revenue. Here, wage income is $20,000 per year, interest income is $10,000 and the bond's value has increased by $10,000. Total income is $40,000. Income of $40,000 less expenses of $35,000 per year yields a budget surplus of $5,000. (263-265)

2. As discussed on page 263, the real deficit is the nominal deficit adjusted for inflation's effect on the debt. The definition of real deficit states: Real deficit = Nominal deficit − (Inflation × Total debt).

a. $0: $100 billion − 0.05 × $2 trillion. (263)

b. $35 billion: $20 billion − (0.03) × $500. (263)

c. Surplus of $200 billion: $100 billion − 0.10 × $3 trillion. (263)

d. $3.4 billion: $5 billion − 0.08 × $20 billion. (263)

3. **a.** $343 billion: Debt service payment = nominal interest rate × nominal debt. The nominal interest rate when expected inflation is fully adjusted is the real interest rate plus inflation (5+2). Debt service payment= 0.07 × $4.9 trillion. (270-271)

b. $543 billion deficit: The nominal deficit is revenues less government expenditures (including debt service), $1.3 trillion − ($1.5 trillion + $.343 trillion). (263)

c. $445 billion deficit: The real deficit = Nominal deficit −(Inflation × Total debt) = $.543 trillion − 0.02 × $4.9 trillion). (263)

d. Since bondholders must be compensated for the loss in the value of their bonds, they demand a nominal interest rate of 9% (5 + 4). Debt service payment is now $441 billion (0.09 × $4.9 trillion). The nominal deficit is higher at $641 billion. ($1.3 trillion − ($1.5 trillion + $.441 trillion)). The real deficit has not changed. It is still $445 billion (The real deficit = Nominal deficit −(Inflation × Total debt) = $.641 trillion (0.04 × $4.9 trillion)). (263, 270-271)

4. **a.** If the economy were at potential, government would collect $160 million more in taxes, reducing the deficit by that amount. There would a structural deficit of $400 − $160 = $240 million. (265)

b. The passive deficit is the deficit that occurs because the economy is below potential. The passive deficit is $800 million × 20 percent, or $160 million. (265)

ANSWERS

ANSWERS

A BRAIN TEASER

1. If the deficit spending is used to increase the productivity of the nation, enabling the nation to experience much higher rates of economic growth, then the income of the nation could expand faster than its debt. If this happens, then the debt-to-GDP ratio gets smaller, the interest expense is less burdensome, and the debt will be easier to pay off. (270-271)

POTENTIAL ESSAY QUESTIONS

The following are annotated answers. They indicate the general idea behind the answer.

1. First, the government's life is unlimited and, therefore, it never has to settle its accounts. Second, it can pay off debt by creating money (which is not recommended however). Third, much of the government's debt is internally held and therefore, on average as a group, people are neither richer nor poorer because of the debt (even though it may redistribute income to upper-income individuals).

2. When a society experiences real economic growth (growth adjusted for inflation), it becomes richer, and, being richer, it can handle more debt. Moreover, since in a growing economy, a continual deficit is consistent with a constant ratio of debt to GDP, and GDP serves as a measure of the government's ability to pay off debt. A country can run a continual deficit. Deficits should be viewed relative to GDP to determine their importance.

THE MONEY MARKET AND THE AD-AS MODEL

CHAPTER AT A GLANCE

Chapters 8 and 9 developed the AE and AD-AS models by considering only the market for goods and services. This chapter expands this discussion to include the money market, which permits us to consider issues such as inflation, interest rates and exchange rate management.

This chapter will help you to develop an understanding of what money is, the various functions of money, and the demand for money. The information presented in this chapter will prepare you for the following chapter, which discusses the tools that the Bank of Canada has to implement specific types of money policy and to change the money supply in order to achieve specific economic goals.

In completely understanding the workings of the money market, it is important to know how much money individual's will desire to hold as cash. This is called the demand for money. Three main motives for holding money – transactions, precautionary, and speculative – and the quantity theory of money explain the demand for money in the macroeconomy.

The chapter finishes with a discussion of how the money market fits into the AD-AS model.

This review is based upon the learning objectives that open the chapter.

1a. Money is any asset that can be quickly exchanged for any other asset, good, or service. (285)

1b. The three functions of money are: (285)

- Medium of exchange;
  As long as people are confident that the purchasing power of the dollar will remain relatively stable over time (by the Bank of Canada controlling the money supply) then people will continue to swap real goods, services, and resources for money and vice versa.

- Unit of account; and
  Money acts as a measuring stick of the relative value (relative prices) of things. Therefore, the value of money itself must remain relatively stable over time.

- Store of wealth.
  Money's usefulness as a store of wealth also depends upon how well it maintains its value. The key is for the Bank of Canada to keep the purchasing power of money (and therefore prices) relatively stable over time. Inflation can be a problem!

2a. The Quantity Theory of Money relates to the fact that, for the aggregate economy, purchases of goods and services must equal sales, that the price level is thought to vary proportionately with changes in the quality of money. (288-290)

It is defined upon the equation of exchange: $MV = PT$

In Canada, the income velocity of money (V) has been relatively stable.

2b. The quantity theory of money can translate into the theory of money demand, whereby $Md = kPY$, where PY is an economy's nominal income, and k, which is a positive number that translates the economy's nominal income (PY) to how much money will be demanded for the aggregate economy. So, kPY becomes the demand for money.

2c. The quantity theory of money can also be written as: $M = (1/k) = MV = PY$ (288-289)

2d. The widespread use of ATMs and credit cards led to an increase in the income velocity of money and a reduction in k and a fall in money demand. Individuals did not need to hold as much cash as before.

3a. There are three motives for holding money: (290-292)

    1. Transactions demand
The need to have money to undertake day-to-day purchases of goods and services. It is strongly influenced by changes in economic activity, or nominal income.

    2. Precautionary demand
Money need to meet unforeseen expenses.

    3. Speculative demand
Indicates the attractiveness of holding money as opposed to other financial assets.

    The opportunity cost of holding money is the interest rate.

3b. Bonds are held instead of money because they yield a rate of return – an interest payment. Money is a non-interest-bearing asset. (291-292)

3c. Liquidity preference is the choice between holding bonds or money. (292)

3d. As interest rates rise, the demand for money falls as individuals switch over to interest-bearing bonds. (291-292)

4a. Interest rates are determined by the interaction of money demand and money supply. (292-293)

4b. To determine the equilibrium interest rate, we use the formula: (294-295)

$$i = \frac{1}{l}\left(Md^o + hY - \frac{ms}{p}\right)$$

4c. The AD curve can be derived from the money market. The AD curve gives combinations of the price level and real income where both the money market and the goods markets are in equilibrium. (295-296)

As the price level changes, the real money supply (Ms/P), the interest rate and autonomous expenditures change, which affects real income. As real income is inversely related to the price level, the AD curve is downward sloping

5a. In Canada, the money supply is strongly correlated with the CPI, so changes in the money supply affect price stability, or inflation. An increase in the money supply lowers the interest rate, which promotes more consumer and investment spending, translating into more economic activity and inflation. (297-298)

5b. In Canada, real money demand is strongly correlated with real income. As an economy recovers or is experiencing strong economic activity, there is a greater level of transactions and a larger demand for money to facilitate these transactions. (297-298)

5c. In Canada, the relationship between real money demand and interest rates is not clear. (297-298.

MATCHING THE TERMS
Match the terms to their definitions

All of these key terms are found at the end of the chapter.

___ **1.** Cambridge k
___ **2.** income velocity of money
___ **3.** liquidity preference
___ **4.** liquidity trap
___ **5.** medium of exchange
___ **6.** money demand
___ **7.** money neutrality
___ **8.** precautionary demand for money
___ **9.** quantity theory of money
___ **10.** real effects
___ **11.** secondary financial market
___ **12.** speculative demand
___ **13.** store of wealth
___ **14.** transactions demand for money
___ **15.** transactions velocity of money
___ **16.** unit of account
___ **17.** yield

a. The physical good that is used in trade.
b. The standard denomination that prices are measured with.
c. A financial asset that can be used to hold one's savings.
d. How much money individuals will desire to hold as cash.
e. For the aggregate economy, purchase of goods and services must equal sales.
f. The average number of times that a dollar is exchanged between a buyer and a seller over a period of time..
g. The average number of times that a dollar is exchanged to generate the observed level of nominal income.
h. Money that is needed to undertake purchases of goods and services.
i. Money that is needed to meet unforeseen expenses.
j. Money is considered as one type of asset in a portfolio of assets, each earning a rate of return.
k. An exchange where holders of existing bonds can sell them to other investors if they wish.
l. The choice between holding bonds or money.
m. Individuals choose to invest all of their portfolio in bonds above the normal rate of interest, and in money below the normal rate of interest.
n. Changes in the money supply have no effect on real income in the long run.
o. Occurs when a change in an economic variable affects the real value of another economic variable.
p. Difference between the face value and the purchase price, calculated as a percentage of the purchase price.
q. A positive number that translates the economy's nominal income to how much money will be demanded in the aggregate.

● MULTIPLE CHOICE

Circle the one best answer for each of the following questions:

1. Which of the following is not a function of money?
   a. Medium of exchange.
   b. Unit of account.
   c. Store of wealth.
   d. Equity instrument.

2. Using economic terminology, when an individual buys a bond, that individual
   a. is investing.
   b. is saving.
   c. is buying a financial liability.
   d. is increasing that individual's equities.

3. If someone places money under a mattress, the money is functioning as a
   a. medium of exchange.
   b. unit of account.
   c. store of wealth.
   d. equity investment.

4. Which one of following coincides with money's function as a medium of exchange?
   a. Transactions demand.
   b. Precautionary demand.
   c. Speculative demand.
   d. Liquidity preference.

5. A secondary financial market is a market in which
    a. currencies are traded.
    b. commodities are traded.
    c. holders of existing bonds can be bought and sold.
    d. small secondary mergers take place.

6. Liquidity is
    a. a property of water stocks.
    b. the ability to turn an asset into cash quickly and exchange for other goods and services.
    c. the ability to turn an asset into liquid quickly.
    d. a property of over-the-counter markets.

7. As bond price rises,
    a. interest rates are unaffected.
    b. its yield falls.
    c. its yield rises.
    d. bond holders realize a capital gain when the bond is sold.

8. In the equation $MV = PT$,
    a. M is the money demand.
    b. V is the velocity of speculation.
    c. T is time.
    d. P is the average price per transaction.

9. An increase in income velocity of money causes
    a. a reduction in the number of transactions and money demand.
    b. an increase in the number of transactions.
    c. a reduction in k and a fall in money demand.
    d. lower interest rates.

10. If a t-bill that matures in 91 days has a face value of $5,000 is purchased today for $42,250, what is its yield?
    a. 4.01%
    b. 4.24%
    c. 23.3%
    d. cannot be calculated with information provided.

11. Keynes' liquidity preference theory suggests that money is held because
    a. its rate of return is higher than that of bonds.
    b. money has liquidity value.
    c. money is an interest-bearing asset.
    d. money increases in value if the price level rises.

12. The slope of the AD curve is flatter when
    a. the money demand curve is flatter.
    b. the investment schedule is flatter.
    c. the smaller the investment multiplier.
    d. the higher the interest rate.

13. The demand for money curve
    a. shows people's preference to substitute money for bonds at higher interest rates.
    b. reflects the preference for money over bonds.
    c. reflects the inverse relationship between the interest rate and the quantity demanded for money.
    d. all of the above.

14. The money demand curve shifts to the right when
    a. interest rates fall.
    b. transactions demand for money falls.
    c. real income increases.
    d. investment spending falls.

15. The interaction of money demand and money supply determines the
    a. aggregate demand curve.
    b. aggregate expenditures curve.
    c. level of economic activity.
    d. interest rate.

16. A higher price level _____ the real money supply.
    a. increases
    b. decreases
    c. does not affect
    d. affects

17. A downward sloping investment function illustrates the fact that
  a. transactions demand for money is rising.
  b. increasing interest rates reduces investment spending.
  c. reducing interest rates reduces investment spending.
  d. reducing interest rates reduces real income.

18. In Canada, the money supply is
  a. inversely correlated with the CPI.
  b. inversely correlated with real GDP.
  c. directly correlated with the CPI.
  d. directly correlated with the nominal interest rate.

19. Money neutrality implies that
  a. changes in money demand change the price level in the opposite direction.
  b. changes in the money supply only changes the price level by the same proportion in the long run.
  c. lower interest rates only change investment spending by the same proportion in the short run.
  d. money demand and money supply only affect interest rates in the long run.

● SHORT-ANSWER QUESTIONS

1. What are the three functions of money?

2. You are having a stimulating lunchtime conversation about money. Your friend says "I know what money is; it's cash, the dollar bills I carry around." What is your response?

3. You continue the conversation and begin to discuss why we have money. Your friend states that the function of money is to buy things like the lunch he has just bought. Another friend says that because she has money she is able to compare the cost of two types of slacks. Still another offers that she holds money to make sure she can buy lunch next week. What is the function of money that each has described? Are there any others?

4. What is the quantity theory of money and how does it relate to money demand?

5. According to Keynes, what are the three motives for holding money?

6. What is the opportunity cost (what is foregone/sacrificed) of holding money?

7. Under what conditions would the money demand curve shift rightward and what is the impact on the interest rate?

8. How do interest rates influence consumption spending and the trade balance?

9. What is the effect of an increase in real GDP on the demand for money curve?

● PROBLEMS AND APPLICATIONS

1. Suppose a Government of Canada t-bill that matures in 91 days has a face value of $20,000 is purchased for $19,750. What is the yield? If the t-bill purchase price rises to $19,900, what is the yield? As the price of the t-bill rises, what happens to the yield?

2. Assume that the sensitivity of money demand to the change in real income is 0.5, and the sensitivity of money demand to the change in the interest rate is -4,000. If real income is currently $2,000 and the money supply is $1,000, the price level is 1.5 and individuals desire to hold, on average, $230 in cash for transactions purposes, what is the equilibrium interest rate?

● A BRAIN TEASER

1. Whenever new loans are made, the money supply expands. Whenever loans are repaid, the money supply decreases. During any given period of time, new loans are being made and old loans are being repaid. On balance, what happens to the money supply depends upon the magnitude of these conflicting forces. We also know that making loans is the principle source of profits to banks. Having said this, how can bankers' collective lending decisions (whether to give loans or not to give loans in order to maximize their profits, or to avoid losses) destabilize the business cycle–cause recessions to get worse and upturns to become more pronounced?

● POTENTIAL ESSAY QUESTIONS

You may also see essay questions similar to the "Problems & Applications" and "Brain Teasers" exercises.

1. Why is it important for the macroeconomy that the financial sector operate efficiently?

2. Why aren't credit cards money? What is the difference between money and credit?

3. What is the major benefit and problem of government guarantees associated with financial institutions?

━━━━━━━ ANSWERS ━━━━━━━

MATCHING

1-q; 2-g; 3-l; 4-m; 5-a; 6-d; 7-n; 8-i; 9-e; 10-o;
11-k; 12-j; 13-c; 14-h;15-f;16-b;17-p.

━━━━━━━ ANSWERS ━━━━━━━

MULTIPLE CHOICE

1. d. Money is not a type of stock so it is not an equity instrument. See page 285.

2. b   In economic terminology, buying a financial asset, which is what buying a bond is, is a form of saving. Investing occurs when a firm or an individual buys a real asset. See page 291-292.

3. c   See page 287.

4. d   Transactions demand for money is strongly influenced by changes in nominal income. As economic activity and income rises, individuals will hold more money to facilitate exchanges. (285, 290)

5. c   See page 292.

6. b   Answers a and c are total gifts to you — water stocks; give us a break — and it's unclear what d means. The b option is the definition given on page 290.

7. b   There is an inverse relationship between a bond's price and its yield. (292)

8. d   M is the money supply, V is velocity, the number of times money changes hands over a specified period of time, and T is the number of transactions. (288-289)

9. c   The introduction of ATMs and credit cards have increased the number of times money changes hands, but not the amount of money as people do not hold much cash anymore. (288-289)

10. c   Using the formula for the bond yield gives (($50,000−$47,750)/$47,250)) * 365/91) *100 = 0.058*4.01 = 23.3% (292)

11. b   Individuals hold money because it serves the three functions of money. Money is a non-interest bearing asset that only experiences a capital gain and an increase in purchasing power when the price level falls. (292)

12. b   The slope of the money demand curve is a function of the value of l – the sensitivity of money demand to changes in the interest rate. The greater the value of l, the greater sensitivity money demand has to changes in interest rates, and the more responsive investment and aggregate demand are to changes in interest rates. (295-296)

13. d   As interest rates rise, there is a preference to hold interest bearing financial assets such as bonds because the rate of return is higher. Therefore, the opportunity cost of holding money falls as the interest rate declines. This translates into a downward sloping money demand curve. (291-293)

14. c   An increase in economic activity and real income, the greater the transactions demand for money. At each level of real interest rates, more money is demanded, so the money demand curve shifts rightward. (290, 295)

15. d   See pages, 288, 295.

16. b   The real money supply is defined as Ms/P. As the price level rises, this ratio falls. (295-296)

17. b   The investment curve is downward sloping reflecting the inverse relationship between interest rates and the level of investment spending. Reduced interest rates reduces the cost of borrowing, making more investment projects profitable, thereby raising investment spending. (295-296)

18. c   Increases in the money supply translates into lower interest rates, which encourages more consumer and investment spending and thus real income, which puts upward pressure on prices. (297-298)

19. b   See page 297.

ANSWERS

SHORT-ANSWER QUESTIONS

1. Medium of exhange, unit of account and store of wealth. (285)

2. In one sense your friend is right; cash is money. But money is more than just cash. Money is a highly liquid financial asset that is accepted in exchange for other goods and is used as a reference in valuing other goods. (285-286, 290)

3. The first friend has described money as a medium of exchange. The second has described money as a unit of account. And the third has described money as a store of wealth. These are the three functions of money. There are no others. (285-288)

4. The theory suggests that for each transaction, the purchase of goods and services must equal sales or total sales must equal the total amount of money in the economy. In essence, the total money demand is a function of income to be used for transactions purposes and to facilitate the total sales. The total amount of money in the economy is the money supply, so aggregate money demand equals the money supply. (288-290)

5. Transactions demand, precautionary demand and speculative demand. (290-292)

6. If one's preference is to hold money, a non-interest bearing asset, one forgoes the nominal interest rate – the opportunity to obtain a higher rate of return than one can obtain from holding money. At higher interest rates, the preference is to switch from money to bonds. (292-293)

7. According to the transactions demand for money, money demand rises when there is an increase in economic activity and real income. More money is demanded to facilitate transactions. This would be reflective of a booming economy where everyone is working and making a lot of money, and people start to buy bigger houses, newer cars, RVs, boats, etc. For any given money supply, a rightward shift in money demand causes the interest rate to rise. (295)

8. Higher interest rates increase the cost of borrowing, which, in turn, reduces consumer spending. Higher interest rates also tends to raise the value of the domestic currency as foreign investors find Canadian investments, particularly bonds with higher rates of return, more attractive. A higher value of the Canadian dollar causes domestically produced goods and services to be more expensive relative to foreign produced goods and services, so exports tend to fall. So, higher interest rates reduce consumption and exports, which lowers real income. (296)

9. The money demand curve shifts rightward. (295)

ANSWERS

PROBLEMS AND APPLICATIONS

1. The bond yield at a purchase price of $19,750 is ($20,000−$19,750)/$19,750 * (365/91) * 100 = .0126 * 4.01 = 5.05%

   The bond yield at a purchase price of $19,900 is ($20,000−$19,900) * (265/91) * 100 = .005 * 4.01 = 2.0%

   When the price of the t-bill increases, the yield falls. (292)

2. $i = \dfrac{1}{l} \left(Md^o + hY - \dfrac{Ms}{p} \right)$

   $= \dfrac{1}{4,000} \left(230 + (0.5 \times 2,000) - \left(\dfrac{1,000}{1.5} \right) \right)$

   $= 14.08\%$

   (294-295)

A BRAIN TEASER

1. An uncontrolled private banking system (where government is not involved in trying to control the money supply) is destabilizing to the business cycle. Why? Because during recessions, bankers are reluctant to grant loans due to the greater probability of default on loans (bankers are simply wishing to avoid losses). Fewer loans made during a recession coupled with the concurrent repayment of old loans (most likely given during the previous upturn in the economy) means that, on balance, the money supply decreases. Less money means less spending. Less spending means the recession gets worse–unemployment rises further and the economy grows even more slowly. Conversely, during an economic expansion, banks make more loans than old loans are being repaid (bankers are happy to make loans when there is a low probability of default–after all, workers are not likely to lose their jobs and businesses' markets and profits are expanding). Therefore, the money supply expands and total spending increases–people spend their loans. The economy expands even more. (290-293)

POTENTIAL ESSAY QUESTIONS

The following are annotated answers. They indicate the general idea behind the answer.

1. Recall that for every real transaction there is a financial transaction that mirrors it. The financial sector's role is to ensure the smooth flow of savings out of the spending stream back into the economy. Whenever the financial sector is not operating efficiently then it is quite possible that the flow of savings out of the spending stream could be greater than the amount of money going through the financial sector and back into the economy. If this happens, we will experience a recession. The opposite would create inflationary (demand-pull inflation) problems.

2. Money is a financial asset of individuals and a financial liability of banks. Credit card balances cannot be money since they are assets of a bank and a liability of the nonbanking public. In a sense, credit card balances are the opposite of money. Credit is savings made available to be borrowed. Credit is not an asset for the holder of the card. However, ready availability of credit through the use of credit cards does reduce the amount of money people need or wish to hold.

3. The benefit is that they prevent unwarranted fears that causes financial crises. People are less likely to create a run on a bank when they know they will be able to get all of their money back even if the bank fails. The problem is that these guarantees can eliminate warranted fears. A bank manager may be more reckless when depositors are less concerned about the financial well-being of the bank.

MONEY, BANKING, AND THE FINANCIAL SECTOR

13

CHAPTER AT A GLANCE

This chapter will help you develop an understanding of what money is, the various measures of money and the players within Canada's banking system. The information presented in this chapter will prepare you for the following chapter, which discusses the tools that the Bank of Canada has to implement specific types of money policy and to change the money supply in order to achieve specific economic goals.

The important concepts that are presented in this chapter include how banks "create" money, the importance of the money multiplier and the issues surrounding the regulation of banks and the financial sector.

This review is based upon the learning objectives that open the chapter.

1a. The financial sector is central to almost all macroeconomic debates because behind every real transaction, there is a financial transaction that mirrors it. (305-306)

If the interest rate does not perfectly translate saving (flows out of the spending stream) into investment (flows into the spending stream), then the economy will either expand or contract.

1b. The financial sector – financial markets and institutions – channels or transfers savings back into spending. (305-306)

Flow from the spending stream is channeled into the financial sector as savings when individuals buy financial assets such as stocks and bonds.

Interest rates are the mechanisms that equilibrate supply and demand in the financial sector.

2a. Money is a highly liquid, financial asset that is generally accepted in exchange for other goods, is used as a reference in valuing other goods and can be stored as wealth. (307)

Money is any financial asset that serves the functions of money.

2b. The Bank of Canada has the right to issue notes which are IOUs. These IOUs are considered cash or money as individuals are willing to accept the Bank of Canada's IOUs in return for real goods and services. (307)

3a. M1 is the component of the money supply that consists of currency in circulation (bills and coins) plus chequing accounts at chartered banks. (308)

M1 is the narrowest measure of the money supply. It is also the most liquid.

3b. M2 is the component of the money supply that consists of M1 plus personal savings deposits and nonpersonal notice deposits (deposits that can be withdrawn only after prior notice) held at chartered banks. (309)

M2 is the measure of the money supply most used by the Bank of Canada to measure the money supply in circulation. This is because M2 is most closely correlated with the price level and economic activity.

Anything which changes M2 changes the money supply!

3c. The broadest measure of the money supply is M2++ . It consists of almost all assets that can be turned into cash on short notice. (309)

3d. The Bank of Canada is Canada's central bank whose liabilities (bank notes) serve as cash in Canada. Everyone accepts the Bank of Canada's liabilities (IOU) in return for real goods and services, which means the Bank of Canada's notes are money. (307)

3e. Banks "create" money because a bank's liabilities, are defined as money. So when a bank incurs liabilities, it creates money. (311)

4a. The money multiplier is the measure of the amount of money ultimately created by the banking system. (314)

A single bank is limited in the amount of money it may create. The limit is equal to its excess reserves–the maximum amount of funds, which it can legally loan out. However, when considering an entire banking system, where any bank's loans, when spent, may end up being deposited back into that bank or another bank, then the entire banking system ends up being able to increase the money supply by a multiple of its initial excess reserves (the initial maximum amount of funds which can legally be loaned out) because of the money multiplier.

Simple money multiplier = 1/r.

(Initial change in money supply) × (money multiplier) = change in the money supply

4b. When people hold cash the approximate money multiplier is 1/ (r + c). (316)

Approximate real-world money multiplier = 1/(r+c) , where c is the ratio of money people hold in currency to the money held as deposits.

The approximate real-world money multiplier is less than the simple money multiplier because some of the funds loaned out are held as cash and, therefore, do not return to the banks as deposits.

4c. Reserves are cash that banks keep on hand to meet daily withdrawls by its depositors (312-313)

Excess reserves are available reserves over and above the level of reserves that chartered banks wish to maintain. These reserves are lent out or invested.

4d. Banks "create" money (increase the money supply) whenever they make loans from their deposits. Whenever a person borrows from a bank they are swapping a promissory note to repay the loan (which is really an IOU; and an individual's IOU is not money because it doesn't meet the criteria of serving the functions of money) in exchange for cash or funds put in his/her chequing account. Cash and chequing account balances are money! Therefore, the money supply increases. (313-314)

Also note: When a loan is repaid, the money supply (M2) decreases.

4e. All that backs the modern money supply are bank loan customer's promises to pay and government guarantees of bank's liabilities to individuals. (316-317)

5a. Financial systems are based on trust that expectations will be fulfilled. Banks borrow short and lend long, which means that if people lose faith in banks, the banks cannot keep their promises. (317-318)

It is important to maintain the public's confidence in the banking system.
Government guarantees of financial institutions can have 2 effects:
* *They can prevent unwarranted fear that causes financial crises.*
* *They can also eliminate warranted fears and hence eliminate a market control of bank loans.*

5b. The Canada Deposit Insurance Corporation (CDIC) provides a guarantee of up to $60,000 on deposits at all banks (318)

Depositors know that the government will see that they can get their currency back even if the bank fails.

5c. Since its inception in 1967, the CDIC has had to deal with more than 20 failed financial institutions. Most recently, it has had to guarantee the deposits of the Northland Bank, the Canadian Commercial Bank and the Central Guarantee Trust Company. (319)

See also, Appendix A: "A Closer Look at Financial Institutions and Financial Markets." and Appendix B: "Valuing Stocks and Bonds."

MATCHING THE TERMS
Match the terms to their definitions

All of these key terms are found at the end of the chapter.

_____ 1. approximate real-world money multiplier

_____ 2. asset management

_____ 3. bank

_____ 4. Bank of Canada

_____ 5. bond

_____ 6. currency drain

_____ 7. deposit multiplier

_____ 8. excess reserves

_____ 9. financial assets

_____ 10. interest rate

_____ 11. liability management

_____ 12. M_1

_____ 13. M_{2+}

_____ 14. money

_____ 15. money multiplier

_____ 16. reserve ratio

_____ 17. reserves

_____ 18. primary deposit

_____ 19. secondary deposit

_____ 20. secondary reserve

a. Cash that a bank keeps on hand to meet daily withdrawls by its depositors.

b. Component of the money supply that consists of M_1 plus personal savings deposits and nonpersonal notice deposits at chartered banks.

c. Component of the money supply that consists of currency in circulation plus chequing accounts at chartered banks.

d. Assets whose benefit to the owner depends on the issuer of the asset meeting certain obligations.

e. How a bank attracts deposits and what it pays for them.

f. How a bank handles its loans and other assets.

g. Measure of the amount of money ultimately created by the banking system, per dollar deposited, when cash holdings of individuals and firms are treated the same as reserves of banks. The mathematical expression is $1/(r + c)$.

h. When individuals do not deposit the entire increase in income that accrues to them.

i. Ratio of reserves to deposits.

j. Available reserves over and above the level of reserves that chartered banks wish to maintain.

k. The Canadian central bank whose liabilities serve as cash in Canada.

l. A highly liquid financial asset that is generally accepted in exchange for other goods, is used as a reference in valuing other goods, and as a store of wealth.

m. Price paid for the use of a financial asset.

n. A financial institution whose primary function is holding money for, and lending money to, individuals and firms.

o. Promises to pay a certain amount plus interest in the future.

p. The dollar value of the bank's portfolio.

q. Does not change the total value of the money stock, however, it does change its composition.

r. A deposit a bank creates when a loan is given.

s. The multiple by which a new primary deposit can expand total deposits.

t. $(1/r) \times$ primary deposit.

● MULTIPLE CHOICE

Circle the one best answer for each of the following questions:

1. For every financial asset
   a. there is a corresponding financial liability.
   b. there is a corresponding financial liability if the financial asset is financed.
   c. there is a real liability.
   d. there is a corresponding real asset.

2. Using economic terminology, when an individual buys a bond, that individual
   a. is investing.
   b. is saving.
   c. is buying a financial liability.
   d. is increasing that individual's equities.

3. Which of the following is not included in the M_1 definition of money?
   a. cheqing accounts.
   b. currency.
   c. bank notes and coins.
   d. savings accounts.

4. Which of the following components is not included in the M_2 definition of money?
   a. M_1.
   b. personal savings deposits.
   c. non-personal notice deposits.
   d. bonds.

5. In an advertisement for credit cards, the statement is made, "Think of a credit card as smart money." An economist's reaction to this would be
   a. a credit card is not money.
   b. a credit card is dumb money.
   c. a credit card is simply money.
   d. a credit card is actually better than money.

6. Using a credit card creates
   a. a financial liability for the holder and a financial asset for the issuer.
   b. a financial asset for the holder and a financial liability for the issuer.
   c. a financial liability for both the holder and issuer.
   d. a financial asset for both the holder and issuer.

7. Modern bankers
   a. focus on asset management.
   b. focus on liability management.
   c. focus equally on asset management and liability management.
   d. are unconcerned with asset and liability management and instead are concerned with how to make money.

8. Assuming individuals hold no cash, the reserve requirement is 20 percent, and banks keep no excess reserves, an increase in an initial $100 of money will cause an increase in total money of
   a. $20.
   b. $50.
   c. $100.
   d. $500.

9. Assuming individuals hold no cash, the reserve requirement is 10 percent, and banks keep no excess reserves, an increase in an initial $300 of money will cause an increase in total money of
   a. $30.
   b. $300.
   c. $3,000.
   d. $30,000.

10. Assuming the ratio of money people hold in cash to the money they hold in deposits is .3, and the reserve requirement is 20 percent, and that banks keep no excess reserves, an increase in an initial $100 of money will cause an increase in total money of _____. (Use the approximate real world money multiplier.)
    a. $50.
    b. $100.
    c. $200.
    d. $500.

11. If banks hold excess reserves whereas before they did not, the relative money multiplier
    a. will become larger.
    b. will become smaller.
    c. will be unaffected.
    d. might increase or might decrease.

12. A sound bank will
    a. always have money on hand to pay all depositors in full.
    b. never borrow short and lend long.
    c. never borrow long and lend short.
    d. keep enough money on hand to cover normal cash inflows and outflows.

13. CDIC is an acronym for
   a. major banks in the Canada.
   b. major banks in the world.
   c. Canadian government program that guarantees deposits.
   d. types of financial instruments.

14. The textbook author's view of government guarantees of deposits is
   a. they don't make sense.
   b. stronger ones are needed.
   c. it depends.
   d. it should be a private guarantee program.

A1. A secondary financial market is a market in which
   a. minor stocks are sold.
   b. minor stocks and bonds are sold.
   c. previously issued financial assets can be bought and sold.
   d. small secondary mergers take place.

A2. Liquidity is
   a. a property of water stocks.
   b. the ability to turn an asset into cash quickly.
   c. the ability to turn an asset into liquid quickly.
   d. a property of over-the-counter markets.

A3. A financial market in which financial assets having a maturity of more than one year are bought and sold is called a
   a. money market.
   b. capital market.
   c. commercial paper market.
   d. commercial bank market.

B1. If the interest rate falls, the value of a fixed rate bond
   a. rises.
   b. falls.
   c. remains the same.
   d. cannot be determined as to whether it rises or falls.

B2. Two bonds, one a 30-year bond and the other a 1-year bond, have the same interest rate. If the interest rate in the economy falls, the value of the
   a. long-term bond rises by more than the value of the short-term bond rises.
   b. short-term bond rises by more than the value of the long-term bond rises.
   c. long-term bond falls by more than the value of the short-term bond falls.
   d. short-term bond falls by more than the value of the long-term bond falls.

● SHORT-ANSWER QUESTIONS

1. At lunch, you and your friends are arguing about the financial sector. One friend says that real fluctuations are measured by real economic activity in the goods market and, therefore, the financial sector has nothing to do with the business cycle. You know better and set him straight.

2. You are having another stimulating lunchtime conversation, this time about money. Your friend says "I know what money is; it's cash, the dollar bills I carry around." What is your response?

3. What are the two most liquid measures of money? What are the primary components of each?

4. What is the broadest measure of money? What does it consist of?

5. Your friends are curious about money. At another lunchtime discussion, they ask each other two questions: Is all the money deposited in the bank in the bank's vaults? Can banks create money? Since they are stumped, you answer the questions for them.

6. Using the deposit multiplier, what will happen to the money supply if the reserve ratio is 0.2 and the primary deposit is increased by $100?

7. Using the equation for the approximate real-world money multiplier, what will happen to the money supply if the reserve ratio is 0.2, cash to deposit ratio is 0.3, and high-powered money is increased by $100?

8. How does the interest rate regulate the flow of saving into the flow of expenditures during normal times?

9. What would happen if everyone simultaneously lost trust in their banks and ran to withdraw their deposits?

10. What is the potential problem with government guarantees to prevent bank-withdrawal panics?

● PROBLEMS AND APPLICATIONS

1. For each, state whether it is a component of M_1 or M_2, both, or neither:

    a. Money market mutual funds.

    b. Savings deposits.

    c. Stocks.

    d. Twenty-dollar bills.

2. Assuming individuals hold no cash, calculate the deposit multiplier for each of the following reserve requirements:

    a. 15%

    b. 30%

    c. 60%

    d. 80%

    e. 100%

3. Assuming individuals hold 10% of their deposits in the form of cash, recalculate the *approximate* real-world money multipliers from question 2.

    a. 15%

    b. 30%

    c. 60%

    d. 80%

    e. 100%

4. While Jon is walking to school one morning, a helicopter flying overhead drops $300. Not knowing how to return it, Jon keeps the money and deposits it in his bank. (No one in this economy holds cash.) If the bank keeps only 10 percent of its money in reserves and is fully loaned out, calculate the following:

    a. How much money can the bank now lend out?

    b. After this initial transaction, by how much has the money in the economy changed?

    c. What's the deposit multiplier?

    d. How much money will eventually be created by the banking system from Jon's $300?

A1. For each, state whether a financial asset has been created. What gives each financial asset created its value?

   a. Your friend promises to pay you $5 tomorrow and expects nothing in return.

   b. You buy an apple at the grocery store.

   c. The government sells a new bond with a face value of $5,000, a coupon rate of 8%, and a maturity date of 2006.

   d. A firm issues stock.

   e. An existing stock is sold to another person on the stock market.

A2. For each of the following financial instruments, state for whom it is a liability and for whom it is an asset. Also state, if appropriate, whether the transaction occurred on the capital or money market and whether a financial asset was created.

   a. First Bank grants a mortgage to David.

   b. First Bank sells David's mortgage to Financial Services, Inc.

   c. Broker McGuill sells existing stocks to client Debreu.

   d. An investment broker sells 100 shares of new-issue stock to client Debreu.

   e. The Canadian government sells a new three-month T-bill to Corporation X.

   f. Corporation X sells a 30-year government bond to Sally Quinn.

B1. Choose which of the following offerings you would prefer having. (Refer to the present value table on page 331.)

   a. $1,500 today or $2,000 in 5 years. The interest rate is 5%.

   b. $1,500 today or $2,000 in 5 years. The interest rate is 10%.

c. $2,000 today or $10,000 in 10 years. The interest rate is 15%

d. $3,000 today or $10,000 in 15 years. The interest rate is 10%.

B2. A bond has a face value of $5,000 and a coupon rate of 10 percent. (A 10 percent coupon rate mans that it pays annual interest of 10 percent of its face value.) It is issued in 2001 and matures in 2006. Using this information, calculate the following:

a. What is the annual payment for that bond?

b. If the bond is currently selling for $6,000, is its yield greater or less than 10 percent?

c. If the bond is currently selling for $4,000, is its yield greater or less than 10 percent?

d. What do your answers to (b) and (c) tell you about what the bond must sell for, relative to its face value, if the interest rate is 10%? Rises above 10%? Falls below 10%?

● A BRAIN TEASER

1. Whenever new loans are made, the money supply expands. Whenever loans are repaid, the money supply decreases. During any given period of time, new loans are being made and old loans are being repaid. On balance, what happens to the money supply depends upon the magnitude of these conflicting forces. We also know that making loans is the principle source of profits to banks. Having said this, how can bankers' collective lending decisions (whether to give loans or not to give loans in order to maximize their profits, or to avoid losses) destabilize the business cycle–cause recessions to get worse and upturns to become more pronounced?

● POTENTIAL ESSAY QUESTIONS

You may also see essay questions similar to the "Problems & Applications" and "Brain Teasers" exercises.

1. Why is it important for the macroeconomy that the financial sector operate efficiently?

2. Why aren't credit cards money? What is the difference between money and credit?

3. What is the major benefit and problem of government guarantees associated with financial institutions?

ANSWERS

MATCHING

1-g; 2-f; 3-n; 4-k; 5-o; 6-h; 7-s; 8-j; 9-d; 10-m; 11-e; 12-c; 13-b; 14-l; 15-t; 16-i; 17-a; 18-q; 19-r; 20-p.

ANSWERS

MULTIPLE CHOICE

1.   a   The very fact that it is a financial asset means that it had a financial liability, so the qualifier in b is unnecessary. See pages 305.

2.   b   In economic terminology, buying a financial asset, which is what buying a bond is, is a form of saving. Investing occurs when a firm or an individual buys a real asset. See page 305-306.

3.   d   See page 308 and Figure 13-2 on page 308.

4.   d   See page 309 and Figure 13-2 on page 308.

5.   a   A credit card is not money and thus *a* would be the best answer. A credit card replaces money, making the same amount of money able to handle many more transactions. See pages 310-311.

6.   a   One is borrowing money when one uses a credit card, thereby incurring a financial liability. See pages 310-311.

7.   c   As discussed on pages 311, banks are concerned with both asset management and liability management. The second part of answer d is obviously true, but it's through management of assets and liabilities that they make money, so the first part is wrong.

8.   d   The simple money multiplier is $1/r = 1/0.2 = 5$, which gives an increase in total money of $500. See page 314.

9.   c   The simple money multiplier is $1/r = 1/0.1 = 10$ which gives an increase of total money of $3,000. See page 314.

10.   c   The approximate real-world money multiplier is $1/(r+c) = 1/0.5 = 2$, which gives an increase in total money of $200. See page 316.

11.   b   Holding excess reserves would be the equivalent to increasing the reserve requirement, which would decrease the multiplier. See page 316.

12.   d   Banks earn income by managing their assets and liabilities. To follow any policy other than d would cost them income. See pages 316-317.

13.   c.   CDIC stands for Canadian Deposit Insurance Corporation. See page 318.

14.   c   For this textbook author, just about everything depends; you can't get him to take a firm position on anything. See pages 318-319.

A1.   c   See pages 325.

A2.   b   Answers a and c are total gifts to you — water stocks; give us a break — and it's unclear what d means. The b option is the definition given on page 326.

A3.   b   See page 326.

B1.   a   The present value formula tells us that the value on any fixed interest rate bond varies inversely with the interest rate in the economy. See page 330.

B2.   a   Since bond values vary inversely with interest rate changes, the answer must be a or b. Judging between a and b will be hard for you at this point unless you have studied present value in another course. Since a long-term bond is not paid back for a long time, it will be much more strongly affected be interest rate changes. See page 330-331.

ANSWERS

SHORT-ANSWER QUESTIONS

1. The financial sector is important to the business cycle because the financial sector channels the flow of savings out of the circular flow back into the circular flow either as consumer loans, business loans, or government loans. If the financial sector did not translate enough of the savings out of the spending stream back into the spending stream, output would decline and a recession might result. Likewise, if the financial sector increased flows into the spending stream (loans) that exceeded flows out of the spending stream (savings), an upturn or boom might result and inflation might rise. It is this role of the financial sector that Keynesians focused on to explain why production and expenditures might not be equal, resulting in fluctuations in output. (305-307).

2. In one sense your friend is right; cash is money. But money is more than just cash. Money is a highly liquid financial asset that is accepted in exchange for other goods and is used as a reference in valuing other goods. (307)

3. The two most liquid measures of money are M_1 and M_2. M_1 consists of currency in circulation and chequing account balances at chartered banks. M_2 consists of M_1 plus personal savings deposits, non-personal notice deposits held at chartered banks. (308-309)

4. The broadest measure of money is M_{2++}. M_{2++} consists of M1 and nonpersonal notice deposits held at chartered banks. (309)

5. No, banks do not hold all their deposits in their vaults. They keep a small percentage of it for normal withdrawal needs and lend the remainder out. Banks' maintenance of chequing accounts is the essence of how banks create money. You count your deposits as money since you can write cheques against them and the money that is lent out from bank deposits is counted as money. Aha! The bank has created money. (311-313)

6. The equation for the deposit multiplier is $(1/r)$ where r is the reserve ratio. Plugging in the values into the equation, we see that the money multiplier is 5, so the money supply increases by $500. (314)

7. The equation for the approximate real-world money multiplier is $1/(r+c)$ where r is the reserve ratio and c is the ratio of cash to deposits. Plugging the values into the equation, we see that the money multiplier is 2, so the money supply increases by $200. (316)

8. Just as price equilibrates quantity supplied and demanded in the real sector, interest rates equilibrate quantity supplied and demanded for saving. The supply of saving comes out of the spending stream. The financial sector transforms those savings back into the spending stream in the form of loans that are then used to purchase consumer or capital goods. (305-306)

9. If everyone lost their trust in banks, a financial panic could occur. The bank holds only a small portion of total deposits as reserves so that if everyone withdraws their money, the bank cannot meet its promises. (316-318)

10. The potential problem with government guarantees to prevent bank-withdrawal panics is that guarantees might lead to unsound lending and investment practices by banks. Also, depositors have less of a reason to monitor the practices of their banks. (319)

ANSWERS

PROBLEMS AND APPLICATIONS

1. **a.** M_2. (308)
   b. M_2. (308)
   c. Neither. (308)
   d. Both. (308)

2. **a.** 6.67. multiplier = (1/0.15). (314)
   b. 3.33. multiplier = (1/0.30). (314)
   c. 1.67. multiplier = (1/0.6). (314)
   d. 1.25. multiplier = (1/0.8). (314)
   e. 1. multiplier = (1/1). (314)

3. a. $4 = 1/(0.10+0.15)$. (316)
   b. $2.5 = 1/(0.1+0.3)$. (316)
   c. $1.43 = 1/(0.1+0.6)$. (316)
   d. $1.11 = 1/(0.1+0.8)$. (316)
   e. 0.91. In reality a multiplier less than one would be highly unlikely. Recall that this is the approximate real-world multiplier. See page 316, especially footnote 2 for the precise money multiplier.

4. a. $270. (316)
   b. $570: the initial $300 in new deposits plus 0.9 300 in loans that are then deposited. (316)
   c. 10: $1/r = 1/0.1$. (314)
   d. $3,000: money multiplier×primary deposit $= 10 \ 300$. (318)

A1. a. A financial asset has been created. Your friend's promise to pay you $5 is what gives that asset its value. (323)
   b. No, a financial asset has not been created, although a financial transaction did occur. (323)
   c. Yes, a financial asset has been created. The government's promises to pay you $5,000 at maturity and $400 each year until then are what give that asset its value. (323)
   d. Yes, a financial asset has been created. A claim to future profits is what gives that asset its value. (323)
   e. No, a financial asset has not been created. The financial asset sold already existed. (323)

A2. a. The mortgage is an asset for First Bank and a liability for David. The transaction occurred on the capital market. A financial asset was created. (326)
   b. The mortgage is an asset for Financial Services, Inc., and a liability for David. The transaction occurred on the capital market. A financial asset was not created. (326)
   c. The stocks are an asset for client Debreu and a liability for the broker's firm. The transaction occurred on the capital market. A financial asset was not created. (326)
   d. The stocks are an asset for client Debreu and a liability for the firm. The transaction occurred on the capital market. A financial asset was created. (326)

e. The T-bill is a liability for the Canadian government and an asset for Corporation X. The transaction occurred on the money market. A financial asset was created. (323)
f. The bond is a liability for the Canadian government and an asset for Sally Quinn. The transaction occurred on the capital market. A financial asset was not created. (323)

B1. Using the table to calculate the present value of $100 to be received in the future, we find that the better value is
   a. $2,000 in 5 years, valued today at $1,568. (330)
   b. $1,500 today. $2,000 in 5 years when the interest rate is 10% is worth only $1,242 today. (330)
   c. $10,000 in 10 years, valued at $2,470 when the interest rate is 15%. (330)
   d. $3,000 today. $10,000 in 15 years when interest rate is 10% is worth only $2390 today. (330)

A2. a. The annual payment for that bond is $500 annually. (331)
   b. If the bond is currently selling for $6000, its yield is less than 10 percent. (331)
   c. If the bond is currently selling for $4,000, its yield is greater than 10 percent. (331)
   d. My answer to (b) and (c) tell me that the bond must sell for its face value if the interest rate is 10%, less than face value if it rises above 10%, and more than face value if it falls below 10%. (331)

A BRAIN TEASER

1. An uncontrolled private banking system (where government is not involved in trying to control the money supply) is destabilizing to the business cycle. Why? Because during recessions, bankers are reluctant to grant loans due to the greater probability of default on loans (bankers are simply wishing to avoid losses). Fewer loans made during a recession coupled with the concurrent repayment of old loans (most likely given during the previous upturn in the economy) means that, on balance, the money supply decreases. Less money means less spending. Less spending means the recession gets worse–unemployment rises further and the economy grows even more slowly. Conversely, during an economic expansion, banks make more loans than old loans are being repaid (bankers are happy to make loans when there is a low probability of default–after all, workers are not likely to lose their jobs and businesses' markets and profits are expanding). Therefore, the money supply expands and total spending increases–people spend their loans. The economy expands even more. (305-307)

POTENTIAL ESSAY QUESTIONS

The following are annotated answers. They indicate the general idea behind the answer.

1. Recall that for every real transaction there is a financial transaction that mirrors it. The financial sector's role is to ensure the smooth flow of savings out of the spending stream back into the economy. Whenever the financial sector is not operating efficiently then it is quite possible that the flow of savings out of the spending stream could be greater than the amount of money going through the financial sector and back into the economy. If this happens, we will experience a recession. The opposite would create inflationary (demand-pull inflation) problems.

2. Money is a financial asset of individuals and a financial liability of banks. Credit card balances cannot be money since they are assets of a bank and a liability of the nonbanking public. In a sense, credit card balances are the opposite of money. Credit is savings made available to be borrowed. Credit is not an asset for the holder of the card. However, ready availability of credit through the use of credit cards does reduce the amount of money people need or wish to hold.

3. The benefit is that they prevent unwarranted fears that causes financial crises. People are less likely to create a run on a bank when they know they will be able to get all of their money back even if the bank fails. The problem is that these guarantees can eliminate warranted fears. A bank manager may be more reckless when depositors are less concerned about the financial well-being of the bank.

THE AD-AS MODEL AND MONETARY POLICY

14

CHAPTER AT A GLANCE

This chapter explains how the Bank of Canada controls the quantity of money within a market economy by conducting monetary policy, in order to achieve specific economic goals, such as price stability and a high rate of economic growth. The transmission impact of monetary policy through the economy will be considered within the AD-AS framework.

The Bank of Canada is responsible for conducting monetary policy as well as issuing bank notes and administering public debt. The Bank of Canada implements either expansionary or contractionary monetary policy by influencing short-term interest rates. This is done primarily by changing the reserves of chartered banks, by either changing the target range for the overnight financing rates or cash management operations.

Cash management operations included open market operations and switching government deposits. Open market operations refers to the buying and selling of government bonds and bills of Canada in the open market, from the public or from chartered banks. If the Bank of Canada wishes to generate more economic activity, it could expand the money supply by purchasing bonds and paying money for them in the open market. These funds will become reserves for the chartered banks, which will enable them to increase the ability to offer loans. As well, the Bank of Canada can switch government deposits from its reserves to chartered banks, thereby increasing their reserves.

The most important stated policy of the Bank of Canada is to maintain long run price stability. To target against inflation, the Bank of Canada has specific tools to gauge how successful it is at implementing monetary policy. These will be discussed in the last section of the chapter

This review is based upon the learning objectives that open the chapter.

1a. Monetary policy is a policy that influences the economy through changes in the money supply and available credit. (334)

Monetary policy is undertaken by the Bank of Canada. Expansionary (contractionary) monetary policy lowers (raises) interest rates, which shifts the AD curve to the right (left), thereby increasing (decreasing) real income.

1b. The Bank of Canada is a semiautonomous organization. It is a Crown corporation, not under the direct day-to-day control of the federal government. The head of the Bank of Canada is the Governor of the Bank. (335-337)

The Bank of Canada is in charge of monetary policy (changing the money supply, credit availability, and interest rates).

1c. The Bank of Canada has four explicit duties. The most important is conducting monetary policy. (340)

4 Functions of the Bank of Canada:
(1) conducting monetary policy,
(2) providing central banking services,
(3) issuing bank notes and ensuring their authenticity, and
(4) administering public debt.

2. The two tools of monetary policy are: (343-345)

   1. Changing the target range for the overnight financing rate.

   The overnight financing rate is the interest rate associated with very short-term loans occurring in the overnight market. When the overnight financing rate changes, we usually see changes in many other interest rates. The Bank of Canada has a target for the overnight financing rate (a 50 basis point range) with the bank rate being at the upper end of this target range.

The bank rate is the interest rate that members of the Canadian Payments Association are charged for borrowing from the Bank of Canada. The Bank of Canada determines whether monetary policy is loose (expansionary) or tight (contractionary) depending upon what's happening to the bank rate and the target bank for the overnight financing rate.

When the overnight financing rate changes, we usually see changes in many other interest rates. Through raising and lowering the target range, the Bank of Canada relies on the term structure of interest rates to filter changes into interest rates across the maturity spectrum.

2. Cash management operations

This is the main tool for implementing monetary policy in Canada. This includes open market operations which is the buying and selling of government bonds and bills as well as the transfer of government deposits between chartered banks and others) and the Bank of Canada. This is the most frequently used and most important tool to change the money supply.

If the economy is in recession, the Bank of Canada should increase the money supply (pursue an expansionary monetary policy) by doing one of the following:

- Lower the target range for the overnight financing rate
- Buy government bonds
- Transfer government deposits to the chartered banks and other financial institutions from the Bank of Canada

3a. In the AD/AS model, monetary policy works as follows: (346)

Contractionary monetary policy shifts the AD curve to the left:
$$M\downarrow \Rightarrow i\uparrow \Rightarrow I\downarrow Y\downarrow$$

Used during an upturn in the economy to close an inflationary gap.

Expansionary monetary policy shifts the AD curve to the right:
$$M\uparrow \Rightarrow i\downarrow \Rightarrow I\uparrow \Rightarrow Y\uparrow$$

Used during a downturn in the economy to close a recessionary gap.

To increase the money supply, the Bank of Canada must first increase banks' excess reserves and therefore bank loans.

3b. Judging monetary policy can be doine by focusing on the interest rates (346)

- A rising interest rates indicates a tightening monetary policy.
- A falling interest rate indicates a loosening of monetary policy.

4. Five problems of monetary policy: (348)

- Knowing what policy to use.
  Need to know the potential income level first.

- Understanding what policy you're using.
  The Bank of Canada only indirectly controls the money supply.

- Lags in monetary policy.
  It takes time to work.

- Political pressure.
  The Bank of Canada is not totally insulated from political pressures.

- Conflicting international goals.
  We live in a global economy. The desired domestic policy may adversely affect the exchange rate value of the dollar and our trade balance.

5a. The primary goal of the Bank of Canada is price stability (low inflation). The Bank of Canada wishes to maintain inflation within a 1 to 3 percent target band. (349-350)

5b. The features of inflation targeting include: (350-351)

1. The principal goal of monetary policy is long-run price stability.

2. The central bank must establish a numerical target for the rate of inflation and establish a realistic time table to reach the target.

3. The central bank undertakes efforts to make monetary policy more transparent.

4. The central bank must be held accountable of the inflation target is not reached.

5c. The Bank of Canada uses the Monetary Conditions Index (MCI) to track just how tight or loose monetary policy is relative to a base period. The higher the value of the MCI, the tighter the monetary policy is. (351)

5d. Many developed countries have adopted inflation targeting including Canada, the United States, New Zealand, and Australia. (351-352)

Developing countries have been slower to adopt inflation targeting because they suffer from historically high inflation rates.

See also, Appendix A: "The Effect of Monetary Policy Using T-Accounts."

MATCHING THE TERMS
Match the terms to their definitions

All of these key terms are found at the end of the chapter.

____ **1.** arbitage

____ **2.** bank rate

____ **3.** cash management operations

____ **4.** central bank

____ **5.** contractionary monetary policy

____ **6.** exchange rate

____ **7.** expansionary monetary policy

____ **8.** monetary base

____ **9.** monetary policy

____ **10.** monetary regime

____ **11.** open market operations

____ **12.** overnight financing rate

____ **13.** term structure of interest rates

____ **14.** yield curve

a. The value of one nation's currency expressed in terms of another nation's currency.

b. A plot of the yield of a bond against its maturity.

c. The rate at which members of the Canadian Payments Association can borrow from the Bank of Canada.

d. The Bank of Canada's day-to-day buying and selling of government bonds and bills.

e. Main technique for implementing monetary policy in Canada.

f. A type of banker's bank; it conducts monetary policy and supervises the financial system.

g. Currency in circulation, vault cash plus deposits of the Bank.

h. Monetary policy aimed at raising the money supply and raising the level of aggregate demand.

i. Monetary policy aimed at reducing the money supply and reducing the level of aggregate demand.

j. A policy of influencing the economy through changes in the financial system's reserves that influence the money supply and the availability of credit in the economy.

k. The structure of yields on financial instruments with similar characteristics (like risk), but different terms to maturity.

l. The buying and selling of similar goods and services across different markets.

m. A predetermined statement of the policy that will be followed in various situations.

n. Interest rate associated with very short-term loans occuring in the overnight market.

MULTIPLE CHOICE

Circle the one best answer for each of the following questions:

1. The central bank in Canada is
    a. the Bank of Canada.
    b. the Fed.
    c. the Bank of the United States.
    d. Old Lady of Threadneedle Street.

2. Monetary policy is
    a. a variation of fiscal policy.
    b. undertaken by the Treasury.
    c. undertaken by the Bank of Canada.
    d. the regulation of monetary institutions.

3. The Governor of the Bank of Canada is appointed for terms of
    a. 5 years.
    b. 10 years.
    c. 7 years.
    d. 17 years.

4. Explicit functions of the Bank of Canada include all the following *except*
    a. conducting monetary policy.
    b. conducting fiscal policy.
    c. providing central banking services to government, banks, and other central banks.
    d. issuing bank notes and ensuring their authenticity.

5. Tools of monetary policy include all the following *except*
    a. changing the target range for the overnight financing rate.
    b. cash management operations.
    c. running deficits.
    d. executing open market operations.

6. If expansionary monetary policy increases real income by 4 percent and nominal income by 6 percent, the price level will rise by:
    a. 2 percent.
    b. 4 percent.
    c. 6 percent.
    d. 10 percent.

7. An exchange rate is
    a. the daily volume of trade in the foreign exchange market.
    b. the price of one good in terms of another.
    c. the price of one currency in terms of another.
    d. the quantity of imports a country receives for a given quantity of exports.

8. The overnight financing rate refers to
    a. the rate of interest the Bank of Canada charges for loans to banks.
    b. the rate of interest on overnight loans.
    c. the rate of interest the Bank of Canada charges for loans to government.
    d. the rate of interest the Bank of Canada charges for loans to individuals.

9. The primary tool of monetary policy is
    a. open market operations.
    b. changing the discount rate.
    c. changing the reserve requirement.
    d. imposing credit controls.

10. If the Bank of Canada wants to increase the money supply, it should:
    a. buy bonds.
    b. sell bonds.
    c. pass a law that interest rates rise.
    d. pass a law that interest rates fall.

11. When the Bank of Canada sells bonds, the money supply
    a. expands.
    b. contracts.
    c. selling bonds does not have any effect on the money supply.
    d. sometimes rises and sometimes falls.

12. An open market purchase
    a. raises bond prices and reduces interest rates.
    b. raises both bond prices and interest rates.
    c. reduces bond prices and raises interest rates.
    d. reduces both bond prices and interest rates.

13. The bank rate refers to
    a. the rate of interest banks charge each other
    b. the rate of interest charged on advances from the central bank
    c. the rate of interest at the bottom of the target range for the overnight financing rate
    d. the rate of interest the federal government is charged by the Bank of Canada

14. In the short run, if the Bank of Canada undertakes expansionary monetary policy, the effect will be to
    a. shift the AD curve out to the right.
    b. shift the AD curve in to the left.
    c. shift the SAS curve up.
    d. shift the SAS curve down.

15. In the short run, if the Bank of Canada undertakes contractionary monetary policy, the effect will be to
    a. shift the AD curve out to the right.
    b. shift the AD curve in to the left.
    c. shift the SAS curve up.
    d. shift the SAS curve down.

16. Which of the following is the path through which contractionary monetary policy works?
    a. Money down implies interest up implies investment down implies income down.
    b. Money down implies interest down implies investment down implies income down.
    c. Money down implies interest up implies investment up implies income down.
    d. Money down implies interest down implies investment up implies income down.

17. A monetary regime is preferred to a monetary policy because:
    a. a monetary policy is too closely related to fiscal policy.
    b. a monetary regime takes into account feedback effects.
    c. a monetary policy takes into account feedback effects.
    d. One is not preferred to the other; the two a essentially the same thing.

18. Expected inflation is 4 percent; nominal interest rates are 7 percent; the real interest rate is
    a. 1 percent.
    b. 2 percent.
    c. 3 percent.
    d. 7 percent.

19. The real interest rate is 3 percent; the nominal interest rate is 7 percent. It is likely that one could deduce an expected inflation rate of
    a. 1%.
    b. 2%.
    c. 3%.
    d. 4%.

20. The Bank of Canada most directly controls
    a. M_1.
    b. M_2.
    c. the monetary base.
    d. the amount of credit in the economy.

SHORT-ANSWER QUESTIONS

1. You have been asked to speak to the first-year economics students. Your talk is about the Bank of Canada. They want to know what monetary policy is. You tell them.

2. To clarify your answer to question 1, you tell them when the Bank of Canada was created and what its specific duties are.

3. Another economics student asks what monetary policy actions the Bank of Canada can take. You answer.

4. You are asked to elaborate on your answer to question 3. Now that you have listed each of the tools of monetary policy, how does each work?

5. One economics student realizes that the Bank of Canada does not have complete control over the money supply. She states that people could demand more cash, which will reduce the money supply. How does the Bank of Canada know whether its buying and selling of bonds is having the desired effect? You answer by explaining the Bank of Canada's intermediate target.

6. Another economics student asks how monetary policy can keep the economy from overheating. You reply from the perspective of the AD/AS model.

7. Suppose the economy is below potential output. Now how can monetary policy boost output? You reply again from the perspective of the AD/AS model.

8. You take one final question at the conference and it is a difficult one: "It doesn't seem that the Bank of Canada is doing a good job. I read in the paper that the Bank of Canada has followed too contractionary a policy and has caused a recession or that it is not even sure what policy it is following." How do you respond to those concerns?

● PROBLEMS AND APPLICATIONS

1. Fill in the blanks in the following table:

	Inflation rate	Nominal Interest rate	Real Interest rate
a.	5%	10%	____
b.	____	15%	7%
c.	−3%	____	9%
d.	4%	____	10%

A1. Suppose the money multiplier is 2.5 and there are no cash holdings. Textland Bank is the only bank in the country. The Bank of Canada wants to decrease the money supply by $10,000. The initial balance sheet is shown below.

Initial Balance Sheet

Assets		Liabilities	
Cash	20,000	Demand Deposits	50,000
Loans	120,000	Net Worth	100,000
Phys. Assets	10,000		
Total Assets	150,000	Total Liabilities and Net Worth	150,000

a. What open market operations must the Bank of Canada execute to reduce the money supply by $10,000?

b. Using T-accounts show the first two steps of the effects of the Bank of Canada open market operation reducing the money supply by $10,000.

Step #1

Assets	Liabilities

Step #2

Assets	Liabilities

c. Show the final balance sheet for Textland bank.

Final Position

Assets	Liabilities

A2. Using T-accounts, show the effect of a decrease in the reserve ratio from .2 to .1 given the following initial position of Textland. Again, Textland is the only bank, no one holds cash, and there are no excess reserves. Show the first two steps and then the final position.

Initial Position

Assets		Liabilities	
Cash	40,000	Demand Deposits	200,000
Loans	230,000	Net Worth	100,000
Phys. Assets	30,000		
Total Assets	300,000	Total Liabilities and Net Worth	300,000

Step #1

Assets	Liabilities

Step #2

Assets	Liabilities

Final Position

Assets	Liabilities

● A BRAIN TEASER

1. Assume the economy is currently experiencing a recessionary gap of $1000. Also assume that the income multiplier is 4, the reserve ratio is 0.1, the ratio of people's cash-to-deposits is 0.4. Investment changes by $100 for every 1% change in the interest rate. The interest rate changes by 1% for every $50 change in the money supply. Generally, what should the Bank of Canada do with its three monetary policy tools? By how much would the Bank of Canada have to change banks' excess reserves if it wished to close the recessionary gap? (Assume all excess reserves are loaned out.)

● POTENTIAL ESSAY QUESTIONS

You may also see essay questions similar to the "Problems & Applications" and "Brain Teasers" exercises.

1. According to the AD/AS model, what is considered to be appropriate monetary policy over the course of the business cycle? What is the cause-effect chain relationship through which a change in the money supply will effect the level of economic activity? How would this cause-effect relationship be reflected graphically?

2. What are some general problems associated with the implementation of monetary policy?

3. Why do economists keep an eye on the Bank of Canada's overnight financing rate in determining the state of monetary policy?

4. How does open market operations affect interest rates through the bond market?

━━━━━ ANSWERS ━━━━━

MATCHING

1-l; 2-c; 3-e; 4-f; 5-i; 6-a; 7-h; 8-g; 9-j; 10-m; 11-d; 12-n; 13-k; 14-b.

━━━━━ ANSWERS ━━━━━

MULTIPLE CHOICE

1. a   See page 335-336.

2. c   The correct answer is "policy undertaken by the Bank of Canada." (334)

3. c   See page 336.

4. b   Fiscal policy is definitely not a function of the Bank of Canada. See page 340.

5. c   Deficits are a tool of fiscal policy. See page 341-342.

6. a   The price level rise is the difference between the change in nominal income (6 percent) and real income (4 percent). 6-4=2 percent. See pages 347.

7. c   See page 337.

8. b   See page 342.

9. a   See pages 344.

10. a   The last two answers, c and d, cannot be right, because the Bank of Canada does not pass laws. When the Bank of Canada buys bonds, it lowers the interest rate but it does not lower interest rates by law. Therefore, only a is correct. See page 344.

11. b   People pay the Bank of Canada for those bonds with money—Bank of Canada IOUs—so the money supply in private hands is reduced. See pages 344-345.

12. a   As the Bank of Canada buys bonds this increases their demand and their prices rise. Since bond prices and interest rates are inversely related, interest rates will fall. See pages 344-345.

13. b   See page 343.

14. a   Expansionary monetary policy reduces interest rates as a result of which investment increases. Hence, AD shifts out to the right by a multiple of the increase in investment. See pages 346-347.

15. b   Contractionary monetary policy increases interest rates which reduces investment, a component of aggregate expenditures. The AD curve shifts to the left by a multiple of the decline in investment. See pages 346-347.

16. a   Contractionary monetary policy increases interest rates which decreases investment, thereby decreasing income by a multiple of that amount. See pages 346-347.

17. b   Monetary regimes are predetermined rules of what the Bank of Canada will do in certain situations; they take feedback effects into account; a regime presets monetary policy. See page 347.

18. c   To determine real interest rate, you subtract expected inflation from nominal interest rates. 7 4=3. See pages 335, 347.

19. d   To determine expected inflation you subtract real interest rates from nominal interest rates. 7 3=4. See pages 335, 347.

20. c   The monetary base is the cash in circulation, vault cash and the reserves banks have at the Bank of Canada. It is the one variable the Bank of Canada can directly control. See pages 341, 348-349.

━━━━ ANSWERS ━━━━

SHORT-ANSWER QUESTIONS

1. Monetary policy is a policy that influences the economy through changes in the money supply and available credit. The Bank of Canada conducts Canadian monetary policy. (334)

2. The Bank of Canada was created in 1934. Its four explicit duties are (1) conducting monetary policy, (2) providing central banking services, (3) issuing bank notes and ensuring their authenticity, and (4) administering public debt. (336, 340)

3. The two tools of monetary policy at the disposal of the Bank of Canada are (1) changing the target range for the overnight financing rate, (2) cash management operations. (341)

4. By changing the target range for the overnight financing rate, other interest rates also get changed. This changes the cost of borrowing for consumers and businesses. Changing the bank rate changes the willingness of banks to borrow from the Bank of Canada. Open market operations changes the reserves banks hold by directly increasing or decreasing cash held by banks and simultaneously decreasing or increasing their holdings of government bonds. This changes the amount of loans banks can make and changes the money supply. (341-345)

5. Economists and policy makers keep a close eye on the bank rate and the announced changes to the bank rate. These act as signals to the Bank of Canada's intended monetary policy stance. A lowering of the bank rate is consistent with an expansion of the money supply (expansionary monetary policy) and a raising of the bank rate is consistent with a contraction of the money supply (contractionary monetary policy). (342-344)

6. The Bank of Canada should decrease the money supply by increasing the bank rate, selling government bonds or transfering deposits from the chartered and other banks to the Bank of Canada. This contractionary monetary policy in the AD/AS model increases interest rates, lowers investment. This shifts the AD curve to the left and reduces income. (344-347)

7. The Bank of Canada should increase the money supply by decreasing the bank rate, buying government bonds or transfering deposits from the Bank of Canada to chartered and other banks. This expansionary monetary policy in the AD/AS model decreases interest rates, raises investment. This shifts the AD curve to the right and increases income. (344-347)

8. You tell the economics student that conducting monetary policy is difficult. Five problems often encountered in conducting monetary policy are: (1) Knowing what potential income is. No one has the magic number. It must be estimated. (2) Knowing whether the policy you are using is contractionary or expansionary. The Bank of Canada does not directly control the money supply. (3) There are significant lags in the effect of monetary policy in the economy. (4) The Bank of Canada is subject to political pressure. And (5) often domestic goals differ from international goals when deciding which policy to follow. (348-349)

━━━━ ANSWERS ━━━━

PROBLEMS AND APPLICATIONS

1.

	Inflation rate	Nominal Interest rate	Real Interest rate
a.	5%	10%	5%:

Real rate = nominal − inflation. (347)

b.	8%	15%	7%:

Inflation = nominal − real rate. (347)

c.	−3%	6%	9%:

Nominal = inflation + real. (347)

d.	4%	14%	10%:

Nominal = inflation + real. (347)

A1. These calculations are based on the formula $M = (1/r) \times MB$, where M is the money supply, r is the reserve ratio, and MB is the monetary base (here it equals reserves).

   a. The Bank of Canada must sell bonds worth $4,000 to reduce reserves by $4,000. We calculate this by dividing the desired reduction in the money supply by the money multiplier. (356-357)

   b. Step 1: An individual or group of individuals buy $4,000 in Treasury bonds from the Bank of Canada. Individuals withdraw the funds from the bank. (356-357)

Assets		Liabilities	
Cash	20,000	Demand Deposits	50,000
Payment to individuals	(4,000)	Withdrawals	(4,000)
Total cash	16,000	Total demand deposits	46,000
Loans	120,000	Net Worth	100,000
Phys. Assets	10,000		
Total Assets	146,000	Total Liabilities and Net Worth	146,000

Step 2: Reserves are now too low to meet the reserve requirement of 0.4. (We calculated the reserve requirement by solving the equation $1/r = 2.5$ for r.) The bank must call in $2,400 in loans ($46,0003.4 - 16,000$). This shows up as loans repaid. But the individuals repaying the loans must get the money from somewhere. Since no one holds cash and Textland bank is the only bank, the individuals must withdraw the $2,400 from the bank. This is shown as a withdrawal on the liability side and a payment to individuals on the asset side. Again reserves are too low, this time by $1,440. (356-357)

Assets		Liabilities	
Cash	16,000	Demand Deposits	46,000
Loans repaid	$2,400	With drawals	(2,400)
Payment to inds.	(2,400)	Total demand deposits	43,600
Total cash	16,000		
Loans	120,000	Net Worth	100,000
Loans called in	(2,400)		
Loans	117,600		
Phys. Assets	10,000		
Total Assets	143,600	Total Liabilities and Net Worth	143,600

   c. Final balance sheet: Banks continue to call in loans to meet reserve requirements until the multiplier process is finished. The money supply is now $10,000 less. At last, the balance sheet is as shown: (356-357)

Assets		Liabilities	
Cash	16,000	Demand Deposits	40,000
Loans	114,000	Net Worth	100,000
Phys. Assets	10,000		
Total Assets	140,000	Total Liabilities and Net Worth	140,000

A2. Step 1: The bank makes $20,000 in new loans. This money is spent and then deposited into Textland by other individuals. (356-357)

Assets		Liabilities	
Cash	40,000	Demand Deposits	200,000
Payments out	(20,000)	New Deposits	20,000
Payments in	20,000	Total Deposits	220,000
Total cash	40,000		
Loans	230,000	Net Worth	100,000
New loans	20,000		
Total loans	250,000		
Phys. Assets	30,000		
Total Assets	320,000	Total Liabilities and Net Worth	320,000

Step 2: Textland still has excess reserves (40,000/220,000 > 0.1) by $18,000 so it makes $18,000 in new loans. Calculate excess reserves by reserves − total deposits × reserve ratio. (356-359)

Assets		Liabilities	
Cash	40,000	Demand Deposits	220,000
Payments out	(18,000)	New Deposits	18,000
Payments in	18,000	Total Deposits	238,000
Total cash	40,000		
Loans	250,000	Net Worth	100,000
New loans	18,000		
Total loans	268,000		
Phys. Assets	30,000		
Total Assets	338,000	Total Liabilities and Net Worth	338,000

Final position: The previous steps continue until the money creation process ends as shown below. (356-359).

Assets		Liabilities	
Cash	40,000	Demand Deposits	400,000
Loans		Net Worth	100,000
Phys. Assets			
Total Assets		Total Liabilities and Net Worth	500,000

ANSWERS

A BRAIN TEASER

1. The Bank of Canada should undertake expansionary monetary policy: 1) Buy government securities on the open market, 2) decrease the discount rate, and/or 3) decrease required reserves. It should do any one or more of these things to increase banks' excess reserves by $75. This is because to close a recessionary gap of $1,000 when the income multiplier is 4 will require an increase in aggregate expenditures of $250. To accomplish this, investment spending will have to increase by $250. This will require the interest rate to decrease by 2.5%. That will require an increase in the money supply of $150. When the money multiplier equals 2, or [1/(0.1 + 0.4)], excess reserves will only have to increase by $75. (344-336)

ANSWERS

POTENTIAL ESSAY QUESTIONS

The following are annotated answers. They indicate the general idea behind the answer.

1. Use expansionary monetary policy (Bank of Canada reduces reserve requirements, reduces the bank rate, or buys government securities.) during a recession; use contractionary policy during an upturn in the business cycle. Expansionary monetary policy will increase the money supply (rightward shift of the supply of money curve), which will reduce the interest rate and increase investment spending. This shifts the AD curve out to the right by a multiple of the initial increase in investment spending and brings about a multiple increase in the income level. (See Figure 14-4, page 347.) Contractionary monetary policy is just the opposite.

2. See the list and the discussion that begins on page 348 of the text.

3. When the Bank of Canada overnight lending rate is above its targeted range many banks have shortages of reserves and therefore money must be tight (credit is tight); and vice versa. The Bank of Canada will buy (sell) bonds when the Bank of Canada overnight lending rate is above (below) its target and monetary policy is too tight (loose).

4. If the Bank of Canada buys (sells) bonds this increases the demand for (supply of) bonds and, thereby, increases (decreases) their price. As the price of bonds goes up (down), the interest rate goes down (up). Hence, the Bank of Canada buying (selling) bonds decreases (increases) interest rates.

THE INFLATION AND UNEMPLOYMENT TRADE-OFF

15

CHAPTER AT A GLANCE

In previous chapters, we discussed the short-run and long-run frameworks to analyze macroeconomic problems. This chapter examines two specific issues that fall within both frameworks. We consider the relationship between inflation and unemployment and the role that expectations play in that relationship.

Inflation can have several different effects on an economy. Inflation reduces a person's purchasing power. However, if wages or prices can be raised to compensate the inflation there is no effect. The losers of inflation are those that can't raise their wages or prices. Borrowers tend to not be hurt by inflation as they enter into contracts that stipulate a fixed interest rate regardless of inflation. Lenders, on the other hand, are hurt as inflation reduces their returns and purchasing power.

Expectations of inflation also influence the behaviour of households and firms as they attempt to compensate for inflation. There are three different types of expectations.

Economists have developed several theories of inflation: the quantity theory of money and inflation and the institutional theory; two different theories related to the relationship between inflation and unemployment; the short-run Phillips curve and the long-run Phillips curve; and a theory describing the relationship between inflation and growth. As with many theories, they tend to breakdown under certain situations and they have certain shortcomings as they can't explain everything.

This review is based upon the learning objectives that open the chapter.

1a. Inflation redistributes income to those who can raise their prices or wages from those who cannot raise their prices or wages. (358-359)

For example, if inflation is unexpected, income is redistributed from:

- workers to firms if workers have fixed wage contracts but firms raise their prices.
- lenders to borrowers since the real interest rate declines when the nominal interest rate is fixed.

On average, the winners and losers in an inflation balance out; inflation does not make a nation richer or poorer.

1b. Three ways expectations of inflation are formed are: (359-360)

1. Rational expectations ⇒ expectations that the economists' model predicts.

2. Adaptive expectations ⇒ expectations based in some way on the past.

3. Extrapolative expectations ⇒ expectations that a trend will continue.

Expectations can change the way an economy operates. Expectations play a key role in policy.

1c. Policymakers use the following equation to determine whether inflation may be coming:

Inflation = Nominal wage increase − productivity growth.

2a. The quantity theory of money basically states that inflation is directly related to the rise in the money supply. It is based upon the equation of exchange: MV = PY. (360-361)

2b. Inflation that results from increases in the money supply works as a type of tax on individuals as purchasing power and the value of cash is reduced. (362-363)

2c. The institutional theory believes that institutional and structural aspects of inflation, as well as increases in the money supply, are important causes of inflation. It sees the causation in the equation of exchange going from right to left. That is, changes in the price level result in changes in the money supply. (365-368)

Firms find it easier to raise wages, profits and rents to keep the peace with employees and other owners of the factors of production. To pay for those increases, firms raise prices. Government then raises the money supply to make sure there is sufficient demand to buy the goods at the higher price.

The "insider" versus "outsider" situation creates imperfect markets. Imperfect markets provide an opportunity for "insiders" to increase their wages and prices even when unemployment and excess capacity exists in the overall economy, thereby creating inflation.

In a nutshell: According to the quantity theory, $MV \Rightarrow PY$

According to the institutionalist theory, $PY \Rightarrow MV$

3a. The long-run Phillips curve is vertical; it takes into account the feedback of inflation on expectations of inflation. (370-371)

In the long run, when expectations of inflation are met, changes in the rates of inflation have no effect on the level of unemployment. This is shown as LR in the accompanying graph.

3b. The short-run Phillips curve is downward sloping. Expectations of inflation are constant along the short-run Phillips curve. (368-369)

The short-run Phillips curve reflects the empirically observed trade-off between inflation and unemployment. It is shown as SR in the graph above. Expectations of inflation are constant along the short-run (SR) Phillips curve. Increases (decreases) in inflationary expectations shift the short-run Phillips curve to the right (left).

In the long run, we have more time to adjust our expectations to actual inflation. In the short run, we may be fooled–we may expect less (more) inflation than actually occurs when inflation is accelerating (decelerating).

4. Quantity theorists believe that inflation undermines long-run growth. Institutionalists are less sure of a negative relationship between inflation and growth. (373-375)

According to the quantity theory, the best policy is policy that leads to price stability.

Institutionalists believe that low unemployment is an important goal that must be balanced with the risk of inflation.

MATCHING THE TERMS
Match the terms to their definitions

All of these key terms are found at the end of the chaper.

___ 1. adaptive expectations
___ 2. extrapolative expectations
___ 3 incomes policy
___ 4. inflation tax
___ 5. insider/outsider model
___ 6. long-run Phillips curve
___ 7. rational expectations
___ 8. short-run Phillips curve
___ 9. stagflation

a. Expectations based in some way on the past.
b. An institutionalist story of inflation where insiders bid up wages and outsiders are unemployed.
c. A policy placing direct pressure on individuals to hold down their nominal wages and prices.
d. A curve showing the trade-off between inflation and unemployment when expectations of inflation are constant.
e. A curve showing the trade-off (or complete lack thereof) between inflation and unemployment when expectations of inflation equal actual inflation.
f. Combination of high and accelerating inflation and high unemployment.
g. Expectations that a trend will continue.
h. Expectations that the economists' model predicts.
i. An implicit tax on the holders of cash and the holders of any obligations specified in nominal terms.

● MULTIPLE CHOICE

Circle the one best answer for each of the following questions:

1. In an expected inflation, lenders will generally:
   a. gain relative to borrowers
   b. lose relative to borrowers
   c. neither gain nor lose relative to borrowers
   d. The effect will be totally random.

2. In an unexpected inflation, lenders will generally
   a. gain relative to borrowers.
   b. lose relative to borrowers.
   c. neither gain nor lose relative to borrowers.
   d. The effect will be totally random.

3. According to the text, if individuals base their expectations on the past we say that their expectations are:
   a. rational.
   b. historical.
   c. adaptive.
   d. extrapolative.

4. If productivity growth is 2 percent and inflation is 5 percent, on average nominal wage increases will be:
   a. 2 percent.
   b. 3 percent.
   c. 5 percent.
   d. 7 percent.

   [handwritten: inflation = Nominal Wage ↑ − Productivity growth
   NW↑ = infl + Prod growth.
   5 = x − 2, −x = −5 −2, x = 5 + 2]

5. Assuming velocity is relatively constant and real income is relatively stable, an increase in the money supply of 40 percent will bring about an approximate change in the price level of:
   a. 4 percent.
   b. 40 percent.
   c. 80 percent.
   d. zero percent.

6. According to the quantity theory,
   a. unemployment is everywhere and always a monetary phenomenon.
   b. inflation is everywhere and always a monetary phenomenon.
   c. the equation of exchange does not hold true.
   d. real output is everywhere and always a monetary phenomenon.

7. The quantity theory is most applicable to:
   a. U.S. type economies.
   b. West European type economies.
   c. developing economies.
   d. Japanese type economies.

8. The inflation tax is
   a. a tax placed by government on inflators.
   b. a tax placed by god on inflators.
   c. a tax on the holders of cash.
   d. a tax on holders of goods whose price is inflating.

9. Which central bank(s) have a strict monetary rule against inflation?
   a. The U.S. and the European central banks.
   b. The European and Russian central banks.
   c. The U.S. and New Zealand central banks.
   d. The European, Canadian and New Zealand central banks.

10. Individuals who hold an institutional theory of inflation argue:
    a. the equation of exchange is incorrect.
    b. the equation of exchange should be read from right to left.
    c. the equation of exchange should be read from left to right.
    d. both the quantity theory and the equation of exchange are incorrect.

11. If an economist focuses on social pressures in his or her discussion of inflation, that economists is likely:
    a. a quantity theory advocate.
    b. an Institutionalist theory of inflation advocate.
    c. an insider theory of inflation advocate.
    d. an outsider theory of inflation advocate.

12. An individual has said that she favours an incomes policy. She
    a. is likely an institutional theory of inflation advocate.
    b. is likely a quantity theory of inflation advocate economist.
    c. could be either a quantity theory or institutionalist theory advocate.
    d. is not an economist, because no economist could ever support an incomes policy.

13. The Phillips curve represents a relationship between
    a. inflation and unemployment.
    b. inflation and real income.
    c. money supply and interest rates.
    d. money supply and unemployment.

14. The short-run Phillips curve shifts around because of changes in:
    a. the money supply.
    b. expectations of employment.
    c. expectations of inflation.
    d. expectations of real income.

15. The slope of the long-run Phillips curve is thought by many economists to be:
    a. horizontal.
    b. vertical.
    c. downward sloping.
    d. backward bending.

16. If the economy is at point A in the Phillips curve graph below, what prediction would you make for inflation?

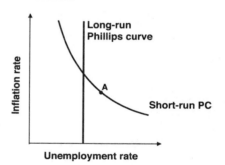

    a. It will increase.
    b. It will decrease.
    c. It will remain constant.
    d. It will explode.

17. If the economy is at Point A in the Phillips curve graph below, what prediction would you make for inflation?

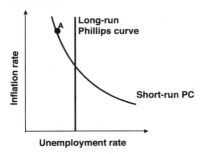

a. It will increase
b. It will decrease.
c. It will remain constant.
d. It will immediately fall to zero.

18. Stagflation is
  a. a combination of low and decelerating inflation and low unemployment.
  b. a combination of low and decelerating inflation and high unemployment.
  c. a combination of high and accelerating inflation and low unemployment.
  d. a combination of high and accelerating inflation and high unemployment.

19. Economists explain the "New Economy" in the last half of the 1990s as:
  a. an example of the stagflation.
  b. an example of the movement from the long run the short run Phillips curve.
  c. an example of the movement from the short run the long run Phillips curve.
  d. a case when productivity grew much faster than expected, negating the standard Phillips curve story.

20. Advocates of the quantity theory are likely to see a tradeoff between inflation and:
  a. unemployment.
  b. distribution.
  c. growth.
  d. money.

● SHORT-ANSWER QUESTIONS

1. Your study partner states that inflation is bad because it makes a nation poorer. How do you respond?

2. What are three ways people form expectations of future inflation?

3. If there is a high inflation, most economists are willing to accept that a rough approximation of the quantity theory holds true. Why?

4. What is the quantity theory of money and how does it relate to long-run growth?

5. How does the institutionalist theory of inflation differ from the quantity theory of inflation?

6. Who is more likely to favour a monetary rule: economists who support the quantity theory or the institutional theory of inflation? Why?

7. Which of the two curves in the graph below is a short-run Phillips curve, and why?

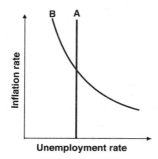

8. Would an economist who supports the quantity theory or one who supports the institutionalist theory of inflation be more likely to see a long-run trade-off between inflation and unemployment? Why?

9. Why would an institutionalist be more likely to support the introduction of an incomes policy than a quantity theorist would be?

● PROBLEMS AND APPLICATIONS

1. With the equation of exchange, answer the following questions:

    a. GDP is $2,000, the money supply is 200. What is the velocity of money?

    b. The velocity of money is 5.60, the money supply is $1,100 billion. What is nominal output?

    c. Assuming velocity is constant and the money supply increases by 6%, by how much does nominal output rise?

2. Suppose the economy is operating at potential output. Inflation is 3% and expected inflation is 3%. Unemployment is 5.5%.

    a. Draw a long-run Phillips curve and a short-run Phillips curve consistent with these conditions.

b. The government implements an expansionary monetary policy. As a result, unemployment falls to 4.5% and inflation rises to 6%. Expectations do not adjust. Show where the economy is on the graph you drew for 3(a). What happens to the short-run Phillips curve? Inflation? Unemployment?

c. Expectations now fully adjust. Show this on the graph drawn for 3(a). What happens to the short-run Phillips curve?

3. Redraw the long-run Phillips curve and a short-run Phillips curve consistent with the conditions of the economy described in question #3 above and explain the effect of the following on inflation and unemployment using the curves you have drawn.

a. The government implements a contractionary monetary policy. As a result, unemployment rises to 6.5% and inflation falls to 0%. Expectations do not adjust.

b. Expectations now fully adjust.

4. For each of the following points that represents the economy on the Phillips curve, make a prediction for unemployment and inflation.

a.

b.

c.

5. Suppose inflation is 12% and unemployment is 5.5% and the natural rate of unemployment is 5.5%. The president believes inflation and unemployment are both too high.

a. Assume you are a quantity theorist. What policy would you recommend to improve the situation?

b. Show the short-run effect of this policy on unemployment and inflation using the Phillips curve analysis. Will the president be satisfied? What is your response?

c. Show the long-run effect of this policy on unemployment and inflation using the Phillips curve analysis. Will the president be satisfied? What is your response? (In that response, discuss the issue of long-run growth).

● A BRAIN TEASER

1. Why do countries increase the money supply enormously even though they know that doing so will lead to high inflation?

● POTENTIAL ESSAY QUESTIONS

You may also see essay questions similar to the "Problems & Applications" and "Brain Teasers" exercises.

1. In what way is inflation a tax? Who pays it?

2. What are the differences between the quantity theorists and the institutionalists with respect to unemployment?

3. What role does government play in the Insider/Outsider model?

ANSWERS

MATCHING

1-a; 2-g; 3-c; 4-i; 5-b; 6-e; 7-h; 8-d; 9-f;.

ANSWERS

MULTIPLE CHOICE

1. **c** In an unexpected inflation borrowers gain and lenders lose because the money they are paying back with will buy less because of the inflation. In an expected inflation the interest rate will have adjusted to compensate lenders for the decrease in the value of money. See page 359.

2. **b** In an unexpected inflation borrowers gain and lenders lose because the money they are paying back with will buy less because of the inflation. See page 359-360.

3. **c** Rational expectations are based on models; extrapolative are based on expectations that a trend will continue. Historical expectations are not mentioned in the text. See page 359-360.

4. **b** Nominal wage increases are the difference between inflation and productivity growth. See page 360.

5. **b** Using the equation of exchange, $MV=PY$, given these assumptions there is a close relationship between changes in M and changes in P. See page 360.

6. **b** The quantity theory directly relates money and inflation. See page 360.

7. **c** The quantity theory is most applicable when there are large increases in the money supply and significant inflation. This is most likely to be the case in developing countries. See pages 360-362.

8. **c** The inflation tax is a tax on the holders of cash because inflation makes their cash worth less. See pages 362-362.

9. **d** As discussed in the text, the European, Canadian and New Zealand central banks have strict rules against inflation. The U.S. does not; Russia is not mentioned in the text. See page 364-365.

10. **b** The equation of exchange is a tautology; it cannot be incorrect; Institutionalists see prices changes causing money and velocity changes so $MV=PY$ should be read from right to left. See pages 365.

11. **b** The book describes two general theories of inflation; social pressures definitely fit with the institutionalist theory. One type of institutionalist theory of inflation is the insider/outsider model, but that is not presented as a choice. See pages 365-367.

12. **a** As discussed in the text, an incomes policy would most likely be favoured by an advocate of an institutional theory of inflation. See page 365-367.

13. **a** The Phillips curve is drawn with inflation on the vertical axis and unemployment on the horizontal axis. See pages 368.

14. **c** The short-run Phillips curve holds expectations of inflation constant. Therefore, it shifts because changes in expectations of inflation cause everybody to build those expectations into their nominal price requests. See page 368-369.

15. **b** As discussed in the text, the long-run Phillips curve is vertical. Actually, there is some debate about whether it is downward sloping, but the text focuses on the vertical nature of the curve so that is the answer that should be given. Remember, one is choosing the best answer relative to what is presented in the text. See page 370.

16. **b** Since Point A is to the right of the long-run Phillips curve, actual unemployment exceeds the natural rate of unemployment. Therefore we would expect inflationary expectations to be decreasing, and hence inflation to be decreasing. See pages 370-372.

17. a   Since Point A is to the left of the long-run Phillips curve, actual unemployment is below the natural rate of unemployment. Therefore we would expect inflationary expectations to be increasing, and hence inflation to be increasing. See page 370-372.

18. d   Stagflation is defined as a combination of high and accelerating inflation and high unemployment. See page 370.

19. d   The last half of the 1990s was a period of low inflation and low unemployment which is not consistent with their Phillips curve story. Economist's explanation of this period centered on the higher than expected increases in productivity. See page 370-371.

20. c   Quantity theory advocates argue that in the long run a non-inflationary environment is conducive to growth and thus there is a long run tradeoff between inflation and growth. See pages 373-375.

ANSWERS

SHORT-ANSWER QUESTIONS

1.   Inflation does not make a nation poorer. It redistributes income from those who can and do raise their prices to those who cannot or do not raise their prices. On average, the winners and losers average out. An example is lenders and borrowers. (358-359)

2.   People formulate expectations in a variety of ways. Three types of expectations are adaptive expectations (expectations based in some way on the past), rational expectations (the expectations that the economists' model predicts), and extrapolative expectations (expectations that a trend will continue). (359-360)

3.   The quantity theory is based on the equation of exchange, $MV=PY$. The quantity theory adds the following assumptions: (1) that velocity is relatively constant; (2) that real output is relatively constant; and (3) that changes in money supply cause changes in prices. In reality, velocity and real output can change sufficiently to make it questionable whether this theory is useful. However, when there is significant inflation—say 100% or more—the relative changes in velocity and real output that are reasonable to assume possible are much smaller than that 100%, leaving a rough correlation between changes in the money supply and changes in the price level.

The debate between economists does not concern the relationships between money growth and inflation; it concerns the direction of causation. Quantity theorists tend to believe that the causation goes from money to prices, and hence they are willing to accept the existence of a long-run vertical Phillips curve. Institutionalists tend to believe that the causation goes from changes in prices and expectations of prices to changes in the money supply—the government is accommodating the higher prices. Thus they favour more institutionally-oriented theories of inflation. (360-362, 365-366)

4.   The quantity theory of money is best summarized by the phrase "Inflation is everywhere and always a monetary phenomenon." Essentially, it is that increases in the money supply are the cause of inflation, and all other supposed causes are simply diversions from the key monetary cause. According to the quantity theory, there is a long-run inverse relationship between inflation and growth. (360-362)

5.   The institutionalist theory of inflation differs from the quantity theory in that it is more likely to include institutional and social aspects as part of the theory. The insider/outsider model is an institutionalist model of inflation. Another way of stating the difference is that the institutional theory of inflation sees the equation of exchange as being read from right to left, rather than from left to right. (365-368)

6.   Economists who support the quantity theory of money are more likely to favour a monetary rule, because they see the economy gravitating toward a natural (or target) rate of unemployment regardless of monetary policy. Thus expansionary monetary policy can lead only to inflation. A monetary rule will limit the government's

attempt to expand the economy with monetary policy and hence will achieve the natural rate of unemployment and low inflation. Institutional economists are less likely to see the economy gravitating toward the natural (or target) rate of unemployment, so they would favour some discretionary policy to improve the operation of the macro economy. (365-368)

7. Curve B is the short-run Phillips curve. The Phillips curve represents a trade-off between inflation and unemployment. It is an empirically determined phenomenon, and based on that empirical evidence economists generally believe that the downward sloping curve (curve B) represents the short-run Phillips curve: Whenever unemployment decreases, inflation increases, and vice versa. They explain that this empirical occurrence is due to slowly adjusting expectations and institutions. In the long run, expectations and institutions can change and hence the reason for the trade-off is eliminated, making the vertical line represent the long-run Phillips curve—it represents the lack of a trade-off between inflation and unemployment in the long run. (370-372)

8. Institutional economists see institutional and social aspects of the price setting process as more important than do quantity theorists. They also see individuals as having a cost of rationality, so individuals may not notice small amounts of inflation. These aspects of the institutional theory make it more likely that there is a long-run trade-off between inflation and unemployment since, in their absence, we would expect that money is essentially a veil and real forces predominate. (365-368, 373-375)

9. An incomes policy is a policy designed to put direct downward pressure on the nominal price setting process. Institutional economists see institutional and social aspects of the price setting process as more important than do quantity theorists. It is these social aspects of the price setting process, which place a direct upward pressure on the price level that will require an incomes policy to offset. Therefore, institutionalists are more likely to support an incomes policy. (368)

ANSWERS

PROBLEMS AND APPLICATIONS

1. a. $V = 10$: $MV = PY$; $200V = \$2,000$; $V = 10$. (363-364)
    b. \$6,160 billion: $MV = PY$; $(5.6)(1,100) = \$6,160$ billion. (363-364)
    c. By 6%. (360-362)

2. a. The long-run Phillips curve is vertical at the rate of unemployment consistent with potential output, here at 5.5%. The short-run Phillips curve is the downward sloping curve shown in the graph below as PC_1. In this case, we drew a short-run Phillips curve where expected inflation equals 3%, actual inflation. It intersects the long-run Phillips curve at 5.5% unemployment and 3% inflation. The economy is at point A. (368-371)

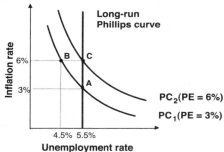

    b. The economy moves along the short-run Phillips curve up and to the left to point B. The short-run Phillips curve does not shift since inflation expectations have not changed. At point B, inflation is 6% and unemployment rate is 4.5%. (368-371)
    c. Now that expectations fully adjust, the short-run Phillips curve shifts to the right to PC_2 so that it intersects the long-run Phillips curve at inflation rate of 6%. The unemployment rate returns to 5.5% and inflation remains at 6%. (368-371)

3. a. The economy moves along the short-run Phillips curve down and to the right to point B in the graph below. The short-run Phillips curve does not shift since inflation expectations have not changed. At point B, inflation is 0% and unemployment rate is 6.5%. (368-371)

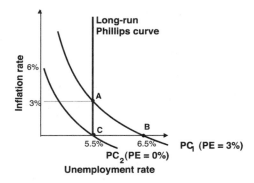

b. Now that expectations fully adjust, the short-run Phillips curve shifts to the left to PC_2 so that it intersects the long-run Phillips curve at inflation rate of 0%. The unemployment rate returns to 5.5% and inflation remains at 0%. (368-371)

4. a. Inflation is below expected inflation and unemployment is higher than the natural rate of unemployment. As expectations adjust, the short-run Phillips curve shifts to the left and both unemployment and inflation will fall. (368-371)

b. Inflation is above expected inflation and unemployment is lower than the natural rate of unemployment. As expectations adjust, the short-run Phillips curve shifts to the right and both unemployment and inflation will rise. (368-371)

c. Inflation equals expected inflation and unemployment equals the target rate of unemployment. Inflation and unemployment will not change. (368-371)

5. a. I assume that in the long run, only inflation can be improved, so I ignore the higher-than-desired rate of unemployment and focus on fighting inflation. A contractionary monetary policy will improve the inflation rate. (368-371)

b. The economy begins at point A in the graph below, where unemployment is 5.5% and inflation is 12%. Inflation expectations equal actual inflation. With contractionary monetary policy, the economy moves along the short-run Phillips curve down and to the right to point B. The short-run Phillips curve does not shift since inflation expectations have not changed. At point B, inflation is lower than 12% and the unemployment rate is higher than 5.5%. The president will be happy that inflation is lower, but disappointed that unemployment is higher. I tell him that in the short run there is a trade-off between the two. Just wait for expectations of inflation to adjust and we will return to 5.5% unemployment. (368-371)

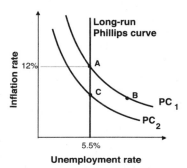

c. Now that expectations fully adjust, the short-run Phillips curve shifts to the left to PC_2 so that it intersects the long-run Phillips curve at inflation rate of below 12% at point C. The unemployment rate returns to 5.5%. The president is now pleased because inflation is lower and unemployment returned to 5.5%. But he wanted the unemployment rate to be below 5.5%. I tell him that 5.5% is the natural rate. If he were to follow an expansionary policy, unemployment would fall in the short run, but would return to 5.5% in the long run and inflation would be higher than it currently is. The higher inflation would undermine the economy's long-term growth. (368-371)

======== ANSWERS ========

A BRAIN TEASER

1. The reasons are complicated. If a government does not have the capability of either taxing or borrowing to finance expenditures (and if the central bank is not independent) the government may rely on its ability to print money to finance government expenditures. For some countries, the choice is between inflation and allowing an economy and its government to fall apart. (362-363)

======== ANSWERS ========

POTENTIAL ESSAY QUESTIONS

The following are annotated answers. They indicate the general idea behind the answer.

1. Inflation can be viewed as a tax because it reduces the value of obligations specified in nominal terms. A simple way to see this is if prices rose at a rate of 5 percent a day, a dollar today will buy only 95 cents worth of goods tomorrow. The holder of the dollar (or any obligation specified in nominal terms) pays the tax.

2. Quantity theorists see a competitive labour market guaranteeing full employment. Institutionalists see an imperfectly competitive labour market. Institutionalists also envision a potential lack of demand for workers because of a lack of aggregate demand for the goods they produce. To institutionalists, this can create some unemployment at any wage.

3. Inflation is a result of *im*perfectly competitive markets. This allows workers and firms (especially "insiders") to raise their nominal wages and prices even during periods of high unemployment and excess production. Other groups, feeling relatively worse off, will push for higher wages and prices too. The government can either ratify this inflation by increasing the money supply or it can refuse to ratify it, causing unemployment (especially for the "outsiders"). In sum, Keynesians emphasize institutional and social causes of inflation.

THE BALANCE OF TRADE, THE EXCHANGE RATE AND TRADE POLICY

16

CHAPTER AT A GLANCE

This chapter delves into the financial side of international trade. More specifically, it addresses issues such as using the balance of payments accounts to account for all transactions (pertaining to goods and services, financial assets such as stocks and bonds, and capital goods) that take place between the domestic economy and its foreign trading partners; how foreign exchange rates are determined; how economies using different currencies are able to trade with each other; and the varieties of trade restrictions.

In our market economy, there are three distinct exchange rate systems – the fixed exchange rate, the flexible exchange rate and the partially (or managed) flexible exchange rate. Each of these systems have their advantages and disadvantages. We will see what the rationale is for the government currently using the partially flexible exchange rate system. The exchange rate section is further expanded to consider how economists estimate the long-run equilibrium exchange rate using the theory of purchasing power parity. There are, however, some shortcomings when used to determine short-run currency movement.

The recent developments surrounding the European Union has prompted considerate debate as to whether Canada and the U.S. should enter into a similar arrangement. This chapter considers several possible options for Canada and the U.S. in adopting a common currency.

This review is based upon the learning objectives that open the chapter.

1a. The balance of payments is a country's record of all transactions between its residents and the residents of all foreign nations. (380-384)

> *It is broken down into the:*
> • *current account*
> • *capital and financial account*

Remember: If it is a minus (plus) sign, money is going out (coming in). Moreover, if foreigners are buying our goods, services, or assets, that represents a demand for the dollar (an inflow) in international exchange rate markets. If we buy foreign goods, services, or assets, that represents a supply of dollars (an outflow).

1b. The balance of goods and services is the difference between the value of goods and services a nation exports and the value of goods and services it imports. (381)

> *The balance of merchandise trade is often discussed in the popular press as a summary of how Canada is doing in international markets. However, it only includes goods exported and imported—not services. Trade in services is just as important as trade in merchandise, so economists pay more attention to the combined balance on goods and services.*

1c. Since the balance of payments consists of both the capital and financial account and the balance of goods and services account, if the capital account is in surplus and the trade and financial account is in deficit, there can still be a balance of payments surplus. (384-386)

> *The capital and financial account measures the flows of payments between countries for assets such as stocks, bonds, and real estate. The current (or trade) account measures the flows of payments for goods and services.*

1d. A deficit in the balance of payments means that the quantity supplied of a currency exceeds the quantity demanded. A surplus in the balance of payments means the opposite. (386-388)

> *Whenever the exchange rate is <u>above equilibrium</u> (below equilibrium) then the country will experience a balance of payments <u>deficit</u> (surplus).*

2a. An exchange rate is the rate at which one currency can be traded for another currency. Exchange rates are typically determined by the supply and demand for the currency in the foreign exchange market. (385-386)

2b. Three important fundamental determinants of exchange rates are prices, interest rates, and income. (387-389)

A decrease in the value of a currency can be caused by:

- *An increase in the nation's inflation rate.*
- *A decrease in the nation's interest rates.*
- *An increase in the nation's income .*

2c. Due to the uncertainty of future exchange rates, particularly when making investments or purchases, there are mechanisms in the market to address this issue. A covered interest parity means that the investor has entered into a derivative market to lock in the exchange rate at which the foreign currency can be traded for the domestic currency. (388-389)

2d. In the short run, normal market forces of supply and demand have a limited, and possibly even perverse, effect on exchange rates. The effect of rumours and expectations, etc. make predicting the exchange rate very difficult. (389-390)

3a. A country fixes the exchange rate by standing ready to buy and sell its currency at any time at the fixed exchange rate. (391)

It is easier for a country to maintain a fixed exchange rate below equilibrium. All it has to do is to print and sell enough domestic currency to hold the value down.

However, if a country wants to maintain a fixed exchange rate <u>above long-run equilibrium</u> then it can do so only as long as it has the foreign currency (official) reserves to buy up its currency. Once it runs out of official reserves, it will be unable to intervene, and must either borrow, use indirect methods (domestic fiscal and monetary policies), ask other countries to buy its currency (to sell their currency), or devalue its currency.

In reality, because a country has a limited amount of official reserves, it only uses strategic currency stabilization (not a fixed exchange rate policy).

3b. Purchasing power parity is a method of calculating exchange rates such that various currencies will each buy an equal basket of goods and services. Those exchange rates may or may not be appropriate long-run exchange rates. (393-395)

Long-run equilibrium exchange rates can only be estimated. The PPP (Purchasing Power Parity) is one method of doing so. However, for many economists, it has serious problems. They contend that the current exchange rate is the best estimate of the long-run equilibrium rate.

4a. Three exchange rate régimes are:
- Fixed exchange rate: The government chooses an exchange rate and offers to buy and sell currencies at that rate.
- Flexible exchange rate: Determination of exchange rates is left totally up to the market.
- Partially flexible exchange rate: The government sometimes affects the exchange rate and sometimes leaves it to the market. (395-398)

Which is best is debatable.

4b. Fixed exchange rates provide international monetary stability and force governments to make adjustments to meet their international problems. (This is *also* a disadvantage.) If they become unfixed, they create monetary instability. (396-397)

Know these advantages and disadvantages!

4c. Flexible exchange rate régimes provide for orderly incremental adjustment of exchange rates rather than large sudden jumps, and allow governments to be flexible in conducting domestic monetary and fiscal policy. (This is *also* a disadvantage.) They are, however, susceptible to private speculation. (398)

Know these advantages and disadvantages!

4d. Partially flexible exchange rate régimes combine the advantages and disadvantages of fixed and flexible exchange rates. (398)

Most countries have opted for this policy. However, if the market exchange rate is below the rate the government desires, and the government does not have sufficient official reserves (to buy and increase the demand for its currency), then it must undertake policies that will either increase the private demand for its currency or decrease the private supply. Doing so either involves using traditional macro policy—fiscal and monetary policy—to influence the economy, or using trade policy to affect the level of exports and imports.

Sometimes the partially flexible exchange rates are referred to as "managed exchange rates" or a "dirty float."

5a. A monetary union has been proposed for North America much like the European Union. There are three possible policy options: (399-400)

- Moving back to fixed exchange rates.
- Creating a new North American currency (the Amero).
- Adopting the U.S. dollar.

5b. Fixed exchange rates force firms to be more innovative and productive, while forcing the closure and failure of uncompetitive industries. It reduces the ability to make domestic goods and services more attractive. (400-401)

5c. A new currency raises the issue as to who will determine monetary policy as well as implement the strategy. The benefits to having a common currency are greatest when the two (or more) nations respond in a similar fashion to disturbances like shifts in commodity prices. (401-402)

5d. Adopting the U.S. dollar is not a feasible option as it eliminates Canada's control over monetary policy. Research shows that Canada benefits significantly from having a separate currency and a floating exchange rate. (402)

6a. Some important international trade restrictions include tariffs, quotas, voluntary restraint agreements, and regulatory trade restrictions. (403-405)

Know the difference between these different trade restrictions as well as embargoes and nationalistic appeals!

6b. Economists generally support free trade because trade restrictions lower aggregate output, reduce international competition, and often result in harmful trade wars that hurt everyone. (405)

The costs of trade restrictions (which include, among other things, higher prices domestic consumers must pay) almost always outweigh the benefits (which include protection from foreign competition that provides higher short-run profits and greater short-run job security to the protected domestic industries).

However, strategic trade policies (threats to implement trade restrictions on another country if it doesn't reduce its trade barriers) can be used to promote free trade (if these threats are credible and the other country reduces its trade restrictions).

7. The three international trade agreements affecting Canada are: (406-409)

- The Canada-U.S. Free Trade Agreement
- The North American Free Trade Agreement
- Free Trade Areas of the Americas

See also, Appendix A: "History of Exchange Rate Systems."

MATCHING THE TERMS
Match the terms to their definitions

All of these key terms, are found at the end of the chapter.

____ **1.** balance of merchandise trade

____ **2.** balance of payments

____ **3.** balance of goods and services

____ **4.** capital and financial account

____ **5.** Canada-U.S. Free Trade Agreement

____ **6.** covered interest parity

____ **7.** currency stabilization

____ **8.** currency support

____ **9.** current account

____ **10.** embargo

____ **11.** exchange rate

____ **12.** fair trade

____ **13.** financial account

____ **14.** fixed exchange rate

____ **15.** flexible exchange rate

____ **16.** free trade

____ **17.** General Agreement on Tariffs and Trade (GATT)

____ **18.** North American Free Trade Agreement (NAFTA)

____ **19.** official reserves

____ **20.** partially flexible exchange rate

____ **21.** purchasing power parity

____ **22.** quota

____ **23.** regulatory trade restrictions

____ **24.** strategic trade policies

____ **25.** tariff

____ **26.** uncovered interest parity

____ **27.** voluntary restraint agreements

____ **28.** World Trade Organization (WTO)

a. A method of calculating exchange rates that attempts to value currencies at rates such that each will buy an equal basket of goods.

b. Agreements in which countries voluntarily restrict their exports.

c. A country's record of all transactions between its residents and the residents of all foreign nations.

d. Taxes governments place on internationally traded goods, generally imports.

e. An exchange rate established by a government that sometimes affects the exchange rate and sometimes leaves it to the market.

f. An exchange rate established by a government that chooses an exchange rate and offers to buy and sell currencies at that rate.

g. An exchange rate for which the determination of its value is left up to market forces.

h. Threatening to implement tariffs to bring about a reduction in tariffs or some other concession from the other country.

i. Policy of allowing unrestricted trade among countries.

j. The difference between the value of goods a nation exports and the value of goods it imports.

k. The part of the balance of payments account that lists all long-term flows of payments.

l. The part of the balance of payments account that lists all short-term flows of payments.

m. The government holdings of foreign currencies.

n. The difference between the value of goods and services exported and imported.

o. The rate at which one currency can be traded for another currency.

p. The investor has entered into a derivative market to lock-in the exchange rate at which the foreign currency can be traded for the domestic currency.

q. The expected return from investing at home and abroad should be identical.

r. The buying of a currency by a government to maintain its value at above its long-run equilibrium value.

s. The buying and selling of a currency by the government to offset temporary fluctuations in supply and demand for currencies.

t. Regular international conference to reduce trade barriers.

u. An organization committed to getting countries to agree not to impose new tariffs or other trade restrictions.

v. Government-imposed procedural rules that limit imports.

w. Restrictions on the import or export of a good.

x. A trade agreement which came into effect in 1989 and set in motion a process in which most tariff and non-tariff barriers would be eliminated over a ten-year period.

y. A trade agreement that came into effect in 1993.

z. The part of the balance of payments that records the amount of its own currency or foreign currencies that a nation buys or sells.

z1. Unlike under free trade, a country is equitably compensated for its products.

z2. Quantity limits placed on imports.

⬤ MULTIPLE CHOICE

Circle the one best answer for each of the following questions:

1. An exchange rate is:
   a. the rate the Bank of Canada charges commercial banks for loans.
   b. the rate the Bank of Canada charges individuals for loans.
   c. the rate at which one country's currency can be exchanged for another country's currency.
   d. the speed at which exchange occurs.

2. If a country has perfectly flexible exchange rates and is running a current account deficit, it is running
   a. a capital account surplus.
   b. a capital account deficit.
   c. an official transactions surplus.
   d. an official transactions deficit.

3. In the balance of payments accounts, net investment income shows up in
   a. the current account.
   b. the capital account.
   c. the official transactions account.
   d. Net investment income is not an entry in the balance of payments.

4. In the balance of payments accounts, all of the following are included in the financial account except
   a. Canadian portfolio investment abroad.
   b. foreign investment in Canadian stocks.
   c. foreign investment in Canadian bonds.
   d. transfer of intangible assets.

5. In 2004, Canada ran a
   a. balance of trade surplus.
   b. balance of trade deficit.
   c. balance of trade surplus sometimes and balance of trade deficit sometimes.
   d. balance of trade equality.

6. In 2004, Canada ran a
   a. capital account surplus.
   b. capital account deficit.
   c. financial account surplus.
   d. current account deficit.

7. All of the following forces influence exchange rates, except
   a. change in a country's income.
   b. changes in a country's prices.
   c. changes in interest rates.
   d. changes in population.

8. If the French demand for Canadian imports increases, one would expect the price of French francs in terms of dollars to:
   a. rise.
   b. fall.
   c. remain unchanged.
   d. sometimes rise and sometimes fall.

9. If the Canadian demand for French imports increases, one would expect the price of French francs in terms of dollars to:
   a. rise.
   b. fall.
   c. remain unchanged.
   d. sometimes rise and sometimes fall.

Use the following graph to answer Questions 10 -12:

10. If Canadian income increases
    a. the supply curve will shift out to the right.
    b. the supply curve will shift in to the left.
    c. the demand curve will shift out to the right.
    d. the demand curve will shift in to the left.

11. If French interest rates increase relative to world interest rates:
    a. only the supply curve will shift out to the right.
    b. only the demand curve will shift in to the left.
    c. the supply curve will shift in to the left and the demand curve will shift out to the right.
    d. the supply curve will shift out to the right and the demand curve will shift in to the left.

12. If French inflation increases relative to world interest rates:
  a. only the supply curve will shift out to the right.
  b. only the demand curve will shift in to the left.
  c. the supply curve will shift in to the left and the demand curve will shift out to the right.
  d. the supply curve will shift out to the right and the demand curve will shift in to the left.

13. If a country runs expansionary monetary policy, in the short run one would expect the value of its exchange rate to
  a. rise.
  b. fall.
  c. be unaffected.
  d. sometimes rise and sometimes fall.

14. Refer to the graph below. If the Canadian government wants to fix its convertible currency at exchange rate P_1, it will have to:

  a. supply official reserves in exchange for dollars.
  b. supply dollars in exchange for official reserves.
  c. disallow currency conversion except at the official rate P1.
  d. supply both official reserves and dollars because excess supply of dollars is so large.

15. Say the Bangladeshi taka is valued at 42 taka to $1. Also say that you can buy the same basket of goods for 10 taka that you can buy for $1. In terms of dollars the purchasing power parity of the taka is
  a. overvalued.
  b. undervalued.
  c. not distorted.
  d. non convertible.

16. Compared to a fixed exchange rate system, a flexible exchange rate system
  a. allows countries more flexibility in their monetary policies.
  b. allows countries less flexibility in their monetary policies.
  c. has no effect on monetary policies.
  d. allows countries more flexibility in their industrial policies.

17. Tariffs are
  a. quantity limits placed on imports.
  b. agreements in which countries voluntarily restrict their exports.
  c. taxes governments place on internationally traded goods—generally imports.
  d. an all-out restriction on the import or export of a good.

18. Which of the following is *not* generally a reason for economists' opposition to trade restrictions?
  a. they lower aggregate output.
  b. they reduce international competition.
  c. they often result in harmful trade wars that hurt everyone.
  d. they increase output of foreign countries relative to the domestic country.

A1. The gold standard is a type of
  a. fixed exchange rate.
  b. partially flexible exchange rate.
  c. flexible exchange rate.
  d. nonconvertible exchange rate.

A2. The gold specie flow mechanism works primarily by flows of
  a. money from one country to another.
  b. services from one country to another.
  c. merchandise from one country to another.
  d. exchange rates from one country to another.

A3. Under the gold standard, if a country has a balance of payments deficit
  a. gold would flow out of the country.
  b. gold would flow into the country.
  c. the country's exchange rate would rise.
  d. the country's exchange rate would fall.

A4. SDRs refers to
   a. Specie Draft Rights.
   b. Specie Drawing Rights.
   c. Special Drawing Rights.
   d. Special Draft Rights.

● SHORT-ANSWER QUESTIONS

1. Distinguish between the balance of payments and the balance of trade.

2. How can a country simultaneously have a balance of payments deficit and a balance of trade surplus?

3. How does each part of the balance of payments relate to the supply and demand for currencies?

4. What are the three fundamental determinants of exchange rates?

5. If the demand and supply for a country's currency depends upon demand for imports and exports, and demand for foreign and domestic assets, how can a country fix its exchange rate?

6. How do market exchange rates differ from exchange rates using the purchasing power parity concept?

7. Define fixed exchange rates.

8. Define flexible exchange rates.

9. Define partially flexible exchange rates.

10. Which are preferable, fixed or flexible exchange rates?

11. Under a fixed exchange rate regime, how can inflation be imported into a domestic economy from abroad?

12. What are a few of the most important international trade restrictions?

13. Why do economists generally support free trade?

● PROBLEMS AND APPLICATIONS

1. State for each whether the transaction shows up on the balance of payments current account or the balance of payments capital account or neither.

   a. An American buys 100 stocks of Mercedes Benz, a German company.

   b. A Japanese businessperson buys Ameritec, an American bank.

   c. An American auto manufacturer buys $20 million in auto parts from a Japanese company.

   d. An American buys 100 shares of IBM stock.

   e. Saturn exports 10,000 cars to Germany.

   f. Toyota Motor Corporation, a Japanese firm, makes a $1 million profit from its plant in Kentucky, USA.

2. For each of the following, state who is demanding and who is supplying what currency:

   a. A French person buys a set of china from a Canadian firm.

   b. A Canadian tourist in Japan buys a Japanese kimono from a department store.

   c. An Italian exchange rate trader believes that the exchange rate value of the dollar will rise.

   d. A Swiss investor invests in Germany.

3. Draw supply and demand curves for British pounds, showing equilibrium quantity and price. Price is shown by price of pounds in dollars.

   a. What is the demand for dollars in this case?

   b. Explain a movement up along the supply curve.

   c. Explain a movement down along the demand curve.

   d. What would be the effect on the price of pounds of an increase in demand for pounds by the British? Show this graphically.

   e. What would be the effect on the price of pounds of an increase in demand for dollars by the British? Show this graphically.

4. For each of the following, show graphically what would happen to the market for British pounds. Assume there are only two countries, the United States and Britain.

   a. Income in the Britain rises.

   b. Income in the United States rises.

   c. The prices of goods in the United States increases.

   d. Interest rates rise in Britain.

   e. The value of the pound is expected to fall.

● A BRAIN TEASER

1. What could cause the U.S. to temporarily experience an increase in its balance of payments deficit even though there is downward movement in the exchange rate value of the dollar? (Hint: Think in terms of demand and supply analysis.)

● POTENTIAL ESSAY QUESTIONS

You may also see essay questions similar to the "Problems & Applications" and "Brain Teasers" exercises.

1. How are a government's exchange rate policy and the financial account in the balance of payments related? Is it easier for a government to push the value of its currency up or down? Why?

2. Explain how fixed, flexible (or floating), and partially flexible exchange rates are determined. What are the advantages and the disadvantages of each? Why do most nations have a partially flexible exchange rate policy?

■ ANSWERS ■

MATCHING

1-j; 2-c; 3-n; 4-k; 5-x; 6-p; 7-s; 8-r; 9-l; 10-w; 11-o; 12-z; 13-z; 14-f; 15-g; 16-i; 17-t; 18-y; 19-m; 20-e; 21-a; 22-z2; 23-v; 24-h; 25-d; 26-q; 27-b; 28-u.

■ ANSWERS ■

MULTIPLE CHOICE

1. c An exchange rate is the rate at which one country's currency can be exchanged for another country's currency. See page 385.

2. a With perfectly flexible exchange rates the balance of payments must sum to zero; thus the capital account must be in surplus if the current account is in deficit. See pages 384-385.

3. a Although net investment income might seem to many people as if it goes in the capital account, it is a return for a service and is considered part of the current account, as is discussed on pages 382-383.

4. d See page 382.

5. a See page 382 and Table 16-1 on page 381.

6. a Running a capital account surplus is the other side of the balance sheet from the trade deficit. See page 384 and Table 16-1 on page 381.

7. d See page 387.

8. b To purchase greater amounts of Canadian products, the French must increase the supply of their currency, pushing down its value relative to the dollar. See pages 385-386.

9. a To purchase greater amounts of French products, Canadian citizens must increase the supply of their currency, pushing down its value relative to the franc. That means, the value of the franc rises relative to the dollar. See pages 385-387.

10. c If Canadian income increases, the Canadian demand for French imports will increase, shifting the demand for francs out to the right. See pages 385-387.

11. c An increase in French interest rates will increase the demand for French assets. As a result, the demand for French francs will shift out to the right. In addition, the French will substitute foreign assets for domestic assets shifting the supply of francs to the left. See pages 385-387.

12. d An increase in French inflation will reduce the demand for French goods. Foreigners will demand fewer francs with which to buy French goods and French citizens will supply more francs as they exchange francs for other currencies to buy cheaper goods abroad. See pages 385-387.

13. b This is a review question from the previous chapter. Expansionary monetary policy decreases interest rates and thereby tends to decrease the exchange rate in the short run. See pages 385-387.

14. a At P_1, there is an excess supply of dollars. To keep the value of the dollar from falling, Canada will have to buy up that excess using official reserves of foreign currencies. Disallowing conversion except at an official rate would make the dollar a nonconvertible currency. See pages 385-387.

15. b Since the purchasing power parity exchange rate is lower than the actual exchange rate, the taka is undervalued. See pages 391-392.

16. a Under a fixed exchange rate system countries must use their monetary policies to meet international commitments. Thus flexible exchange rate policies allow them more flexibility in their monetary policies. Flexible exchange rates *may* allow them more flexibility in their industrial policies, but flexible exchange rates *definitely* do allow them more flexibility in their monetary policy, so a is the preferred answer. See pages 391-399.

17. c   See page 403 of textbook.

18. d   Trade restrictions hurt all countries. See page 405.

A1. a.   See page 413.

A2. a.   When there is an imbalance of trade in the gold system, gold—which is money—flows from the deficit country to the surplus country, pushing the price level down in the deficit country and up in the surplus country. This process brings about a trade balance equilibrium, eventually. See page 414.

A3. a   See pages 413-414 about the flow of gold. The last two answers could be eliminated since the gold standard involves fixed exchange rates.

A4. c   As discussed on page 415, SDRs refers to Special Drawing Rights.

ANSWERS

SHORT-ANSWER QUESTIONS

1. The balance of payments is a country's record of all transactions between its residents and the residents of all foreign nations. It is divided into the current account, the capital account, and the official transactions account. The balance of trade is one part of the balance of payments—specifically that part dealing with goods. It is not all that satisfactory a measure of the country's position in international markets since it does not include services. Generally, economists pay more attention to the combined balance on goods and services account. (380-385)

2. As discussed in question 1, the balance of trade is one part of the balance of payments. Thus, if other parts of the international payments—for example, the capital account—are in deficit, the balance of trade could still be in surplus. (380-385)

3. The balance of payments records the flow of a currency in and out of a country (1) in order to buy and sell goods and services in the current account, (2) in order to buy and sell assets along with payments resulting from previous purchases of assets in the capital account, and (3) in order to affect the value of a country's currency in the official transactions account. To buy foreign goods and assets one must supply domestic currency and demand foreign currency. Therefore, the balance of payments records the demand and supply of a country's currency during a given period of time. (380-386)

4. Three fundamental determinants of the value of a country's exchange rate are (1) domestic income, (2) domestic price level and (3) domestic interest rates. (387)

5. The current account and capital account reflect private demand and supply of a country's currency. If a country wants to fix the value of its currency to maintain its value at the fixed value, the government must buy and sell its currency using official reserves. Buying (selling) one's own currency shows up as a positive (negative) in the financial account. (381, 391-392)

6. Market exchange rates are determined by the demand and supply of a country's currency. Since not all goods, services and assets produced in a country can be traded internationally, the value of an exchange rate may not reflect the relative prices in each country. The purchasing power parity concept adjusts the value of a country's currency by determining that rate at which equivalent baskets of goods can be purchased in each country. (393-395)

7. A fixed exchange rate is an exchange rate that the government chooses and then holds at the chosen rate, by standing ready to buy and sell at that rate. (396-397)

8. Flexible exchange rates are exchange rates that are determined by the market without any government intervention. (398)

9. Partially flexible exchange rates are exchange rates that are determined by the market but are sometimes also affected by government intervention. (398)

10. It depends. Each has its advantages and disadvantages. Flexible exchange rates give a country more control over domestic policy, but it can experience large fluctuations in the value of its currency, hurting trade. But with fixed exchange rates, such fluctuations can be avoided. (398)

11. Assume that the U.S. increases its money supply. This will eventually lead to higher inflation in the U.S., thereby making its currency less attractive to hold. The low inflation environment in Canada will lead to increased interest by foreigners, thereby pushing up the demand for the Canadian dollar. If the Bank of Canada is maintaining the Canadian dollar at a pegged value, the increased demand for the Canadian dollar can be offset by selling Canadian dollars in the foreign exchange market and buying U.S. dollars. The lower valued U.S. dollar means that more U.S. dollars will have to be spent by Canadians in order to buy American goods and services. This leads to higher inflation being imported from the U.S. (400-401)

12. The most important international trade restrictions include tariffs, quotas, voluntary restraint agreements, and regulatory trade restrictions. (403-405)

13. Economists generally support free trade because restrictions in trade lower output, reduce international competition (raising prices to consumers), and often result in harmful trade wars that hurt everyone. (405)

ANSWERS

PROBLEMS AND APPLICATIONS

1. a. Capital account. This is a long-term outflow. (381)
    b. Capital account. This is a long-term inflow. (381)
    c. Current account. This is merchandise imports, a short-term flow. (381)
    d. Neither. It is a domestic transaction. (381)
    e. Current account. This is merchandise exports, a short-term flow. (381)
    f. Current account. This is net investment income. (381)

2. a. The French person supplies francs and demands dollars because the French person sells francs to get Canadian dollars to purchase the china. (385-386)
    b. The Canadian tourist supplies dollars and demands Japanese yen because the tourist has to sell dollars to get yen. (385-386)
    c. The Italian trader will supply Italian lire and demand Canadian dollars because the trader wants to purchase that exchange that is believed to rise, the dollar. The trader must sell lire to get the dollars. (385-386)
    d. The Swiss investor will supply Swiss francs and demand German marks because the Swiss investor needs German marks to invest in Germany. (385-386)

3. A market for British pounds is shown below. Price of pounds in Canadian dollars is on the vertical axis and quantity of pounds is on the horizontal axis. Equilibrium price and quantity is determined by where they intersect. (385-386)

Quantity of British pounds

    a. If only two countries exist, the United States and Britain, the demand for dollars is the supply of pounds. (385-386)
    b. As the dollar value of the pound rises, individuals will supply more pounds. (385-386)
    c. As the dollar value of the pound declines, individuals will demand more pounds. (385-386)

d. An increase in the demand for pounds by the British would shift the demand for pounds as shown in the graph below. The price of pounds in dollars would rise. (385-386)

e. An increase in the demand for dollars by the British is equivalent to an increase in the supply of pounds. The supply curve for pounds would shift to the right as shown in the graph below. The price of pounds in dollars would fall. (385-386)

4. a. Demand for imports by the British rises; hence demand for dollars (supply of pounds) rises. This is shown in the graph below. (385-386)

b. Demand for imports by Americans rises; hence demand for pounds rises. This is shown in the graph below. (385-386)

c. Demand for imports by the British falls; hence demand for dollars (supply of pounds) falls. This is shown in the graph below. (385-386)

d. Demand for British assets will rise; hence the demand for the pound rises. This is shown in the graph below. (385-386)

e. The demand for the pound falls. This is shown in the graph below. (385-386)

A BRAIN TEASER

1. A decrease in the demand for the dollar and/or an increase in the supply of the dollar in international exchange rate markets will create a temporary balance of payments deficit (because the quantity of dollars supplied will exceed the quantity demanded—imports will exceed exports). The balance of payments deficit will also put downward pressure on the exchange rate value of the dollar. (384-385)

POTENTIAL ESSAY QUESTIONS

The following are annotated answers. They indicate the general idea behind the answer.

1. If a country is experiencing a balance of payments deficit (the quantity supplied of its currency exceeds the quantity demanded at the current exchange rate) then its currency will fall in value over time. A country's government could prevent its currency from falling (depreciating) by buying its own currency in exchange rate markets. If it does, then this shows up in the financial account as a plus sign and we say that the government is supporting the value of its currency. The opposite is also true. Because a country can create and then sell its own currency it is easier for a country to push the value of its currency down, than up.

2. See pages 391-398. Also, notice the "margin list" on pages 395-399. Most nations have opted for a partially flexible exchange rate policy in order to try to get the advantages of both a fixed and a flexible exchange rate.

FISCAL AND MONETARY POLICIES IN THE OPEN ECONOMY AD-AS MODEL

CHAPTER AT A GLANCE

As domestic economies become more globalized and see the merits of entering into more international trade agreements, domestic economic goals may have to be altered along with how and when monetary and fiscal policies should be conducted. Economic goals could include whether an economy should have a high or low value for its currency; a fixed or flexible exchange rate system; or whether it should maintain a trade surplus or trade deficit. Each of these have their own advantages and disadvantages. This chapter uses the models developed so far (the AD-AS model and the money market) to analyze the transmission effect of various policies.

The next issue raised is once the economic goals are determined, how can an economy use its domestic monetary and fiscal policies to successfully achieve them and what is the net effect on income, price, interest rates, and the trade balance. This chapter uses the models developed so far – the AD-AS model and the money market – to analyze the transmission effects of policy.

This review is based upon the learning objectives that open the chapter.

1a. There is significant debate about what Canadian international goals should be because exchange rates have conflicting effects and, depending on the state of the economy, there are arguments for high and low exchange rates. (417)

A high exchange rate (strong value of the Canadian dollar) helps hold down the prices of imports and therefore inflation. However, it creates a trade deficit and that has a depressing effect on aggregate demand and therefore the income level.

1b. Running a trade deficit is good in the short run, but presents problems in the long run; thus there is debate about whether we should worry about a trade deficit or not. (417-418)

Trade deficit ⇒ imports > exports.

Short-run benefit: We are able to consume more than we would otherwise be able to.

Long-run cost: We have to sell off Canadian assets because we are consuming more than we are producing. All the future interest and profits on those assets will thus go to foreigners, not Canadian citizens.

1c. Canada has developed an inflation targeting initiative as its overriding objective of monetary policy. As a result, the Bank of Canada pursues a proactive exchange rate policy or a trade balance policy. (418-419)

2a. A country that has fixed exchange rates is limited in its ability to use fiscal and monetary policy to address domestic policy goals. (419-421)

A country with fixed exchange rates must give up any attempt to target domestic interest rates to achieve domestic goals.

2b. If a country wants to fix the value of its currency higher than the market value, a country can increase the private demand for its currency by implementing contractionary monetary policy. This type of monetary policy raises the interest rates which attracts foreign investors to purchase domestic securities (interest-bearing assets such as bonds) which now yield a higher rate of return. This increases the demand for the domestic currency and raises its value. The country can also decrease the private supply of its currency by implementing contractionary monetary policy. (419-420)

2c. In a closed economy, fiscal policy causes higher interest rates, which leads to a crowding-out effect of reducing private sector investment spending. So, the positive effects of increased government spending and/or reduced taxes are offset to some extent by reduced investment spending. The resulting equilibrium real income depends on the magnitude of the crowding-out effect and the multiplier effect.

In an open economy, the central bank can implement expansionary monetary policy to restore interest rates and increase real income as long as real income is below potential GDP. (420-421)

3a. Monetary policy affects exchange rates through the interest rate path, the income path, and the price-level path. (422-423)

Expansionary monetary policy (increasing the money supply and lowering the interest rate) lowers exchange rates. It decreases the relative value of a country's currency. Contractionary monetary policy has the opposite effect.

Be able to explain why!

3b. Monetary policy affects the trade balance through the income path, the price level path, and the exchange rate path, as shown in the diagram on page 425. (424-425)

Expansionary monetary policy makes a trade deficit larger.

Contractionary monetary policy makes a trade deficit smaller.

Be able to explain why!

3c. Fiscal policy affects exchange rates through the income path, the interest rate path, and the price-level path. (426)

The net effect of fiscal policy on exchange rates is ambiguous.

Be able to explain why!

3d. Fiscal policy affects the trade deficit though the income path and the price-level path, as shown in the diagram on page 428. (427-428)

Expansionary fiscal policy increases a trade deficit.
Contractionary fiscal policy decreases a trade deficit.

Be able to explain why!

4. Governments try to coordinate their monetary and fiscal policies because their economies are interdependent. (429-430)

Each country will likely do what's best for the world economy as long as it is also best for itself.

5. While internationalizing a country's debt may help in the short run, in the long run, it presents potential problems, since foreign ownership of a country's debts means the country must pay interest to those foreign countries and that debt may come due. (430-431)

We have been internationalizing our debt since the early 1980s, which means that we must, at some point in the future, export more than we import (consume less than we produce) to pay for this.

● MULTIPLE CHOICE

Circle the one best answer for each of the following questions:

1. In Canada, the overriding objective of monetary policy is
   a. exchange rate targeting.
   b. trade balance targeting.
   c. inflation targeting.
   d. interest rate targeting.

2. If a country has fixed exchange rates
   a. the government need not worry about the exchange rate.
   b. governments are committed to buying and selling currencies at a fixed rate.
   c. the exchange rate is set by law.
   d. the exchange rate has a fixed component and a flexible component.

3. If a country has a flexible exchange rate, the exchange rate
   a. is determined by flexible government policy.
   b. is determined by market forces.
   c. fluctuates continuously, changing by at least 1 percent per year.
   d. fluctuates continuously, changing by at least 10 percent per year.

4. Countries prefer
   a. a high exchange rate.
   b. a low exchange rate.
   c. sometimes a low and sometimes a high exchange rate.
   d. a fixed exchange rate.

5. Countries prefer
   a. a trade deficit.
   b. a trade surplus.
   c. sometimes a trade deficit and sometimes a trade surplus.
   d. a trade equilibrium.

6. If a country wants to maintain a fixed exchange rate above equilibrium, but does not have the necessary official reserves, it can:
   a. increase demand for its currency by running contractionary monetary policy.
   b. reduce the supply of its currency by running expansionary monetary policy
   c. increase demand for its currency by running contractionary fiscal policy.
   d. increase supply of its currency by running expansionary fiscal policy.

7. Expansionary monetary policy has a tendency to
   a. push interest rates up and exchange rates down.
   b. push interest rates down and exchange rates down.
   c. push income down and exchange rates down.
   d. push imports down and exchange rates down.

8. Contractionary monetary policy has a tendency to
   a. push interest rates up and exchange rates down.
   b. push interest rates down and exchange rates down.
   c. push income down and imports down.
   d. push imports down and exchange rates down.

9. If the exchange rate has gone up, it is most likely that the government ran
   a. an expansionary monetary policy.
   b. a contractionary monetary policy.
   c. an expansionary fiscal policy.
   d. a contractionary fiscal policy.

10. If the trade deficit has gone up, it is most likely that the government ran
    a. an expansionary monetary policy.
    b. a contractionary monetary policy.
    c. a contractionary fiscal policy.
    d. an expansionary monetary policy and a contractionary fiscal policy.

11. Expansionary monetary policy tends to
    a. push prices up and the trade deficit down.
    b. push prices down and the trade deficit down.
    c. push income up and the trade deficit down.
    d. push income up and the trade deficit up.

12. Expansionary fiscal policy tends to push
    a. income up and exchange rates up.
    b. income up and exchange rates down.
    c. income up and imports up.
    d. income up and imports down.

13. If the exchange rate has gone up, it is most likely that the government ran
    a. an expansionary fiscal policy.
    b. a contractionary fiscal policy.
    c. Who knows?
    d. an expansionary monetary policy.

14. Contractionary fiscal policy tends to push
    a. income down and imports up.
    b. income down and the trade deficit up.
    c. prices down and the trade deficit down.
    d. prices down and imports up.

15. Assume that Canada would like to raise its exchange rate and lower its trade deficit. It would pressure Japan to run
    a. contractionary monetary policy.
    b. contractionary fiscal policy.
    c. expansionary monetary policy
    d. expansionary fiscal policy.

16. According to the textbook, generally, when international goals and domestic goals conflict
    a. the international goals win out.
    b. the domestic goals win out.
    c. sometimes it's a toss-up which will win out.
    d. international monetary goals win out but international fiscal goals lose out.

17. When a country runs a large trade deficit, the amount of crowding out that occurs because of fiscal policy is
    a. increased.
    b. decreased.
    c. unaffected.
    d. sometimes increased and sometimes decreased.

● SHORT-ANSWER QUESTIONS

1. What should Canadian international goals be?

2. Why can a country achieve an interest rate target or an exchange rate target, but generally cannot achieve both at the same time?

3. Which dominates for a country: domestic or international goals? Why?

4. If a country runs expansionary monetary policy, what will likely happen to the exchange rate?

5. If a country runs contractionary monetary policy, what will likely happen to the trade balance?

6. If a country runs expansionary fiscal policy, what will likely happen to the exchange rate?

7. If a country runs contractionary fiscal policy, what will likely happen to the trade balance?

8. Given the difficulty of doing so, why do countries try to coordinate their monetary and fiscal policies with other countries?

9. Canada in recent years has run a large capital account deficit. What are some of the potential problems that this presents?

● PROBLEMS AND APPLICATIONS

1. You observe that over the past decade, a country's competitiveness has improved, reducing its trade deficit.

    a. What monetary or fiscal policies might have led to such results? Why?

    b. You also observe that interest rates have steadily fallen along with a fall in the exchange rate. What monetary or fiscal policies might have led to such results?

2. You have been hired as an adviser to Fantasyland, a country with perfectly flexible exchange rates. State what monetary and fiscal policies you might suggest in each of the following situations. Explain your answers.

    a. You want to increase domestic income and to reduce the exchange rate.

    b. You want to reduce interest rates, reduce inflation, and reduce the trade deficit.

    c. You want lower unemployment, lower interest rates, a lower exchange rate, and a lower trade deficit.

● A BRAIN TEASER

1. Suppose a country has been running a significant expansionary fiscal policy for many years. Monetary policy has been neutral. What can you expect to have happened to this country's trade balance? What are the benefits and costs of this trade imbalance? If this country wishes to correct for its trade imbalance, what fiscal and monetary policies would you suggest this country pursue now? Will your recommended polices coincide or conflict with any of the country's domestic goals? If so, which goals?

● POTENTIAL ESSAY QUESTIONS

You may also see essay questions similar to the "Problems & Applications" and "Brain Teasers" exercises.

1. If there was initially a trade balance, what kind of trade imbalance would be created by an increase in the exchange rate value of the dollar (a stronger dollar)? Why?

2. What are the benefits and costs to Canada of having a strong dollar–a high exchange rate value of the dollar?

3. Why do domestic economic goals usually dominate international economic goals?

■ ANSWERS ■

MULTIPLE CHOICE

1. c.   See pages 418-419.

2. b   To keep the exchange rate at the stated amount, governments must be willing to buy and sell currencies so that the quantity supplied and quantity demanded are always equal at the fixed rate. See pages 419-421.

3. b   There are no predetermined levels of change with a flexible exchange rate. See page 417.

4. c   The answer is "sometimes a low and sometimes a high exchange rate" because, as discussed on page 417, there are rationales for both.

5. c   The domestic economy's needs change over time and as they do, so does the country's preferred trade situation. Both a deficit and a surplus have their advantages and disadvantages. See pages 417-418.

6. a   Contractionary monetary policy will increase the demand for one's currency and increase its value. Contractionary fiscal policy will reduce the supply of one's currency and increase its value. Contractionary monetary and fiscal policy is one way to fix one's exchange rate without intervening in the exchange market. See pages 419-420.

7. b   See the diagram on page 423-424.

8. c   See the diagram on page 423-424.

9. b   As discussed on page 423-424 the b answer is definitely correct. As discussed on pages 426-427, fiscal policy has an ambiguous effect on exchange rates.

10. a   Expansionary monetary policy and expansionary fiscal policy increase the trade deficit. See the diagrams on pages 425 and 428.

11. d   See the discussion on pages 424-425 and the diagram on page 425.

12. c   The effect of expansionary fiscal policy on exchange rates is ambiguous, which eliminates a and b. Increased income increases imports, not decreases them. See pages 426-427 and the diagram on page 427.

13. c   The effect of expansionary fiscal policy on the exchange rate is ambiguous, as shown on the diagram on page 427, eliminating a and b. As discussed on pages 424-425, an expansionary monetary policy pushes the exchange rate down, eliminating d, leaving only c.

14. c   See diagram on page 428 and the discussion on pages 427-428.

15. c   The effect of fiscal policy on the exchange rate is ambiguous, so the only sure option is c. See the "Knowing the Tools" box on page 430.

16. b   As discussed in the text on pages 429-430, usually, because of political considerations, domestic goals win out.

17. b   Since the trade deficit means capital is flowing into the country, the capital usually ends up buying some government debt, which reduces crowding out, as discussed on pages 430-431.

■ ANSWERS ■

SHORT-ANSWER QUESTIONS

1.   By "international goals", economists usually mean the exchange rate and the trade balance that policy makers should shoot for. There is significant debate in Canada about what our international goals should be, and there are arguments for both high and low exchange rates, and for both trade deficits and trade surpluses. The argument for a high exchange rate is that it lowers the cost of imports; the argument against it is that it raises the price of exports, making Canadian goods less competitive. The argument in favour of a trade deficit is that it allows a country to consume more than it produces; the argument against is that a trade deficit will have to be paid off at some point. (417-418)

2. Because monetary policy affects the value of one's currency, a country cannot target both interest rates and exchange rates simultaneously. Suppose one's currency is at its desired level, but interest rates are too high. Expansionary monetary policy would lower the interest rate, but a lower interest rate reduces foreign demand for the country's interest-bearing assets. The demand for one's currency will shift inward to the left and its exchange rate will fall. Likewise, citizens of the country will invest elsewhere and the supply of one's currency will shift out to the right. The value of one's currency will be lower than its target. (418-424)

3. Generally, domestic goals dominate for two reasons. (1) International goals are often ambiguous, as discussed in answer 1 above and (2) international goals affect a country's population indirectly and, in politics, indirect effects take a back seat. (418)

4. Expansionary monetary policy tends to push income and prices up and interest rates down. All these phenomena tend to push the exchange rate down. Contractionary monetary policy has the opposite effect. (421-423)

5. Contractionary monetary policy tends to push income and prices down and interest rates up. The strongest effect of these phenomena on the trade balance in the short run is the effect on income, which causes a fall in imports and a fall in the trade deficit. (421-423)

6. Expansionary fiscal policy pushes interest rates, income, and prices up. The higher income and higher prices increase imports and put downward pressure on exchange rates. The higher interest rate pushes exchange rates in the opposite direction so the net effect of fiscal policy on exchange rates is unclear. (426-427)

7. Contractionary fiscal policy pushes income and prices down. This tends to decrease imports and increase competitiveness, decreasing a trade deficit. (427-428)

8. The policies of one country affect the economy of another. So it is only natural that they try to coordinate their policies. It is also only natural that since voters are concerned with their own countries, that coordination is difficult to achieve unless it is in the interest of both countries. (429-430)

9. While internationalizing a country's debt may help in the short run, in the long run it presents potential problems, since foreign ownership of a country's debts means the debtor country must pay interest to those foreign countries, and also, that debt may come due. (430-431)

■─────── **ANSWERS** ───────■

PROBLEMS AND APPLICATIONS

1. a. An increase in competitiveness and a decrease in the trade deficit are probably due to contractionary fiscal policy. Contractionary fiscal policy reduces inflation, improves competitiveness, and decreases income which reduces imports. Improved competitiveness and decreased income both work to reduce the trade deficit. Contractionary monetary policy would also reduce the trade deficit, but its effect on competitiveness is ambiguous. (424-425, 427-428)

    b. If interest rates have also fallen, it is likely that fiscal policy has been very contractionary because contractionary monetary policy would have led to higher interest rates and a higher exchange rate value of the dollar. (421-428)

2. a. Expansionary monetary policy will reduce the exchange rate through its effect on interest rates and will increase domestic income. Expansionary fiscal policy will increase domestic income. The increase in income will increase imports, which will tend to decrease the exchange rate, but higher interest rates will tend to lead to a higher exchange rate. The effect of expansionary fiscal policy on exchange rates is ambiguous. (421-428)

b. Contractionary fiscal policy will tend to reduce inflation and interest rates. The reduction in inflation will improve competitiveness and a reduction in income will reduce imports. Both work to reduce the trade deficit. (421-428)

c. Expansionary monetary policy will reduce unemployment and reduce interest rates. Lower interest rates will tend to make exchange rates fall. Expansionary monetary policy, however, will make the trade deficit higher. Expansionary fiscal policy will also reduce unemployment. Interest rates, however, will rise and so will the trade deficit. This mix of goals is difficult to attain. (421-428)

ANSWERS

A BRAIN TEASER

1. Because of the expansionary fiscal policy, this country will have moved in the direction of a trade deficit. The benefit of the trade deficit is that the country has been able to consume more that it has produced. The cost, however, is that it has had to sell off some of its assets. All the future interest and profits on these assets will now go to foreigners, not the country's citizens.

   To reduce the trade deficit the country should pursue contractionary fiscal and monetary policies. This will reduce imports and increase exports and increase the country's competitiveness in the global economy. That's good. However, even though fewer imports and greater exports should help stimulate aggregate expenditures, the effects of the contractionary fiscal and monetary policies are also simultaneously at play. Aggregate demand may fall on balance. If it does, then you may have created a recession. That's bad. Sometimes, countries can find themselves "in a pickle." (There could be other effects associated with the prescribed contractionary policies.) (421-428)

ANSWERS

POTENTIAL ESSAY QUESTIONS

The following are annotated answers. They indicate the general idea behind the answer.

1. A stronger dollar means that a single dollar will now buy more units of a foreign currency. This makes foreign products cheaper to Americans. Canada would import more. At the same time, a stronger dollar means it will now take more units of a foreign currency to buy a single dollar. This will cause Canadian goods to become more expensive to foreigners. Canada would export less. The combined effects of more Canadian imports and fewer Canadian exports means a trade deficit will be created or get larger in the U.S.

2. A strong dollar holds down the price of imports and, therefore, inflation. However, the cost is a trade deficit that would have a depressing effect on total spending and, therefore, the nation's income level (there would be an especially depressing effect on the nation's exporting industries).

3. First, there is more agreement on domestic goals. Second, domestic goals affect people within one's country more directly. Finally, pursuing domestic goals is politically more appealing.

TOOLS, RULES, AND POLICY

18

● CHAPTER AT A GLANCE

The chapter adds a new element into the macro-economic models that have been discussed so far – the expectations of consumers and firms. Central banks and governments must consider the effect that rational expectations plays on the effectiveness of fiscal and monetary policies.

The short-run aggregate supply (SAS) curve must be derived in a more formal manner by incorporating the labour market. Workers with rational expectations can adjust their expectations quickly to new information regarding economic variables such as the price level and the wage rate. As a result, owners of firms have no informational advantage over their workers.

This chapter considers the Keynesian and Classical monetary response towards temporary and permanent shocks to aggregate demand and aggregate supply to determine which policy is more appropriate.

The effectiveness of government policy will also depend on time-consistency – the extent to which policymakers have no incentive to deviate from their policies in the future. Policies are time-consistent and creditable if everyone knows about it, that it is transparent, enforceable and predictable.

This review is based upon the learning objectives that open the chapter.

1a. Rational expectations is the value of an economic variable that utilizes all available information and is correct on average. (435)

Rational expectations is a method to include expectations in an economic model when expectations cannot be easily measured. As a result, we need to have an economic process, a method by which the value of an economic variable is determined.

A basic example of a process are the equations that have been used throughout this textbook.

1b. Consumers who form rational expectations act as if they know the process that is generating the value of the economic variable. Their forecasts are correct on the average, but can be too high or too low in any single period. The forecast errors exhibit no pattern. (435-436)

1c. Some economists criticize the assumption of rational expectations on the grounds that consumers cannot learn the process determining an economic variable, or be able to acquire the information needed to use it. (435-437)

It can be acquired, however, if consumers or firms make the best decisions available to them, regardless of knowing the process. Their actions are consistent with the predictions of the theories. It is also reasonable to assume that access to information is getting cheaper and more accessible.

2a. The SAS curve can be derived through the labour market using the demand and supply for labour which affects the wage rate. If the price level rises, it is a signal for firms to hire more labour. The demand for labour rises, causing the wage rate to rise and the SAS curve to shift vertically. Real output rises and labour is fooled into providing more labour at a lower real wage. As workers find out that their real wage rate (W/P) has actually fallen, they withdraw their services and the labour supply curve shifts leftward, causing the nominal wage to rise further until the initial real wage is restored. (437-440)

2b. The SAS curve shifts vertically to a new higher price level to reflect the adjustment of expectations. (437-439)

2c. Workers with rational expectations adjust their expectations quickly to new information. They cannot be fooled into providing more output temporarily. With rational expectations, there will be no effect on real output, not even a temporary effect. (439-440)

3a. Monetary policy, through changes in interest rates and the money supply, causes shifts in the AD curve. Monetary policy can be used to deal with unexpected shocks to the AD and LAS curves. (441)

3b. An AD shock is an unexpected shift in the AD curve that can be temporary or permanent. (442)

3c. An AD shock can come about in 4 ways: (442)
- An unexpected change in any of the autonomous expenditure components.
- An unexpected change in autonomous money demand.
- An unexpected change in the stock of factors of production.
- An unexpected change in the productivity of factors of production

3d. There are 2 broad monetary policy methods: (441)
- Keynesian monetary policy which pursues cyclical monetary policy to offset fluctuations in the business cycle.
- Classical monetary policy which advocates that money supply should grow at a constant rate, ideally equal to the rate of growth of real output.

3e. In the case of a temporary AD shock, Keynesian monetary policy might overshoot the original price level and real GDP, causing the price level to be more variable than it should. The Classical monetary policy response avoids this problem but can result in a temporary recession. (442-443)

3f. A Keynesian monetary policy is preferable if the Bank of Canada can evaluate the shock quickly and not overshoot potential income. This will minimize fluctuations in the price level and real GDP. (443)

3g. The classical monetary policy response is to not react to the shock at all and let adjustments in the labour market (a rightward shift in the SAS curve) restore potential output. This results in a

period of stagflation and after expectations adjust to the new higher price level, there is no further adjustment. (443-445)

3h. The Keynesian policy response results in a prolonged increase in the price level that is greater than it should be. An effort to maintain real output at the original level results in accelerating inflation and stagflation. (443-445)

3i. In the case of a permanent AD shock which reduces the level of potential real GDP, Keynesian monetary policy can avoid a recession if the policymaker has superior information. (443-445)

4a. An aggregate supply shock is an unexpected shift in the LAS curve that changes the productive capacity of the economy. It can be caused by a rapid increase in the price of a factor of production, such as energy prices. (445)

4b. A negative LAS shock shifts the production function downward, thereby making labour less productive, which lowers the wage rate and the demand for labour. (445-446)

4c. The Classical monetary policy response to a permanent supply shock is to do nothing, which results in a one-shot increase in the price level and a period of stagflation. After expectations adjust to be a new higher price level, there is no further change. (447-450)

4d. The Keynesian monetary policy response to a permanent supply shock results in a prolonged increase in the price level that is greater than it should be. Expansionary monetary policy shifts the AD curve rightward resulting in accelerating inflation and a prolonged period of stagflation. (450-451)

4f. The Classical monetary policy is preferable if price stability is a priority. (451)

5a. A time-consistent policy is one from which the policymaker has no incentive to deviate from the future. Consumers and firms with rational expectations will know that it is. (451-452)

5b. It is usually the case that the socially optimal economic policy is not time-consistent, while the sub-optimal poicy is time-consistent. (452)

5c. An example of a time-consistent policy is where housing developers want to build a subdivision in an area subject to flooding. If the government allows the development on the flood plain, the policy is time-consistent, but not socially optimal. (452)

5d. Another example would be the case of a government promising to offer investment tax credits to firms would bring new investment projects today. If the government continues this policy after the projects have been completed, it reflects a sub-optimal policy that is time-consistent. (452)

MATCHING THE TERMS
Match the terms to their definitions

All of these key terms, are found at the end of the chapter.

____ **1.** aggregate demand shock
____ **2.** aggregate supply shock
____ **3.** Classical monetary policy response
____ **4.** diminishing returns
____ **5.** economic process
____ **6.** Keynesian monetary policy response
____ **7.** myopic expectations
____ **8.** random error
____ **9.** rational expectations
____ **10.** reservation wage
____ **11.** time-consistent policy

a. A forecast of the value of an economic variable that utilizes all available information and is correct on the average.

b. The unpredictable component of an economic variable.

c. As more labour is added to a fixed amount of other factors of production, output rises at a diminishing rate.

d. The minimum wage that each person requires to induce him or her to work at a given price level.

e. It takes one time period for workers to adjust their expectations to the new price level.

f. Pursuing counter cyclical monetary policy to offset fluctuations in the business cycle.

g. The money supply should grow at a constant rate, ideally just equal to the rate of growth of real output.

h. An unexpected shift in the AD curve that can be temporary or permanent.

i. An unexpected shift in the LAS curve that changes the productive capacity of the economy.

j. A policy from which the policymaker has no incentive to deviate in the future.

k. The method by which the value of an economic variable is determined.

● MULTIPLE CHOICE

Circle the one best answer for each of the following questions:

1. A forecast of the value of an economic variable that utilizes all available information is called a(n)
   a. adaptive expectation.
   b. extrapolative expectation.
   c. inflationary expectation.
   d. rational expectations.

2. A random error is
   a. not part of the economic process.
   b. an error that occurs once in a while.
   c. a forecasted value of a variable that is too high or low.
   d. predictable.

3. One criticism of rational expectations is that
   a. it makes no sense most of the time.
   b. it is too costly for consumers to obtain the information needed to use the economic process.
   c. adaptive expectations is more relevant in "real-world" situations.
   d. policy tools such as monetary and fiscal policy are ineffective.

4. The forecast errors of a rational expectations
   a. are easy too predict.
   b. are typically small.
   c. do not exhibit any pattern over time.
   d. are positive on the average.

5. The SAS curve with rational expectations must consider the
   a. goods markets.
   b. money market.
   c. labour market.
   d. capital market.

6. When considering rational expectations, the upward slope of the SAS curve arises due to
   a. a lowering of productivity.
   b. hiring more labour by firms in response to an increase in the price level.
   c. lower wages translating into more workers hired.
   d. firms adjusting both price and quantity in response to changes in aggregate demand.

7. Workers with rational expectations of the price level will
   a. work more overtime to earn more wages.
   b. increase their productivity.
   c. immediately recognize a higher price level.
   d. immediately recognize that nominal wages are too high.

8. Which policy pursues a counter cyclical monetary policy to offset fluctuations in the business cycle?
   a. Keynesian monetary policy.
   b. Classical monetary policy.
   c. Monetarist monetary policy.
   d. expansionary monetary policy.

9. An aggregate demand shock can come about because of all of the following, except
   a. unexpected change in the stocks of factors of production.
   b. an unexpected increase in energy prices.
   c. an unexpected change in money demand.
   d. an unexpected change in any of the aggregate expenditure components.

10. A temporary negative aggregate demand shock causes
   a. the AD curve to shift rightward causing the price level and real output to rise.
   b. the AD curve to shift leftward causing the price level to rise and real output to fall.
   c. the AD curve to shift rightward causing the price level to fall and real output to rise.
   d. the AD curve to shift leftward causing the price level and real output to fall.

11. You have been appointed advisor to the governor of the Bank of Canada. A negative AD shock has taken place. You would suggest
   a. expansionary monetary policy.
   b. contractionary monetary policy.
   c. to take a wait and see approach.
   d. combining expansionary monetary policy with contractionary fiscal policy.

12. A Keynesain monetary policy is preferable in the face of a temporary negative AD shock if
   a. the expansionary monetary policy is followed by contractionary fiscal policy.
   b. the Bank of Canada can evaluate the shock quickly and not overshoot potential income.
   c. the Bank of Canada does nothing.
   d. the Bank of Canada implements contractionary monetary policy.

13. In the case of a permanent AD shock,
   a. Classical monetary policy can avoid a recession.
   b. Keynesian monetary policy can avoid a recession.
   c. there is a possibility of the Bank of Canada to overshoot the original price level and real output.
   d. the variation in real output is greater with Classical monetary policy.

14. A negative aggregate supply shock affects real output and the price level by affecting all of the following, except
   a. interest rates.
   b. the production function.
   c. the labour market.
   d. the productive capacity of the economy.

15. In the case of a negative aggregate supply shock, the Classical monetary response is to
   a. implement expansionary policy.
   b. to do nothing that would be considered discretionary.
   c. get the economy out of a recession.
   d. negotiate with the federal government.

16. Optimal policies are usually
   a. not rational.
   b. not time-consistent.
   c. only optimal in the long run.
   d. second-best policy choices.

● SHORT-ANSWER QUESTIONS

1. What is a rational expectation?

2. What are the characteristics of a rational expectation?

3. Explain the Lucas critique of discretionary macroeconomic policy.

4. What are the two types of monetary policy available to address issues within the macroeconomy?

5. Assume that an economy experiences a temporary negative AD shock. What are the consequences of this shock and the impact of implementing Keynesian and Classical monetary policy?

6. How does an aggregate supply shock affect the economy?

7. Assume that an economy experiences a permanent negative aggregate supply shock. What are the consequences of this shock and the impact of implementing Keynesian and Classical monetary policy?

8. What is a time-consistent policy? What can policymakers do to make a policy time-consistent?

● PROBLEMS AND APPLICATIONS

1. Explain how each of the following unexpected shocks would affect the AD or AS curves. Also note whether a temporary or permanent shift in the AD or AS curve is expected.

    a. Consumers are worried about their debt levels and the impending higher interest rates.

    b. Strong economic activity, brought on by increasing oil and natural gas production, creates more high paying jobs for the economy.

    c. The Government of Alberta announces a reduction in business taxes.

ANSWERS

A BRAIN TEASER

1. In our globalized and integrated economy, the ability to attract foreign firms and investors into an economy becomes important. One way of encouraging foreign direct investment is to create a climate conducive to research and development and the development of technology. To accomplish this, government has to ensure that firms can reap the benefits of taking risks and innovating. Legislation related to patent rights, copyrights, trademarks, private property protection and contract enforcement becomes important. Discuss how time-consistency applies to this legislation.

ANSWERS

POTENTIAL ESSAY QUESTIONS

You may also see essay questions similar to the "Problems & Applications" and "Brain Teasers" exercises.

1. Explain how rational expectations affects the effectiveness of monetary policy in response to a temporary negative AD shock.

ANSWERS

MATCHING

1-h;2-i;3-g;4-c;5-k;6-f;7-e;8-b;9-a;10-d;11-j.

ANSWERS

MULTIPLE CHOICE

1. d   See page 434.

2. c   A random error is the unpredictable component of an economic variable. It reflects the fact that forecasters cannot always make perfect predictions as the random error is unpredictable. (437)

3. b   The theory of rational expectations requires individuals have information about the economic process determining the economic variable in order to make predictions of that variable. Information is costly, yet it is becoming more readily available – through the Internet, Statistics Canada, the Bank of Canada, and other private sector forecasting agencies. (435-437)

4. c   Forecast errors are unpredictable and vary over time. They are zero on the average – being positive, negative, or zero in any time period, but canceling each other out over many time periods. (437)

5. c   The labour market determines the number of employed workers. As the price level changes, it is a signal for firms to hire more or less labour, thus changing real output. (438-439)

6. b   See pages 437-438.

7. c   With a higher price level, workers observe the increase in the price level as their real wage (W/P) has fallen and their nominal wage has not risen by enough to maintain their initial real wage. See Figure 18-1 on page 438 and 440.

8. a Keynesian monetary policy advocates a monetary response that offsets a demand or supply shock. Classical monetary policy advocates following a rule and not using discretionary policy. Monetarist monetary policy is the same as Classical monetary policy. d is just incorrect. (441)

9. b Changes in energy prices would influence the SAS and LAS curves. (442)

10. d See pages 442-443.

11. a Expansionary monetary policy results in reduced interest rates and increased money supply which leads to a rightward shift in AD and a higher price level and real output. (442-443)

12. b See pages 442-443.

13. b Keynesian monetary policy can avoid a recession if the Bank of Canada responds quickly and applies it in each period. The Classical response seems superior if price and output stability are the priorities of expectations are rational. (444-445).

14. a See pages 445-446.

15. b See page 448.

16. b Optimal policies are usually not time-consistent, while time-consistent policies are usually not optimal. (452)

ANSWERS

SHORT-ANSWER QUESTIONS

1. A rational expectation is a forecast of the value of an economic variable that utilizes all available information and is correct on the average. It relates to a theory of how expectations can be formed for a wide range of economic variables that one encounters in macroeconomic models. It can influence the outcome or the magnitude of the impact of economic policy if the implementation of the policy does not consider rational expectations.(434-435)

2. The forecast error of rational expectation is zero on the average and do not exhibit any pattern over time. (437)

3. Robert Lucas attempted to show how traditional Keynesian economics falls apart when consumers form rational expectations. Lucas showed that many macroeconomic models that rely on statistical estimates of macroeconomic functions to formulate its optimal policy, the policy is doomed to failure. (441)

4. The two types of monetary policy are Keynesian monetary policy and Classical monetary policy. Keynesian monetary policy pursues counter cyclical policy to offset fluctuations in the business cycle. For example, expansionary monetary policy is used to offset a recession where real GDP is below potential. Classical monetary policy advocates that the money supply grow at a constant rate, ideally, just equal to the rate of growth of real output. (441)

5. A negative AD shock causes the AD curve to shift leftward resulting in a lower price level and real output level. Classical economics would suggest the Bank of Canada do nothing, resulting in a recession, and waiting for the AD curve to shifty back to its original price level and output level. Keynesian economics would implement expansionary monetary policy, which lowers interest rates and shifts the AD curve rightward. The concern is the possibility of overshooting the original price level and level of real output. (442-443)

6. A supply shock affects real output and the price level by affecting the production function. Firms react by using less labour and reducing production. The demand for labour falls, resulting in lower nominal wages, lowering the productive capacity of the economy. In the long run, both the SAS ands LAS curves shift. (445-447)

7. The Classical monetary policy response is to do nothing. This results in leftward shifts in both the LAS and SAS curves, causing a higher price level and lower level of real output – a prolonged period of stagflation. The Keynesian monetary response is to implement expansionary monetary policy after the LAS and SAS curves have both shifted leftward. The AD curve shifts rightward so that the original level of potential output is restored. With rational expectations, workers immediately recognize the new price level and adjust their expectations and wage demands, causing the SAS curve to shift leftward. The Bank of Canada repeats its expansionary monetary policy, which causes further acceleration of inflation. The Classical monetary policy is preferable to the Keynesian monetary policy if price stability is a priority. (449-451)

8. A time-consistent policy is one from which the policymaker has no incentive to deviate from its policy in the future. If a policy is time-consistent, consumers and firms with rational expectations will know that it is. Optimal economic policy is usually not time-consistent, however, it is possible to construct time-consistent polices if policymakers follow policy rules that are known to everyone. Time-consistent monetary policy does not change radically and unexpectedly over time, thereby giving the central bank creditability. (451-452)

PROBLEMS AND APPLICATIONS

1   **a.** A lack of confidence that interest rates will remain low may cause consumers to retrench on their spending. Since consumer expenditures are an AE component, the AD curve shift leftward. If the historically low interest rates are considered a thing of the past, the shift could be permanent. (442-445)
b. Strong employment and income growth leads to higher consumer confidence and a greater transactions demand for money. This results in a rightward shift of the AD curve which could be permanent depending on the level of energy prices. (442-445)
c. Taxes is a factor affecting supply. The cost of production for producers has fallen, providing an incentive to hire more labour to produce more output. This would be deemed a permanent shock, causing the SAS to shift rightward. 442-445)

■ **ANSWERS** ■

A BRAIN TEASER

1. To provide a safe and secure environment to attract foreign direct investment and encourage research and development requires legislation that is predictable, transparent and enforceable. Time-consistent policies becomes extremely important in reducing uncertainty and encouraging risk taking. (451-454)

■ **ANSWERS** ■

POTENTIAL ESSAY QUESTIONS

The following are annotated answers. They indicate the general idea behind the answer.

1. Rational consumers and firms could incorporate the Bank of Canada response to the shock into their expectations of the price level. The negative AD shock would be viewed as temporary by the Bank and individuals so there would be no need to alter labour demand or supply.